Pilot and Pacifist:

a World War Two History

by

Esdaile Carter

Second edition

2014

All rights reserved © Esdaile Carter 2013

Second edition © Esdaile Carter 2014

Cover painting by Imogen Rigden

Second edition, with added illustrations and information

ISBN-13: 978-1503166813

ISBN-10: 1503166813

Every effort was made to locate copyright holders but I am currently unable to locate any contractual information indicating who controls the rights with reference to *Third Time Down* and *Never so Young Again* by Dan Brennan; *Till the Lights of London Shine Again* by E. Pola and T. Connor, *How About You?* by R. Freed; *Friends Ambulance Unit* by A. Tegla Davies; *Their Past* by Grantown Museum. I am awaiting replies from *The Aeroplane* and *Flight*.

Please contact me about omitted credits at http://esdailecarter.wordpress.com/

All profits from the sale of the paperback go to Christian Aid in memory of Jack and to The Brunswick Club, which John helped to found and which Freda always supported.

Table of contents

Dedication

Introduction

Chapter 1: Freda

Chapter 2: Jack

Chapter 3: March

Chapter 4: April

Chapter 5: May

Chapter 6: After Jack

Epilogue

Acknowledgments

List of figures

Further information

Bibliography

Index

Notes

Dedication

This book is written for my children and grandchildren and dedicated to all lost family members:
"For here in this thinking they will live a little longer"

Introduction

A carved solid oak chest, bought in Harrods, lived under the landing window, upstairs in my aunt's house. Now, at the end of February 2009, it was bequeathed to me and was on my sitting room floor, waiting to be examined. I dragged it over to the light and knelt down to open it. My aunt's favourite ball gown, chestnut coloured lace over satin, wrapped in black tissue paper, rustled among WW2 magazines about Tunisia and Tobruk, old Labrador retriever club circulars and copies of *The Friend*, a Quaker newsletter. I shook out the dress, and laid it over an armchair. Somewhere was her Will, along with dozens of letters and postcards.

Freda became crippled by arthritis in her eighties but regularly insisted that I help her up the stairs to visit the trunk where she would draw my attention to one thing or another, so the contents looked familiar but I had never examined them on my own. I picked out a squashy brown paper packet, tied with string. Within this was a voluminous quilted green and cream make-up bag. As soon as I opened it, the smell of my aunt's face powder filled the room. I closed it quickly and sat back on my heels for a bit, then bent towards it again, opening it very slowly to hold for as long as possible the perfume, the emotions. Inside the make-up bag was a folding leather photograph frame and a bundle of letters bound tightly with faded red ribbon.

In the frame, on one side, a postcard of an airplane, with a glinting blue and gold RAF pin clasped through one corner and opposite, the photograph of a man I did not recognise. He had a high forehead, thick hair parted on the left, deepset dark eyes, a mouth slightly open, with the beginnings of a smile or maybe he was nervous and telling the photographer to hurry up. Wearing an air force uniform with sergeant's stripes he had to be Jack. Surely the letters couldn't be from Jack? There were also two smaller photographs in the frame, contact prints, one of Freda and the other of my uncle John. He too was in uniform and it was taken before they met and before he was captured at Tobruk. I balanced the frame on her dress so that

I could see the pictures and sat back on the floor, cross-legged, to untie the bow and release the letters.

Some of the letters were sent to an unfamiliar address in Yorkshire and some were addressed to my aunt in Gordon Square and the dates on the postmarks? – yes, war time, 1943. When I found the letters, I read through each one, carefully sorting them into date order. As I slid each from its envelope, there was the smell of face powder again.

As Freda lay dying, I told her that Jack was waiting for her. Now it seemed that she and Jack were waiting for me.

The story which follows is taken from the letters of Freda, a conscientious objector, and Jack, the pilot of a heavy bomber. Many of their letters are reproduced and some of Freda's are edited for length. A few typos have been corrected. I have imagined some episodes which are inspired by their letters and supported by contemporary accounts. Where possible, I trod in their footsteps so the story is also mine.

There are no long gaps in the story of Freda and Jack but what gaps there are, cover the most important episodes in their friendship: the times they were together. Their story begins in York in mid-February 1943 when they dance at the De Grey Rooms, and fall in love. They meet on three subsequent occasions, once in London in March when Jack is on a 48hr pass, and again in April, when he is on annual leave in Norwich for ten days and spends four of them with Freda in London. In May, they spend a few hours together in York. Later, Freda is posted to the Near East and she works in Egypt, Syria and then Italy.

Figure 1 The leather frame with photographs of Jack, Freda and John

Chapter 1: Freda

YORK, SURROUNDED BY AIRFIELDS, was a good place for aircrew to meet and relax together. Many drank in Betty's Bar and then went on to the De Grey Rooms but on Friday 10th February, 1943, Jack a bomber pilot, and Maxie his engineer, made straight for the De Grey Rooms because Maxie had fallen in love again.

The ornate staircase up to the assembly rooms was blue with airmen, some in groups, laughing and fooling around, and some in couples, he with his arm around his girl, she proud to be with him. One boy leant over the banisters and wolf whistled, trying to catch a pretty girl's eye. A couple of girls had left the dance floor and stood at the top of the stairs, deciding whether to go back in for another dance. Jack and Maxie began to edge their way up the staircase.

"I only hope the girl I met last week isn't here. You will give her a dance, Jack, won't you? If she is?"

"Look here, Maxie, old man, I'm tired of sweeping up after you." Maxie was eighteen and Jack just twenty.

"Be a sport. Wait till you see her! She's a real princess."

But Jack had already glimpsed a princess near the top step, waiting to come down but not yet looking towards him. He ran his fingers through his blonde hair, straightened his jacket, automatically straightening his tie and, leaning against the banister, he polished each shoe in turn on his calf, through his blue serge trouser, never lowering his gaze. No longer listening to him, he touched Maxie lightly on the shoulder and left him to push his way up through the throng towards her.

Freda was finding the noise and the smoke overpowering but Marjorie wanted to stay a bit longer. This was Marjorie's first visit to York; she and Freda were on leave together from their jobs in London, and staying with Freda's family. Marjorie was in the mood for dancing.

"We'll go downstairs for a breather and then come back for the last few dances, all right?" Freda smiled back at Marjorie, nodded slowly and turned to go down the staircase.

"Hello," said Jack and smiled.

This is how Jack and Freda met. They danced only twice more in the De Grey Rooms before she had to return to London, on St. Valentine's Day, but she could not get him out of her mind.

Back in Whitechapel, Freda wrote the first of twenty six letters to Jack.

Figure 2 Freda Smith

Dear Jack,
I did not ask you for your number and full address lest it gave me the temptation to be most unladylike and write you before you wrote to me. The temptation is proving too strong, however, and I am

writing this because even if I do not hear from you (and I hope that I shall)

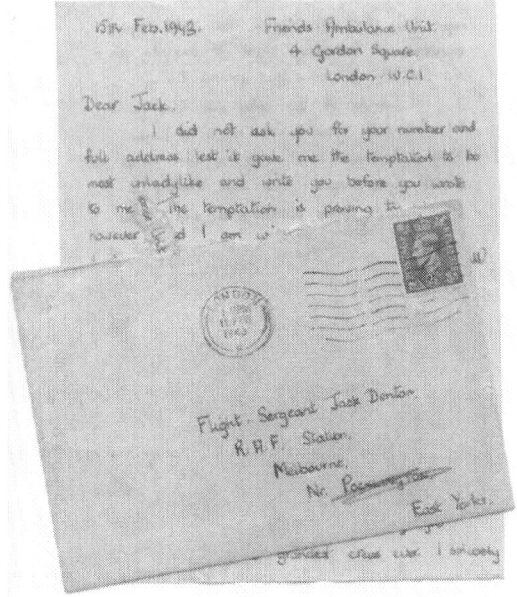

Figure 3 Freda's first letter to Jack

I would like to say how much I enjoyed the time I spent with you last week, and how sorry I was that I had to meet you at the wrong end of the week and thus be unable to see more of you.

Jack replied promptly to Freda's first letter.

My Dear Freda,
I am so sorry for not having replied to your letter earlier – actually it has been at Melbourne for 3 or 4 days now but unfortunately I have been on another station during this time & so did not have the pleasure of reading it until this morning.

I was exceedingly flattered by your remarks concerning myself & crew & hardly dared to tell Wally and George of them in case they went to their heads.

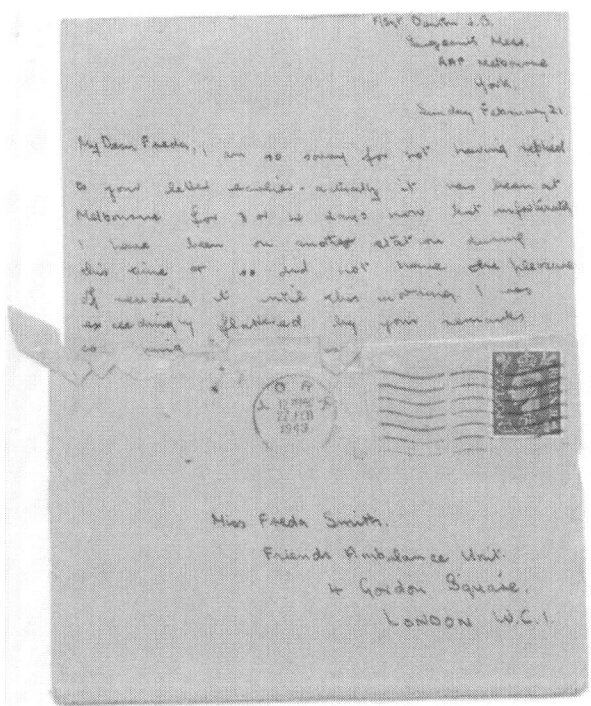

Figure 4 Jack's first letter to Freda

Seriously, I am afraid my chances of a visit to London in the near future are pretty slim at the moment (owing to pressure of work Ahem!) but I assure you that if ever I do find myself in the vicinity I will surely look you up as I promised.

Perhaps you will tell me when you reply (hopefully) if you would like to keep up a fairly regular correspondence. I am sure we would be able to find enough to talk about even if we only tell each other about ourselves & our doings. If you would like some of my personal data for a kick-off –: I am 20 ½ years old, single of course & and not particularly accomplished in anything at all but always full of good intentions (very brief but I should hate to bore you!)

Maxie looked up the meaning of your name today & found it meant Peaceful – is it appropriate? Maxie is the name of my engineer who you saw on the first night we met. Do you remember him?

I have been writing this letter during a lecture & it is just about coming to a close now & so I shall have to bring this letter to a close also as it is now time to start something more industrious.

Before I close please accept my regrets that my handwriting is so poor (such a contrast to your own)

& please don't forget to pass on best wishes of self & boys to Marjorie. And to yourself.
Sincerest Good Wishes,
Jack Xxx

As a child in York, Freda worked hard at school and she won a scholarship to Mill Mount. She walked to the school along the top part of the Knavesmire, past grazing cattle. Sometimes she walked up and over the hill at Scarcroft and down by the infant's school, crossing the road by one of the Rowntree mansions. From her home in Knavesmire Crescent, it was a thirty minute walk to York station, passing the Bar Convent and Mickelgate Bar. Aged 14, she became a Quaker and joined York Meeting. If she walked to the Friends Meeting House near the bus station, then she entered the city by Bishopgate Bar but she rarely walked because there was a bus stop close to home. She had to leave school at 16; she needed to get paid work.

The job she found was with Rowntree's Cocoa Works in York. As Rowntree's was owned and run by Quakers, it is not surprising that Freda should join the company. The engine works for L.N.E.R., where her father was a Works foreman, along with Terry's and Rowntree's chocolate factories, were the main employers in York at the time. At Rowntree's she worked for Arnold and Philip Rowntree and then for Roland Whiting in the social services department of the organization, from which she took a short-hand and typing course. Already a member of the Peace Pledge Union, Freda sold copies of Peace News in the town. Begun in 1934 by Dick Sheppard of St. Martin's in the Fields on Trafalgar Square, the Peace Pledge Union was not an official organization. Advertisements in the Manchester Guardian encouraged people to send postcards to Sheppard with a pledge to "renounce war" (Farson, *Bomber's Moon*, p. 12). Within a few weeks 30,000 people had pledged peace and by 1939, 1000,000 people had added their names, including Jack Denton in Norwich.

Shortly after war was declared both Rowntree's and Terry's were ordered to join the military effort. Rowntree's continued to make chocolate and cocoa along with tinned dried egg but the factory was forced to make bomb fuses as well. All staff were given the choice to leave and Freda, by now already a Quaker, chose to join the WarVics, the Friends War Victims' Relief Service, a Quaker organisation for the relief of refuges based in London. Later she moved over to the Friends Ambulance Unit (F.A.U.) also in London.

Freda says herself that she "writes yards and yards, or pages & pages or sheets & sheets, or lines & lines, or words & words" which is true, but because I want you to hear her voice, this is one of the few long letters I have left unedited.

       Friends Ambulance Unit.
       4 Gordon Square.
       London. W.C.1
       Tuesday & Wednesday. Feb. 23rd

       Dear Jack,
       I can see from your (literally) one-sided letter
that the Ministry of information salvage campaign
does not seem to have penetrated the Sergeant's Mess!
Here is the whole world engaged in a well-nigh

superhuman struggle & you contrive to write letters on one side of the paper only -, fie! fie!.

It was very nice indeed to have news from you this morning, and Marjorie was terrifically pleased to receive your good wishes. We have managed by now to more or less settle into the old routine, and get our noses down to the grindstone once again.

I expect you are wondering just what sort of a stone we grind in the F.A.U. I just did not want to spend what little time there was at the dance telling you about the Unit, and as everything would take ages to explain I thought you might like to see a copy of our Annual Report and so get the low-down on us. We've got lots here. So there is no need to return it.

As for the part Marjorie & I play, it's rather more difficult to say just what our function is. We joined originally to do Shelter Work in blitzes, but as there aren't blitzes any more, and the difficulties in finding openings for women overseas are pretty enormous so we do various other jobs of a social service nature in the meantime and train for post-war relief work on the continent. Being a short-hand typist I actually spend most of the week except Sunday at our H.Q. at Gordon Square, where I am assistant to our Executive Officer for Overseas Work in the M. East, Ethiopia & Syria. India & China is covered by someone else. I find it all very interesting, and though I should very much like to do more field-work and get further training (hospital training etc) we are so short of s/typists that at the moment I am more use there than anywhere else. We all do six-weeks hospital training after we have been to camp – the men do much more. Marjorie is toying with the idea of doing a further 3 months nursing training shortly.

On 3 evenings a week (Mon. Wed. Fri.) I finish my work at the Square at 5.0 pm and come down to Wapping where I run a play centre with another girl. I wish you could see it. We call it "The Sugar Loaf", this being the name of the pub which was on the premises before it was blitzed. The room is very small – about 12ft x 12 ft, and in it up to 30 kids paint and read & sew and tease & fight and throw things around, & believe me 1 ½ hrs of keeping 30-40 kids of ages from 2 to 12 in order is some going.

Marjorie also does Play Centre work on 5 evenings a week. Her kids are Gibraltar evacuees who live in a Bloomsbury hotel which the Govt. has taken over for some 400 families. The kids are of course of Latin extraction, and speak only broken English. In the day-time she does various other things. So there you have (I hope) some idea of what we do down here.

If you would like to drop me in a line whenever you feel that way inclined, I very much hope you will do so, and we shall certainly have to go dancing again when I come home in May – I'm 22 by the way, almost 23, and far too busy down here to get around London as one feels one ought. Anyway, Marjorie and I are usually broke before the month is half-way through, as this is voluntary work & our only payment is 25/- a month pocket money, which does not get us very far. However, we manage to have a very happy time withal, and get many laughs from our poverty.

The address on the back of the envelope, London Hospital Students Hostel, is where we live, though we are leaving here in April (the students are moving in again). I use the H.Q. address because I always leave here before the post comes, and Gordon Square is a much more stable address anyway. Incidentally, the phone no. is Museum 5986 after all – I was right first time.

London is a very fascinating place, you know, and it's amazing how it grows on one. On Sunday I went for a walk along the embankment, and then through St. James Park and up to Hyde Park, where I spent about an hour listening to the Speakers – I like doing that. The Embankment is a favourite walk of mine – on a windy day when I feel somewhat homesick and longing for the country it's a god-send, and about the nearest place from the East End. I like living in Whitechapel, and love going down to Wapping, which, as any London Map will show you, is down by the Thames about 10 mts walk from the hostel, but the East does acquire a rather unwholesome smell.

 We are having a dance here on Thursday – we usually have one every month, and they are quite good fun. Anyway, they are the only ones we go to here in London. We don't go out o' nights except at week-ends, & not always then. Our main form of amusement is toasting bread and drinking tea. Marjorie & I were only saying the other evening how nice it would be if you and your crew could come to the dance.

 Now that the days are lengthening I often cycle to the Square. Its rather good cycling through the city. I came back through Fleet Street to-night for a change. We had a nice quiet time at the Play Centre by way of a change, too.

 Our only furniture there is a table and about 8 chairs and a very ancient, toothless piano which has to be propped up. But on the whole we get along very well. We've only just got some windows in – the original one's being blown out way back in 1940, though even now most of the windows are boarded up.

 Wapping is so fascinating though, and one gets some very pleasing sights of the river as one goes along the High Street which runs parallel to the Thames, and sometimes one sees in the docks the river barges with their lovely red sails silhouetted against the evening sky.

 In the event of raids & alerts I go down to a shelter underneath one of the warehouses alongside the river. It holds some 300 folk & we staff the Medical Aid Post there, but of course nothing ever happens now, fortunately. Most of the kids at the Play Centre go there when there are raids – they all live nearby – most of them in Jubilee Buildings, which is a pretty grim block of flats. Heavens, how I run on about these things – sorry.

 Marjorie and I are hoping to go to the New Theatre on Saturday to see "Merchant of Venice" if we can get in the gallery [Gods crossed out]. I shall try and slip out and get some stools on Saturday morning.

    I hope my script does not give you an inferiority complex – I can write very badly sometimes. I shall be interested to learn what the character-reading-through-handwriting crew member has to say about me from my writing – then I will tell you if he is right! For a girl who is what the army would term a (Pygmalion) conshie I should think my name was very appropriate, but maybe you wouldn't agree!

    Yes, I remember Maxie quite well – how is his friend from the shoe-shop?

    Incidentally, I do hope that the fact that I am, so to speak, of a different persuasion, won't bar our writing. You know, I don't know anyone in the R.A.F. bar a cousin, and meeting you all and knowing you made me feel very small and humble. Please tell me more about yourself and your activities when you write.

    As you have probably observed earlier in this letter, girls do talk and this one seems no exception – I write yards and yards, or pages & pages or sheets & sheets, or lines & lines, or words & words (take your pick) once I pick up a pen, and realise how easy it must have been for Margaret Mitchell to write "Gone With The Wind".

    I hope you won't reply to this during another lecture or I can see myself being charged with sabotaging the war effort; I hope you will be able to find time to reply between lectures however.

    I wonder where you all are now (its 9.15 p.m.). I never let an evening go by without wondering & wishing you all Good Luck and Happy Landings.

    Remember me to the boys, and also F. for Freddie or whatever machine you are flying – what type of 4-engined is it anyway? I'd like to know, when you write.

    Best wishes, Jack.
    Freda.

    Freda's work in London needs some explanation, so what follows is a description of the London Freda knew in 1943 along with a description of the organisation Freda worked for, the Friends

Ambulance Unit. The F.A.U. was a volunteer relief organisation, staffed by Quakers, which had grown out of the carnage of the Western Front in the First World War, when its members worked mainly in field hospitals and dressing stations. The Unit was relaunched in January, 1940. Members were not necessarily Quakers but they needed to share outlook and be willing to serve in the most extreme conditions. Freda joined the Unit in London in 1941. She was fed and given lodgings and was paid 25/- a month, of which 5/- was Philip Rowntree's donation, and which in 1943 would have the buying power of £43 in 2010.

I have used two books to describe the Friends Ambulance Unit. Both books tell the history by quoting members' recollections. A. Tegla Davies published his account *Friends Ambulance Unit: the Story of the F.A.U. in the Second World War 1939-1946* in 1947, from inside the F.A.U., while memories were fresh. He does not attribute quotations but some sound like Freda's voice. Freda's copy of the book is inscribed with her name and address in York and the dates she belonged to the Unit: 5.10.41-31.1.47. She marked some sections with a line in the margin and inserted letters, photographs and notes at other sections.

Lyn Smith interviewed as many members of the F.A.U. as she could in the last years of 20th century for her book, *Pacifists in Action: the Experience of the Friends Ambulance Unit in the Second World War* (1998). Freda wrote in a self-deprecating manner, and persuaded Lyn not to add her recollections:

> I wasn't one of the F.A.U. intellectuals – working class background, typist at Rowntrees where I worked for Arnold Rowntree (Mike's father) and also Philip Rowntree, to whom I have a life-long debt for encouraging me to join the F.A.U. and supporting me with extra pocket-money as I knew I could not get by on the 5/- a week we were given (could not expect parental backing).
> However, I have filled in the Form as best I can – the really interesting work was done by the women on relief work at home and abroad.

Freda's own letters provide the third source of information, along with her collection of Unit publications. Part of her job in

London was to write regularly to fellow Unit members who were now overseas. Some of the overseas workers were isolated and grappling with almost overwhelming poverty and disease and their replies to her letters show how valuable this unofficial contact was to them. Some of these letters are about Freda's personal life and observations but most are general Unit gossip and news.

Her correspondents are in Ethiopia, the Near East and China, with one in Bengal. She tended to write to them all in the first week of every month but the date slips with time. Each typed original is on bright yellow flimsy paper. She kept all her carbon copies because it would have been hard to recall what she had written to whom and when. All the same, she repeats herself to some people almost word for word, but each letter is surprisingly fresh and reads almost as though she had not written on the same subject four or five times already.

Freda herself could have been a fourth source of information. When at Queen Mary College in 1970, I used to skip paying tube fares by getting out two stops early at Whitechapel, where there was rarely a ticket collector and then I'd walk up the Mile End Road to college. When I told this to Freda, I paid little attention when she said she'd lived over the road at the London Hospital in the war. We talked about Petticoat Lane market and how lively it was, and Stepney library, but I was not interested in her history and, anyway, she downplayed it. I walked by the river near the Tower but never in Wapping. I drank in the Students' Union and went to a pub frequented by the Kray twins but never to the Prospect of Whitby or the Town of Ramsgate. The students' union and demonstrations led by Jack Straw were far more interesting subjects than wartime memories. The student who was attacked opposite college and whose head was cracked open by an axe was of immediate concern, not WW2 air raid shelters. So, when I read that long letter from Freda, written at the end of February 1943, I am ashamed to say, little of it was familiar.

I looked in books, on maps and on the internet for the shelter where Freda worked, called Colonial Wharf in her letter dated March 3rd 1943, but with no luck at all. I discovered much about Jack the Ripper territory and the scene of Communist and Anarchist groups in Conrad's *Confidential Agent* as well as ugly Blackshirt marches and earnest Peace Pledge Union meetings, the Sidney Street siege and the largest of the large London hospitals but never a mention of Colonial

Wharf. Freda mentions Jubilee Buildings and, finally, I found the Tower Hamlets library photograph collection, which includes a picture of Royal Jubilee Buildings. Freda's description in 1943 remained accurate for the 60's: "a pretty grim block of flats". Looking more closely, what did I see to my delight? Painted on an overpass at second storey level – many of the streets in Wapping still have these walkways between warehouses – on literally the next building to Jubilee, "Colonial Wharves". Result!

Photographs of Wapping in the war years held in Tower Hamlets library present a discrete area of London. Wapping, like the Isle of Dogs, is an island in the Thames. More than waterways separated it from near-by London, and to an extent still do; customs were different from the surrounding areas and most of the inhabitants were originally Irish Catholics. Areas to the north of Whitechapel Road were mainly Near Eastern. "Where is it? It might be Cairo, Bagdad, Jerusalem, Aleppo, Tunis or Tangier, but, as a matter of fact, it is Petticoat Lane in Whitechapel," writes E.V. Morton in 1925 and it was still exotic in 1943 (Morton, 1940, p. 10).[1]

The island of Wapping is accessed by five bridges threaded with waterways and dotted with wharves. To the north, towards the Tower and jutting out into river is the self-explanatory Execution Wharf and down-river is Shadwell pool and one of the oldest pubs in London, the Prospect of Whitby. Opposite Wapping, over the river, is Bermondsey.

The area between Whitechapel Road and Wapping is partly Shadwell and partly Whitechapel. Here were Eastern European enclaves, full of politics and dotted with committees, often revolutionary, usually left wing, and Jewish groups, who were very active in the community, and which by 1943 ran most of the local play centres and refuges. Between Shadwell and the river, the other side of old St. George's Street, lay Wapping, a stone's throw from the Tower, a cat's cradle of canals and wharves.

Writing in 2000, Peter Ackroyd describes Wapping as "blasted by decay". He says "The area of Wapping itself is hard to find, with its high street running beneath the walls of the old warehouses, while the adjacent streets seemed to wish to conceal themselves behind gasworks and tenements" (Ackroyd, p. 553). Today, only a decade later, Wapping, and other dilapidated docklands now house the wealthy, mostly in converted warehouses, while the less wealthy still live in their shadows in modern developments.

In March 2010 I took this information to Wapping and walked from the site of Freda's lodgings in the London Hospital Students' Hostel on Philpot Street, south to Wapping. I tried to find the post office on Philpot Street where there had been a heist early in 1943: "There was a hold-up at the Post Office in Philpot Street last Saturday afternoon – some fellows in a car. They dashed off but ran into a wall in Stepney Way and were caught" Freda wrote at the end of January. The bomb shelter, or a building which could have been a shelter, at the bottom of Philpot Street was not visible. The cinema on Commercial Road may be one that Freda visited. I walked on past Shadwell tube and under the railway at Cable Street.

At night, when the siren sounded, Freda got out of bed, threw on clothes lying ready, grabbed her helmet, torch and gas mask and raced down stairs. In "black nothingness, in which you move gingerly for fear you will meet something" (Farson, *Bomber's Moon*, p. 15), the road lit only by searchlights, flares or fires, she found her way to Wapping.

She cycled or ran down Philpot Street, past the post office and the remains of the synagogue, across Commercial Road by the cinema, and skirted the railway along to Cable Street, scene of the so-called massacre when Oswald Mosley's Blackshirts marched provocatively in 1936. If it was too dangerous to cross St. George's park, or if she was cycling, she took the long way round by Shadwell station, in fact I believe that's her route because she mentions passing the underground. Once past St. George's she crossed the Highway over to Wapping Lane, which winds down to the river. Or she might have taken Garnet Street, along Shadwell pool, and then turned right at Wapping Wall to follow the High Street along the curve of the river to Colonial Wharves. Or she cut through to the High Street via Reardon Path, passing St John's graveyard and school. Looking back from St John's towards Whitechapel, she saw St. George's spire on moonlit nights, often caught in a web of searchlights. Colonial was a few minutes away, via Hermitage Wall, down Hellings Street.

Her route depended on where the bombs were landing that night, where shrapnel was falling from anti-aircraft batteries, whether any roads were blocked with rubble or barred by ARP wardens because of dangerous buildings, gas leaks or fires: she took whichever route appeared to be the safest.

Royal Jubilee Buildings and Colonial Wharves no longer stand.[2] Jubilee Buildings were replaced in 2002 by peculiarly shaped, interestingly coloured apartment blocks called Halcyon Wharf. No mention is made of the buildings which used to stand there, so when I went looking for them in 2010, I walked up and down, asking in shops, and estate agents if anyone had heard of Royal Jubilee Buildings and Colonial Wharves, the photo from Tower Hamlets Library getting more and more battered as I showed it to everyone.[3] The search led me to P&J Bakers for a Wapping Whopper[4] and to the Best One convenience stores opposite, where even Tom, the oldest local historian, did not remember Royal Jubilee Buildings.

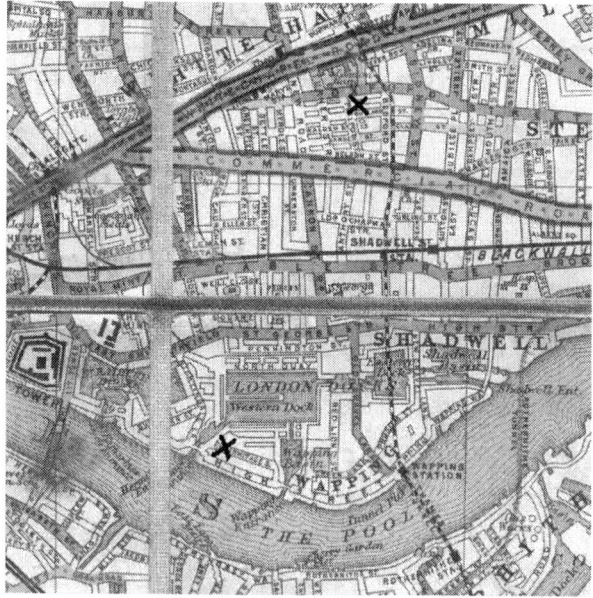

Figure 5 Batholomew's pre-war map

I took a long walk up to Whitechapel and along the Mile End Road to the Bancroft library, where the librarians produced Kelly's directories for 1943, which list all the businesses and many of the houses along Wapping High Street. Armed with this information, I walked back down to the river. Now I knew where Freda had done her relief work but all I found of the old buildings was one length of brick wall in an alley between apartment blocks, along what was in 1943, Orange Court.

The shape of roads has stayed more or less the same, though a few have been added and one, Bushell Street, remains only as a driveway into a car park under one of the new blocks of flats.

Walking east from the Ministry of Labour for Port Workers, down the High Street, there are many older buildings which Freda would have known but I could not find anywhere fitting the description of the Play Centre, the old Sugar Loaf pub before it was bombed. The building was very small, 12'x12', no bigger than a two-up, two-down terraced house. Wapping was full of gigantic wharves and warehouses with extensive tenement blocks for the dockworkers, cut by narrow lanes and lined with older buildings and small stores. There were 29 pubs along Wapping High St. I walked and imagined the old Sugar Loaf somewhere between Execution Wharf and the Town of Ramsgate or the Captain Kidd, near one of the numerous small businesses listed in Kelly's Directory: Frederick Tomlinson's coffee rooms near Plough Alley, Frederick Garratt's and Ernest Dunkley's dining rooms on opposite sides of the High Street; Mrs. Florence Johnson's dining rooms on Reardon Path, near to Mrs. Ellen Elizabeth Walsh's tobacconists, close by Alfred Backler: hairdresser's; A.B. Mackay, a baker near Orange Court, Leslie Symon's grocery near Sampson Street, and the Globe public house, owner: Mrs. Sarah Want.

I sat near the Old Stairs to imagine Wapping in blackout, the river glinting through narrow gaps between the wharfs. When Freda describes seeing "barges with their lovely red sails silhouetted against the evening sky". She may have sat near the gardens at East Pier or near one of the many beaches revealed at low tide but she is probably seeing them through blitzed buildings, possibly through Hermitage Steam Wharf, or from Hermitage steps, because the river cannot be seen from most of the original narrow or winding gaps which remain.

Hermitage Wharf was immediately opposite Royal Jubilee Buildings. Bombed in the Blitz, it provided a clear view over the Thames from Jubilee Buildings to the Bermondsey wharves and church spires, St James' still standing proud and to the right is Tower Bridge. Hermitage Memorial Park now stands on the site of the wharf and Royal Jubilee Buildings stood to the left of the dove sculpture in the photograph below. The park is dedicated to the memory of East London civilians killed during the war. Looking left, down river, the wide Thames snakes East, round to the Isle of Dogs and Canary Wharf, and on out to the Channel. The river was the Luftwaffe's path to London.

When Freda and Mary Shaw worked in Wapping during 1943, many of the larger buildings were bombed-out shells and many houses had been reduced to rubble in the Blitz, forming an adventure playground for children. Some buildings were turned into temporary accommodation, as the Sugar Loaf pub became the Play Centre. Organisations such as the F.A.U. provided necessary equipment, which in the case of the Sugar Loaf was intriguing: "a very ancient, toothless piano, which has to be propped up" Freda tells Jack. Brenda Friedrich, who joined the Unit after Freda, remembers Wapping with affection.[5]

Figure 6 Hermitage Wharf park in 2010

There was an eerie feeling about Wapping High Street in the moonlight: the stark moonlight against one side of the warehouse and the deep, deep shadows on the other side – I could almost paint it. Very often at the end of my shelter round we would stop off at the Prospect of Whitby, which was the first time I had ever been to a pub or seen anyone drink alcohol. But a lovely fraternity developed between all the people in the area and for years after I would go down there and someone in the street would say 'Hi Brenda!' It was a very warm feeling. (Smith, p. 86-7)

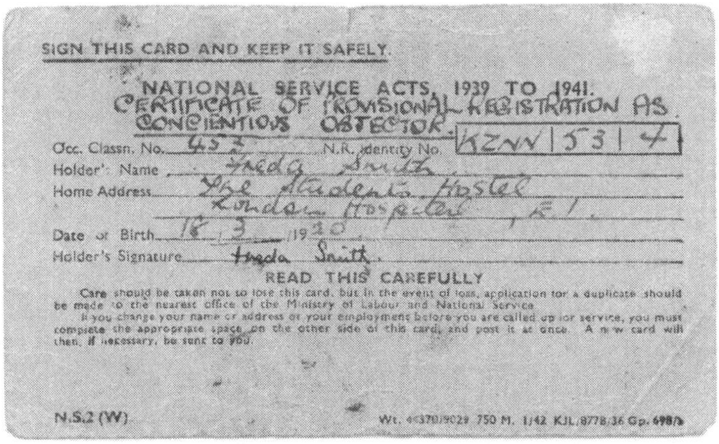
SIGN THIS CARD AND KEEP IT SAFELY.

NATIONAL SERVICE ACTS, 1939 TO 1941.
CERTIFICATE OF PROVISIONAL REGISTRATION AS CONSCIENTIOUS OBJECTOR.

Occ. Classn. No. 453 N.R. Identity No. KZNV | 53 | 4
Holder's Name Freda Smith
Home Address The Students Hostel London Hospital, E.1.
Date of Birth 18 3 1920
Holder's Signature Freda Smith.

READ THIS CAREFULLY

Care should be taken not to lose this card, but in the event of loss, application for a duplicate should be made to the nearest office of the Ministry of Labour and National Service.

If you change your name or address or your employment before you are called up for service, you must complete the appropriate space on the other side of this card, and post it at once. A new card will then, if necessary, be sent to you.

N.S.2 (W) Wt. 46370/9029 750 M. 1/42 KJL/8778/36 Gp. 698/5

Figure 7 Freda's Conscientious Objector identification card

The first letter Freda wrote to Jack says hopefully that there is now no blitz, but only a week later she mentions nightly bombing. In fact, nobody knew what night would bring and the members of the Friend's Ambulance Unit were always on the alert in case another 7th September 1940 came along and a new Blitz began.

Marjorie's youth work was in a shelter under Lloyds of London but in the day she worked with Gibraltar refugees. These children were housed near the British Museum and had been forcibly evacuated when Gibraltar defences were reinforced by the British government early in the war.

As soon as conscription for women was introduced in December 1941, women like Freda, who already worked in a pacifist organisation, or belonged to the Peace Pledge Union and did not want to fight or work in armaments factories, had their pacifist beliefs cross-examined in courts called Tribunals. Freda, as far as I can find out, did not have to be examined by Tribunal but most conscientious objectors in WW2 had to undergo sometimes harsh questioning. 1,072 women were sent to Tribunal in WW2. The judges of WW1 Tribunals were generally military men and very harsh but in WW2 Tribunals consisted mainly of civilians. Some judges from the earlier

Tribunals, such as Harold Macmillan, influenced later judgments. Some Tribunals were more strict than others, for instance those in London, Coventry, Plymouth and Bristol. During WW2 257 women were imprisoned for their beliefs, according to Virginia Nicholson (Nicholson, *Millions Like Us*, p. 171).[6] Communism, linked in many people's minds to pacifism, was feared. It was thought that after intense bombardment, when people were depressed and felt let-down by the government, Hitler might offer a peace which pacifists and communists would then accept (McLaine, *Ministry of Morale*, p. 114). Davies recalls that "Some conscientious objectors, some members of the Unit, went to prison, but for the majority the battle of the prisons had been won by the steadfastness of their fathers in the previous war" (Davies, p. 2).

When her pacifism had to be proved, Freda was recuperating in hospital from an attack of measles but she, along with all other pacifists, had to provide letters to prove her good character, and her old boss at Rowntree's not only supported her financially but encouraged her course of action; however his personal reply to Freda is reproduced below. I am shocked at the language used in this letter to Freda and not only because the Cocoa Works was run by Quakers. However, Philip Rowntree believed the Nazis had to be stopped; as a Quaker he was well aware of Nazi treatment of non-Aryans and especially Jewish people and was not a pacifist.[7] Freda presented the letter he wrote to the Tribunal and it was presumably acceptable.

The Unit may also have written in support of her work with shelters and playgroups. Marjorie is quoted in *Pacifists in Action* saying that the Unit would have supported her in her tribunal but she never thought to ask. The experience was "awful. I was terribly nervous," she writes (Smith, p. 53). Once passed by Tribunal, the conscientious objector was issued an identity card by their Ministry of Labour district office. Freda's was in Settles Street, Stepney.

Written on the reverse of Philip Rowntree's letter to Freda is a transcription of the letter he sent to the Tribunal:

> Dear Sir,
> Miss Smith has asked me to make a statement in connection with the hearing of her case by your Tribunal. I have known her for 6 years as she was on my staff for 2 years and I kept in touch when she went to senior work for

other managers at the Cocoa Works. During the whole of that time she has to my knowledge been an active pacifist spending a large part of her own time on pacifist propaganda before the war & otherwise taking a leading part in the young persons group connected with the Society of Friends. Whilst I, personally, am not a member of the Society of Friends, nor do I feel that pacifism is the way to meet the political & social difficulties that confronted this country in September 1939, I do nevertheless respect the sincerity & purpose of the views held by Miss Smith.

She is a competent shorthand-typist and was in a job in a comparatively safe area where she might with reason have expected to be deferred, but Miss Smith preferred to do work which involved personal danger and hardship and which would help to mitigate the distress of people who were suffering in the blitz. Consequently, while the blitz on London was still in progress, she gave in her notice, thereby terminating very good employment, and went to the F.A.U. there to do unpaid work in shelters and rest centres. Fortunately, there have been no raids since Miss Smith went to London, but I understand that she has been doing work in connection with Rest Centres, Day Nurseries, etc.

Yours faithfully

Pacifists who had proved their beliefs were allowed to join the Red Cross or a similar reserved occupation and sometimes the Friends Ambulance Unit was asked to take them. Some objectors were thought to be dishonest and were forced to work for the armed forces or a factory or for the war effort in one way or another.

Being allowed to stay with the F.A.U. was one of Freda's very lucky breaks in life. Though the F.A.U. was not exclusively Quaker, being a pacifist was a condition of service, and being at ease with the Quaker ideals, so Freda felt she belonged in the Unit. Men and women sent to the Unit by Tribunals were refused if they were simply not dynamic enough for the work, or not in sympathy with the main aims of F.A.U., which was to work unpaid and sometimes very hard indeed. Each member helped form the organization, and a degree of social responsibility was demanded which not everybody felt able to offer. During the war 97 women joined the FAU out of a total 1,314 members and in doing so became members of a close-knit self-governing society: "young workers with young leaders… it was indeed our unit, for it was our responsibility to make it what we wanted it to be" (Davies, p. 1).

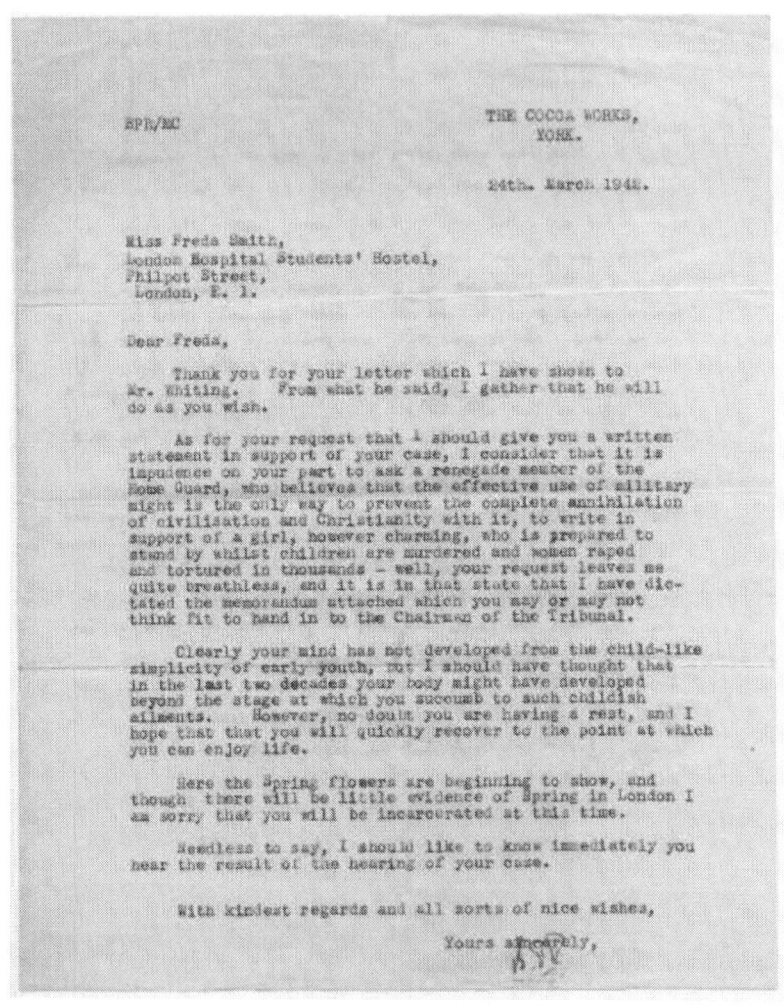

Figure 8 Letter written by BPR, once Freda's manager at Rowntree's

The Friends Ambulance Unit moved into the London Hospital students' hostel for a couple of years when staff were evacuated during the Blitz, 1940-41. The Transport section of 50 men and various vehicles, the Works section who kept the shelters and play centres equipped and in good repair, and a Canteen section who helped various other groups deliver food and drink to the shelters and Rest Centres, were all based at the London Hospital. By the end of 1941, rest centres for bombed-out families no longer took priority and children who had been evacuated were now coming back to London's East End, so when Freda joined in 1941, shelter and play centre work had gained in importance.

Little or no schooling for a year or more caused "moral deterioration in the children of the East End" according to Farson in *Bomber's Moon* (p. 101) published at the end of 1941, the same time the F.A.U. published their manual, *Shelters*. The F.A.U. realised that they could help to occupy bored children who needed to be safe in the early evenings, elsewhere called "the problem of urchins", which is why play centres and clubs like the Sugar Loaf and the Old Mahogany Bar in Wapping came into being. Shelter work began in Limehouse, Whitechapel, Mile End, Poplar, Wapping and Bow, the area collectively known as Tower Hamlets. The F.A.U. provided medical aid workers with first aid kits for air-raid shelters by arrangement with the ARP, all night, every night. Tilbury was the most important local shelter holding 14,000 people each night of raids. Colonial Wharves held 2-300 people.

According to *Shelters*, an internal F.A.U. publication, there were over 80 shelters in the Tower Hamlets area. The F.A.U. provided 50-60 shelter workers, all of them under 25 years old. The major problem at the time was that shelters, built and/or furnished as temporary accommodation, had become second homes as raids continued night after night in the Blitz. Some families, even once the Blitz was over, felt safe at night only when in a shelter. Tickets were distributed for the nearest shelter so that workers would not have to hurry home after work, not knowing whether they would be able to find a space in their local shelter. Visitors were actively discouraged. At dawn or when the raid stopped, before going to work, people would rush home to wash or eat, if they still had a home to go to. If their home had been destroyed, they could eat at a mobile canteen. Washing was more of a problem. Travelling to places of greater safety at night and returning to work in the day was widespread, called "trekking" and it was officially frowned upon. Ian McLaine found that trekkers were thought to be "of a weaker constitutional mental make-up than the rest." The department of Home Intelligence was worried that trekkers would not continue to go back to work but the Department of Home Security thought trekking eminently reasonable behaviour (McLaine, p. 121).

The F.A.U., and eventually local government, had to accept by the end of 1941 that shelters were more than a temporary retreat, and had become places of entertainment and of learning.

> Many adolescent girls appear to read only two-penny weeklies and novelettes, though they sometimes take an interest in the better magazines that deal with domestic life when these are provided for them. Boys, who have recently left school, on the other hand are often the most energetic readers in a shelter and should be given every encouragement. (*Shelters*, p. 23)

Some shelters provided their own entertainments and local bands or theatre troupes visited others. Families were taught about basic hygiene, children were given painting lessons and there were often singing and dancing lessons too, though pianos in East End shelters "received unnecessarily rough treatment" (*Shelters*, p. 28). After the Blitz began, the L.C.C. tried to run their usual evening classes but in the shelters instead of schools. Over 300 subjects were taught with varying success.

The aim in most shelters was to provide a normal life for children as well to try to stop them running riot among the adults, so shelter wardens tried to encourage reasonable bedtime hours by providing separate children's play and sleeping areas. However most shelters were noisy, dirty and smelly, with few flush lavatories. Some still had metal pails in the sleeping areas which rapidly filled up and many had no washing facilities to speak of. A shelter for 8,000 people, diplomatically described in *Bomber's Moon* as somewhere in the East End, still had only bucket lavatories and two water taps. The L.C.C. "are urged" in *Shelters* to provide public baths and the public were urged to use public lavatories before entering their shelter.

Freda and the others were dedicated to the children they worked with in the play centres. As with most F.A.U. projects, the play centres were often equipped and staffed by the F.A.U. to begin with but then passed on to local groups. Unit members had to be self-starters. The ideal Shelter worker is, one who has a patient application to the details of medical work, a cool head and a certain amount of dash in a blitz, sufficient bonhomie to get on with everyone, sufficient sense to organize a shelter committee and to be friendly with wardens without criticizing the authorities too dangerously. The female shelter worker, in addition to possessing these qualities, must be able to tolerate amicably plenty of coarse banter and be able to look after herself. She should be fond of children and able to interest them without indulging them. (Davies, p. 49)

Working overtime was not an F.A.U. concept and members often volunteered extra duties. So, in April 1943 Freda writes to Jack that

> I've let myself in for a nightmare next Saturday afternoon in that I've promised about 14 little girls to take them to St. James & Buckingham Palace. Fortunately Marjorie is coming with me, so it might be worse.
> I hope none of them fall in or get lost or anything. They are all 7 yr. olds, and it seems too ridiculous that they have not seen Buckingham Palace or anywhere, when they have lived in London so long. I had thought of Kensington Gardens, but its rather an awkward Tube journey when there are so many of them.

Freda's mother always wanted her daughter to have "proper work". She should have stayed at Rowntree's or got well-paid work in an armaments factory, like other girls so Freda felt the need to justify her course of action and towards the end of April 1943, she tried to describe to Jack her reasons for working in the Friends Ambulance Unit and why the work was inspiring.

> I know we're a crazy organisation in many ways, & not always terribly efficient, but on the Unit & similar organisations are pinned all my hopes for humanity and reconstruction after the war, as well as at the present time, and while the war is on, I'd like to feel that I was taking a share in its work.

Figure 9 The Middle East Section Office, Gordon Square

    I'm not expressing myself very well, I'm afraid, but hope you will understand me, Jack. Anyway, even if I did not want to remain in the Unit, there would be nothing else much I could do, and you know I would sooner see myself dead than on munitions or any war labour. I hope that doesn't sound terribly dramatic, dear, I didn't mean it to be, but when an individual goes against all that is precious within him, then he is dead indeed and has no contribution to make to the world as a citizen.

    I'm getting terribly serious, aren't I? I'm terribly proud of the fact that I live in this time of great upheaval, and feel that we should say, with Rupert Brooke, "Now God be praised, Who matched us with this hour", and to be young and to be among the rest of the world's youth, who have so much on their shoulders at this time.

    And not only while the war is on, but afterwards, Jack. There's going to be so much to do. I know that time will not be easy or comfortable, but I can fight as well as the next in my own way.

Freda's began work in London with the Quaker organisation, Warvics, the War Victims Relief Service. She worked in the Warvics offices in the London Hospital hostel but lodged in their Cannonbury building. After joining Unit headquarters, "the seats of the mighty" as she called it, in January 1943, she lived in the London Hospital hostel but worked in Gordon Square. Freda's employment at 2-4 Gordon Square was separate from her duties at the Students' Hostel, the Sugar Loaf and Colonial Wharf. The Unit offices were divided into various sections each of which administered working parties, or convoys, whether they were based at home or abroad – Finland, China, Ethiopia, Syria, Egypt, Coventry, Bristol and so on. Initially working for Michael Barratt-Brown and David Tait, from Spring 1943 she began to work exclusively for the Middle East Section under Ronald Joynes, Executive Officer for Overseas Work in the M. East, Ethiopia & Syria. Bill Spray later described Ronald as well-built and larger than life. Freda transcribed airgraphs from outlying medical teams and typed up reports and letters and regularly wrote to colleagues abroad. She tells Jack in April that she's writing to the Archbishop of Canterbury for funds and support of some sort, and "I toil away sending cables and airgraphs to the uttermost ends of the earth with now and then a letter to the War Office thrown in!"

The office photo shows the Middle East section at 4 Gordon Square, with its large picture window. The head of section, which at the time was either Barratt-Brown or Tait, is sitting by the window and Freda sits straight-backed, as always. The map on the wall by Freda's desk is of Syria and the Middle East.

Her desk in Gordon Square allowed her to gaze at the world going by, as she wrote to a colleague in January:

> I have a large desk here – as I type I can look
> right down the street on to Euston Road at the bottom,
> and it's nice to be able to watch the world go by.
> Usually there is a continual stream of taxis – I should
> imagine for most part carrying uniformed individuals
> to and from King's X and Euston and leave. Often a
> rumble of wheels and the jingle-jangle (see latest
> song-hit from U.S.A., a dreadful thing "I've got spurs
> that jingle-jangle-jingle" runs the first line, and babes
> in their cradles even, are crooning it all over the place)

of reins and harnesses gives warning of an approaching horse and van. A dispatch rider has just raced down on a motor-bike and so on.

In March she describes her busy office to Jack, crowded with F.A.U. doctors, who she and Ronald entertain later that evening. They are bound for Addis Ababa and will have to travel there via South Africa:

> Our office is crowded just at the moment as we've got five very excited newly qualified doctors in, busy reading all the dope on Ethiopia before they go out to join the unit there, and they are somewhat noisy at times.
> It's going to be ages before we get them fully equipped, and the poor blighters have to take not only their own equipment but lots of drugs and medical instruments, and also equipment for the others including six saddles, and if the boat goes down, its going will just be too sad.

On February 24th Freda posted to Jack the *Third Report of the Friends' Ambulance Unit: October 1941-September 1942*. Convoys to the Middle East and China, Burma, Ethiopia and Finland are described. Jack would have been familiar with the some of the subject matter of the Finland report, as it was one of the first major operations for his RAF squadron. 10 Squadron bombed the Tirpiz from Lossiemouth in March and April 1942, shortly before Jack arrived there with his unit, 20 OTU. Ronald Joynes later described his time in Finland for *Pacifists in Action*. He arrived in Norway with the Finnish relief expedition of 1940. "When we arrived in Oslo," Ronald says, "we caused a bit of a sensation as we were wearing British Red Cross khaki with jackets from the First World War which were buttoned to the neck." Once the Finland Convoy arrived near the Russian border to help with the evacuation of Finnish nationals, they had to paint over red crosses on the ambulances because the Russians used them as targets: "we were machine-gunned by the 'Molotovs' – the Russian planes." Ronald describes Finns silently skiing up to the front and knifing Russian soldiers: "It was a very bloody war – the slaughter was very bad on both sides" (Smith, p. 96).

The Norwegian campaign was "a complete disaster" Ronald declares, an example being officers taking more fishing rods than guns and "aeroplanes lined up on frozen lakes" like sitting ducks ready for the Germans to destroy (Smith, p. 99). Both stories are corroborated by other sources. Unpublished photographs taken by Captain Hughes, a fighter pilot of 263 Squadron, show aircraft parked on ice, unable either to take off or to land. His notes about the Norway campaign tell of the terrible loss of life among all the services, but especially the pilots of 263 Squadron, many of whom sank with HMS Glorious as they tried to return to Scapa Flow when their transport was bombed by the Scharnhorst and the Gneisenau (sometimes known as The Ugly Sisters or Salmon and Gluckstein).[8]

Ronald also became mixed up in a peculiar situation which involved negotiating for Goering, whose first wife was Swedish, to meet Duff Cooper in England, and make peace. It all sounds rather thrilling, and may have been officially recognised for a time because the defeat of Finland and Norway caused panic in the Government, but the adventure sounds very naive and was nipped in the bud (Smith, p.104-5).

Working as a relief worker, Ronald reached Greece from Denmark via Russia, Egypt and Libya. In Greece, he contracted dysentery and he joined the Greek retreat and the evacuation from Kalamata under German fire, still kitted out in the serviceable WW1 tunic he had worn since the Norway campaign. Roald Dahl describes the same retreat in *Going Solo*, but from an RAF base east of Kalamata. All Roald knew was that the retreating army and rescuing navy were being dive-bombed by Stukas. Ronald writes,

> We hid in olive groves by day, trying to escape the dreaded Stukas and were told to march down to the beach at night in an orderly fashion ... I had a problem because I had my account books tied round my middle. I was also wearing a pair of high riding boots I'd had made in Egypt and was determined not to lose any of this. ... I am indebted to one of my colleagues who, as I was disappearing under the water, hauled me up into the back of a landing craft – by that time I wasn't feeling too good as I had a mild attack of dysentery (Smith, p. 113-114)

The report Jack read also mentions six Unit POWs captured in Greece, and a member captured in Hong Kong and how, as prisoners, they continued their relief work. The China Convoy reports on the hardship of moving heavy hospital equipment along the Burma Road, as Unit trucks race just ahead of the Japanese, saving American medical supplies worth £120,000 bound for Free China. The Transport section frequently has to strip engines mid-journey, cobbling them back together to keep going just a bit longer. They used wood as fuel most of the time. Dr. Seagrave, an American doctor working in a mobile hospital in Burma at the time, recalls men of the China Convoy as "some of the funniest Englishmen I ever met. They pick those blood-covered patients up in their arms as if they were sweet and lovely" (quoted in Davies, p. 249). There are also descriptions of poverty found in war-torn China and India and of dangers faced by relief workers: cholera, typhus and malaria. China was already partly occupied by the Japanese, who were threatening the whole of South Asia. India was under threat of invasion by the Japanese overland from Burma, as well as from Bengal via the sea. Bengal was also beginning to suffer from one of the worst famines of the century.

F.A.U. members attached themselves to any purely medical organisation in need of help and these included the Anglo-French Syrian Hadfield-Spears Mobile Hospitals, also described in the *Report*. One of these mobile hospitals moved to North Africa with the French Division to support Tobruk, where my uncle John, Freda's future husband, was taken prisoner. The Hadfield Spears men view the defence of Tobruk as chaotic and dirty:

> The wounded are brought in fully clothed, in dirty blood-stained uniforms, and their clothes are cut away on the table. Further aggravating factors are the presence of dust during fierce sandstorms, and the constant attention of flies. Theatre staff frequently have to operate non-stop for twenty-four hours with hardly a break, and there is the added strain of working through the noise made by 'enemy' planes and bombs as they attack military objectives nearby.
> (*F.A.U. Third Report*, p.12-13)

The hospital was so close to the front line at Tobruk that two operating theatre trucks were lost in the evacuation. The description in the *Report* is confirmed by the *Imperial War Museum Book of the Desert War 1941-1942*. The flies which covered the sick apparently laid eggs, which became maggots, which helped clean wounds but dust, on the other hand, had no use: it might hide you from the enemy but it also hid the enemy from you. I have Freda's copy of the book and she has marked a page quoting Ronald Joynes, remembering treatment of the enemy in a chapter called 'Casualties'.

> We saw examples of man's inhumanity to man. Some of the Egyptian orderlies were dreadfully uncaring towards those poor Libyans ... There I saw one of the best left hooks ever – delivered by a Quaker from Bristol, to an Egyptian orderly who deliberately picked up a Libyan with a broken arm by the broken arm. (*Desert War*, p. 48)

Jack barely had time to read the F.A.U. report, and certainly had no time to reply to Freda's letter, when Freda wrote again. To be concerned personally about a member of the armed forces was new for Freda – in her letters she certainly never mentions close friends and only once mentions a cousin in any of the services – and this letter to Jack was not the last time she expressed concern but she knew, probably immediately after posting it, that her worries should stay controlled and hidden, at least from Jack himself. She had to tread a fine line between letting him know she was attached to him while not allowing him to worry about her fears. She would not boost his morale or make his job easier by allowing herself the luxury of emotional outbursts.

> Wednesday. March 3rd 1943
>
> My dear Jack,
> This is not meant to pass for a letter, and is really more of a P.S which I should have liked to add to the one I wrote you last week. What I wanted to say then was please don't let too long an interval pass before you write to me, will you? I know you must be having a very busy time, but when I hear the news or look at the papers in the morning I can't help wondering what part you have played in the R.A.F. activities, and wondering if you have returned safely.
> Ought I to worry like this? ... I hope you will not think me exceedingly stupid for doing so, but all this

round the clock bombing is very worrying when I know you all. So I do hope that you will write at regular intervals.

I'm writing this at 11.0 p.m. having just returned from my shelter at Colonial Wharf after the rather pathetic reprisal raid. There were not very many folk down – about 200, bless 'em.

I do hope you are all well, Jack, and the rest of your crew – you had better be, because I'm certainly looking forward to tripping the light fantastic with you once again in May.

- - So treat me gently if I worry now & then!
Good Luck, Jack.
Freda.

Chapter 2: Jack

Figure 10 Jack Denton at home in Norwich

JACK BANFIELD DENTON was born at Bulford army camp near Salisbury. When Jack was a baby his father, a career soldier who had fought on the Western Front in WW1, was posted to Egypt with the Royal Artillery. The family spent almost four years in Cairo, which is where his sister Beryl was born. Back in England, the family were posted to Norfolk but Jack spent most of his youth in a leafy suburb of Norwich. The family had quarters in Norwich Barracks, an imposing red brick building built on Mousehold Heath, high over the city. From the ramparts on a hot summer day it is silent until gorse buds explode open. Swallows fly high against the sun, wheeling, whistling and diving in search of insects or for the mere fun of flying. Shade your eyes to see the whole city spread out below. The river clutches the town, glinting where it catches the sun. The massive castle, the cone-shaped spires of the Anglican cathedral, St. Peter's and the Catholic cathedral all break the horizon.

Jack was the oldest boy, the second of six children. Close to his younger sister Beryl who had just left school, he was a steadying influence on his younger brother William who was now a teenager; Sylvia, his youngest sister, was four years old. Esme, his step sister, was slightly older than Jack. She died in her twenties, not many months after Jack and Freda met. Before the war, Jack's father resigned from the army to work in Norwich prison, situated immediately behind the barracks. The family moved to a permanent house close by, with a garden which bordered the Heath in a rural part of Norwich. Jack and his friends spent long summer days on the Heath with sandwiches and a drink. Sylvia remembers taking lunch to her father at work a couple of blocks away, so Jack probably did so too. She also remembers prisoners locked in their cells, screaming during bombing raids.

Jack was an altar-boy and sang in the choir at St. Leonard's Thorpe, over the road and past the gasworks. He was a quiet, gentle, rather unadventurous and adored child. On leaving school, he worked in a grocery and in the evenings he went to night school to learn draftsmanship. He designed posters for local events and sometimes took his pens and coloured papers onto the Heath to draw the city from above. He joined the Peace Pledge Union when Italy invaded Abyssinia, while it was thought war with Germany could be avoided. After war was declared and once he was old enough, in a move rather out of character but to please his father, he volunteered to serve with the forces but he chose the air force, not the army. His training began on 5th December 1940, shortly after his 18th birthday.

Norwich was close to many major airfields and air force blue would have been the commonest uniform about town. Some of the first raids of the war were flown from Norfolk and Cambridgeshire airports, so maybe it was natural that once he had decided to volunteer to join-up, it would be the air force. If he aimed to be a solitary fighter pilot, he did not make the grade, though his navigator said later that "there wasn't a pilot like Jack". Being part of a tightly knit bomber aircrew probably suited his personality better.

In joining the R.A.F. Jack joined an elite force, one of the few, as Churchill described airmen. It was brave indeed to volunteer to serve with Bomber Command because losses among bomber crews from September 1939, were very high. However, as Freda felt fortunate to be with the F.A.U. so Jack, whatever his initial reservations, felt lucky to be able to do what he learned to love most: to fly.

Jack's first long letter is, like Freda's first long letter, quoted in full. I find it hard to imagine the Jack I know from his letters, piloting a bomber so his letters made me begin to reassess my opinion of Bomber Command. He was calm, gentle, unassuming and could be annoying but never cruel or careless. He comments on Freda's "interesting" work, so he must have read the F.A.U. *Annual Report* Freda sent him on February 24th.

> Sergeant's Mess
> RAF Melbourne
> E. Yorks.
> 5.3.43
>
> My Dear Freda,
> This time you will be pleased to hear that I am not disposing of my correspondence during a lecture period. Your letter has been in my hands for some time now & I hope you will believe me when I say that I really have not had a sufficiently long off-duty period in which to reply until now.
> I don't know whether the weather has been as good in London as it has in Yorks. recently – it really has been wizard here & so of course there has been plenty of flying for me to do. However in spite of the fact that the weather has decided to continue, the powers that be have decided to give us today off. It is now after noon but we have only just risen as we were flying last night.
> Unfortunately we all have to spend the afternoon in camp as we have before us the task of making up our log-books for February's flying – each one of us invariably leaves this job until far in the following month so that the high-ups are just about tearing their hair with rage before F.Sgt Denton and crew finally condescend to submit their log-books for checking.
> Another job that will help me to fill up the afternoon is darning socks & sewing on buttons – a job I am inclined to shirk until the need becomes so desperate that I just have to do something about it. So far the service has not sufficient personnel to provide

each member of air-crew with a W.A.A.F. to do these jobs for us – but we are ever hopeful!!!

I seem to have written a lot of rot so far & I don't expect you will find it very easy to interpret – on top of my poor phraseology you have the added difficulty of deciphering my hopeless handwriting & so on the whole I really do feel quite sorry for you. How much more pleasant to read your legible handwriting (or script to be more accurate] – the mention of your letter reminds me to thank you for the low-down on yourself and the stone you grind – your work really is interesting – it seems such a pity that you are so poor in spite of your worthy work. However you surely must get an angle on life which is different from that which every other Tom Dick & Harry is getting. Most of the people one meets these days are either in the services or doing some other form of so-called war work & it is a pleasant change to hear of someone who is doing something different.

Our job is pretty monotonous although of course you would not think so if you pay too much attention to the newspaper boys. For a start there is a vast difference between London & Melbourne as you would probably imagine.

My crew have been feeling very fed-up with life lately as we have had no opportunity of getting out of camp for many days now so you can imagine how happy everyone will be to get out this evening. It is not yet decided where or how we shall spend the evening but I expect we shall get along to a show of some sort & not a dance as we have so many non-dancers in the crew.

The time I met you at a dance my primary reason for dancing was to give Maxie moral support but he has since quarrelled with his girl friend from the shoe shop & so is not particularly interested in dancing at present. Then again we have George & Wally who are both married men & who therefore have to exercise a great deal of self-discipline in their social activities. George also has the added responsibility of an 8 months old daughter – I'll bet this surprises you as I don't think either of them appear to be the "hen-pecked husband" type.

The rest of the boys are either too faithful to their girl-friends at home or else they are not interested in females at all. My wireless operator, Peter, is in the latter category, his only interests apart from radio being red hot swing & politics. The two other members of the crew are the navigator & and the bomb-aimer. The navigator is of a very serious & systematic nature as most navigators are & as he represents the bigger percentage of the brains of the crew he commands a great deal of respect.

The bomb-aimer is of a very different nature – being a Londoner he is a very happy-go-lucky soul but very good at his job for all that.

In spite of the fact that the 7 of us make up such a peculiar mixture we are quite famous as a crew in that we are always seen together. On such occasions as we have to spend an evening in camp we all occupy ourselves in very diverse ways. For instance since I have been writing this letter the sound effects alone have been alternating between operatic extracts from Maxie & swing numbers from Peter both accompanied by a violent argument between the two gunners.

However I will persevere in spite of the fact that I have just received an ultimatum from the crew that it is time for me to be getting ready for York. I am also beginning to experience a slight difficulty in finding something to say. I think my best plan would be to read through your letter again for inspiration –

How did your dance go off? With a big bang I hope. It has just struck me that I have not been out of camp pleasure-bent since I last went dancing with Marjorie & yourself – I can't imagine how long ago that was but it must have been about 3 weeks now –

Your mention of toasting bread etc. has reminded me of the "Bean-Feasts" we often have here in the hut. We take it in turns to be "duty stooge" & the duties are to light the fire, toast the bread & cook & serve cheese or tinned beans etc, which the rest of us have previously pinched from the mess. Our supplies are also enhanced by the fact that after a night operation we have to pass a poultry farm whilst walking back from the air field to our billets. I am afraid not one of us is saintly enough to walk past at dead of night without pinching one egg each – actually it doesn't seem like stealing as there are so many eggs there. Who am I trying to convince – you or myself?

I notice you have asked me "what sort of a 4 Engined is it anyway" Well, in view of the Official Secrets Act I am afraid I am not allowed to disclose this so I will send you a picture of it instead – that's not telling. I hope you are not a beautiful spy!!!

I really feel that I could go on writing for ever in spite of the fact that nothing ever happens here – however I have just received final notice from the boys that the bus is due to leave in a desperately short space of time so I am sadly afraid I shall have to call it a day this time.

I hope you will not follow my bad example by waiting as long as I did to reply. Well – I would like to linger longer but this must really be finished as my life is endangered if I continue to write!

Sincerely Yours.
Jack.

Jack's letter mentions starting "something more industrious". I knew nothing and as a pacifist myself, never imagined wanting to know anything about bombers in WW2. I despised Arthur 'Butcher' Harris and his Command and I was one of many who thought the actions of Bomber Command shameful, and the only command not to deserve a medal or memorial, the way Fighter and Coastal Command aircrew most obviously did. All the same, Jack's comment was intriguing. A letter written to Freda by Jack's flight engineer in June 1943 recommends *The Aeroplane* as a good source of information and so I took his advice and found that by comparing Jack's letters with reports in *The Aeroplane*, I could begin to work out which bombing missions he had flown. Other sources which have helped me work out what kept Jack so busy, are the RAF station operation record books in the National Archives, now thankfully online, and Freda's own library. Dan Brennan, a mid-upper-gunner in 10 Squadron, an American who trained and flew at the same time as Jack, wrote novels I found on Freda's shelves which gave an idea of how it felt to fly in a WW2 bomber. Brennan's account rarely differs from the first-hand accounts of other aircrew on, for example, BBC Wartime Memories Project, or in books of memoirs such as Martin W. Bowman's *Bombs Away: Dramatic First Hand Accounts of British & Commonwealth Bomber Aircrew in WWII* or on television programmes such as John Sergeant's celebration of the Bomber Command memorial.[9] Conversations with knowledgeable people have often filled in gaps in information gleaned from other websites and books, some of which are listed in the bibliography.

Jack's first letter is dated Sunday, 21st February and when I looked up the date, I found that the target that night was "Bremmen (in heavy raid)" (*The Aeroplane*, March 5, 1943, p. 269). The squadron ORB, operations record book (AIR 27) in the National Archives, confirmed that 10 Squadron had flown on that mission, so this was Jack's "something more industrious". The more I learned, the more I was intrigued by details of bombing raids, impressed by the unequivocal bravery of bomber crews and saddened by wartime and post-war propaganda which scrubbed out Churchill's complete support of Bomber Command and disparaged the part played by area bombing in WW2. Churchill told Stalin in 1942 that "We looked upon [German] morale as a military target," and "We sought no mercy and we would show no mercy."[10]

Jack was undoubtedly inspired by Churchill's praise of bomber crews in his "never so few" speech on the radio at the end of August, 1940. At almost 18 years old he must have dreamed of becoming one of the airmen who with barely restrained "unflinching zeal" will win the war. The role of Bomber Command was cut out of Churchill's speech subsequently because it was thought that to persuade America to join the war, the impression had to be given that England and specifically London, was fighting Germany like David against Goliath. The result is that even now "the few" has come to mean only fighter pilots of the Battle of Britain. Here is the speech, the relevant section quoted in full. Bomber Command, Churchill says, can take a position of pride, unsurpassed even by Fighter Command.[11] It is the bomber crews who will bear the brunt of the war in the air:

> The gratitude of every home in our Island, in our Empire, and indeed throughout the world, except in the abodes of the guilty, goes out to the British airmen who, undaunted by odds, unwearied in their constant challenge

and mortal danger, are turning the tide of the world war by their prowess and by their devotion.

Never in the field of human conflict was so much owed by so many to so few. (Prolonged cheers.) All hearts go out to the fighter pilots, whose brilliant actions we see with our own eyes day after day; but we must never forget that all the time, night after night, month after month, our bomber squadrons travel far into Germany, find their targets in the darkness by the highest navigational skill, aims their attacks, often under the heaviest fire, often with serious loss, with deliberate careful discrimination, and inflict shattering blows upon the whole of the technical and war-making structure of the Nazi power. (Cheers.)
(Winston Churchill's address to Parliament, reported in *The Manchester Guardian*. ©Winston S. Churchill)

Crews training after mid-1941 will also have read *Bomber Command: the Air Ministry's Account of Bomber Command's Offensive Against the Axis September, 1939 – July, 1941* published by the Ministry of Information (MofI).[12] Due praise is given to Fighter Command and fighter production is given priority, but the importance of bombers who can attack Germany's heartland is recognised. The MofI describes the role each bomber crewman plays and the pilot is described as a type of superman.

> The Bomber Pilot differs in training from his colleague flying a Spitfire or a Hurricane. The fighter pilot is in action for an hour and a half to two hours at most, often for less. …. [The Bomber Pilot] must be capable of considerable physical and mental endurance, for it may be necessary for him to remain nine, ten, eleven even twelve hours in the air … They are of necessity subjected to strain." (MofI, p. 10)

An editorial in *The Aeroplane* notes that

> Captains of aeroplanes must develop presence of mind and the ability to control both aircraft and crew, but they can rely on others for navigation, gun-firing and so on, in contrast to the fighter pilots, whose training is not so specialist. (*The Aeroplane*, May 8, 1943, p. 615)

Air crew losses were indeed perceived to be very great, but the public only knew about losses over enemy territory because aircraft lost over the sea or over Britain or in training were not at this stage reported. John Sweetman gives the example of a raid in early 1941 in *Bomber Crew: Taking on the Reich* when eleven Wellingtons were lost, but only three crashes were publicly announced because the other eight crashed in bad weather, when aircraft ran out of fuel trying to land back at base. Sweetman does not fail to remind readers that each heavy bomber carried seven men or more.

Land crew losses are not often remarked but air bases were easy targets. By the close of war over 55,000 air crew had died, but more than 8,000 land crew had also died. When on reconnaissance in Yorkshire in 2010, I spoke to the widow of an engineer who had been ground crew at Melbourne at the same time as Jack. She spoke of his intense disappointment at not being able to join an air crew even though his job was calibrating compasses and without him, night missions would have been jeopdised and more aircrew would have died. The job of ground crew was indeed less glamorous because less dangerous. In his letter posted on 16th March Jack explains that erks (land crew and WAAFs) do all his domestic duties. Apart from that he rarely mentions the erks who looked after his aircraft and his crew, and who manned the canteen and drove the buses and who also stood and waited by the Control Tower, their ambulances, fire engines and crash wagons, the meat wagons, at the ready, praying for the heavies to return and if they did, that they would land safely with all their crew unharmed.

Training a pilot was a long process and initially took around two years, therefore it took 14 years to train the crew of a heavy bomber.[13] In 1943, pilots achieved around 300 flying hours before becoming operational. The process became streamlined as losses increased and aircrew were sent abroad to train in the uncluttered airspace of one of the Colonies – Canada and South Africa, for instance. Of Jack's crew, Derrick, Norman and Peter trained in Canada but Jack seems to have stayed in England. Training included theory of flying, navigation, mechanics, etc, but also drilling and frequent inspections to instill unthinking obedience in the event of emergencies in the air. Jack appears to have been on operations by Autumn 1942 and it was

Figure 11 Sprogs training in Canada, Derrick top left

during operations training that the crew became a team. They became familiar with each other's voices and behaviour patterns and learned how to work as one; all-important when caught in flak or search lights, or if an engine failed and each had to react immediately to the relevant command, and when all commands had to be immediately understood.

Bomber aircrew teams were not assigned by desk boffins but self-selected. There were 25 training stations in the UK and at each, a hangar or large mess was set aside regularly and all trainee aircrew attended. The Long Room at Lords was one but most Operations Training Units used a hangar. Groups or couples or chaps singly milled around and chatted to the other recruits, weighing up their reliability or quick wits. Civilisation is best achieved by allowing men to "pile up and arrange themselves by moving and shuffling about, just as a group of objects thrown into a bag find their own way to join and fit together, often better than they could have been arranged deliberately" comments Sennett discussing Montaigne in the *Guardian* (11 December 2011). The pilot might hook up with an engineer he'd been working with, or a navigator, and then they would work the crowd chatting to all the men until they had a full crew. There are stories of recruits wondering whether they would ever get chosen, as crews formed and they were left unattached. Two of Jack's crew came from his part of the world: his engineer was from March in Cambridgeshire and his wireless operator was from Wroxham, a few miles from Norwich, three of the crew had training in Canada, but who knows why he chose the other four, or why they chose him.

Jack's service record states that he began his training at Uxbridge in December 1940 as an Air Cadet.[14] There, men learned formation flying: men on tricycles with a radio in one hand, pedalled hell-for-leather around the runways. He spent some time in the pilot's reception wing in Torquay, followed by a couple of months with 81 Training wing and at Yeadon near Leeds with 51 Group pool, where his character is deemed to be "V.G.". He became a Leading Aircraftman on 12th July 1941 and from August he learned to fly at Brize Norton. Based with 2 SFTS (Service Flying Training School), he probably flew Oxfords and Harvards, 25 of which were based there. Harvards were squat single-engined bombers. The station was large and also varied because it housed 6 MU (Maintenance Unit) where Gladiators for Norway and Blenheims for Yugoslavia were prepared and serviced. Handley Page Hampdens, precursors of the Halifax, and Supermarine Spitfires were also handled by 6 MU, along with the now obsolete, romantically named Fairey Battles. A couple of weeks before Jack arrived, Oxfordshire airports were targeted by two Junkers 88 of the Luftwaffe which destroyed hangars and 46 aircraft as well as damaging the barrack block and other buildings at Brize. From that date, aircraft were not stored in hangars but were dispersed singly on turning circles at the end of narrow concrete ribbons linked to the edges of runways.

On 29th November 1941 Jack was made a Sergeant. In December that year he was trained, also at Brize, by the AGS (Air Gunnery School) and then in July 1942 he was with the HGCU (Heavy Glider Conversion Unit). In *Action Stations: Military Airfields of Oxfordshire*, Michael Bowyer includes a photograph of a Whitley glider tug landing over Horsas at Brize. The Whitley appears thin and antiquated compared to the massive Halifaxes Jack was soon to fly. Army glider pilots also came to Brize to learn how to fly "the hefty Horsa, intended backbone of the airborne forces" (Bowyer, p. 85). Glider flying was no simple skill and the training was complicated but pilots would be needed for the invasion of Fortress Europe, for the operation which eventually took place in September 1944, called Market Garden. "It took time to marshal the glider, attach the tow rope and position the tug. Accidents were frequent; night training difficult" (Bowyer, p. 85-6). Jack became T/F/SGT or Trainee Flight Sergeant on 1st August 1942 and was posted to 3 (P)AFU (Pilots Advanced Flying Unit) the following month, when he was based at South Cerney, near to Brize Norton. While training with 3 (P)AFU he attended B.A. (beam approach) school at Feltwell back in Norfolk – the skill was necessary for night landing without standard approach lights. Jack gained his Wings at Feltwell.

Having completed his advanced flying training very quickly, in October 1942 he was posted to 20 OTU (Operations Training Unit) at Lossiemouth, the main training unit for the Free French, where he probably flew Avro Ansons and twin-engined Whitleys, still being flown on ops at that time, and Wellingtons.[15] Mac, a Mid-Upper-Gunner from the same squadron as Jack, recently described Whitleys as flying coffins and said, laughing, that it was most unsettling to watch them in the air because their noses pointed down, earthwards. Jack's flying experience now included dropping leaflets over Germany and occupied France, which was called nickelling, and probably mine-laying in the North Sea, called gardening. His aircraft would have carried two bombs as well as 20 packets of leaflets. Accidents were frequent and often fatal and they happened normally because the aircraft being used were damaged or old and not because the trainee pilots were careless or inefficient.

It was recognised early that training new crews was hardly a safe option for crew who had flown a complete tour and were taken off operations. In fact Bowyer writes that 870 aircraft were written off or seriously damaged during training at OTUs between January and December 1941, which inspired "shock and strong words" and caused Command to initiate pilot training in the Colonies, where there were clear skies and little or no air traffic (Bowyer, p. 29). Dai, a pilot in Brennan's *Third Time Down* says

'You live through O.T.U. you live through the war, mate.' He blinked and smiled. 'They kill more crews than the Germans.' (Brennan, 1953, p. 56)

However, this was not the general perception at the time, which must be the reason why, though Freda tried to persuade him to tell them, Jack refused to tell his family when he was transferred from training to active duty on 25th January 1943. He was posted to 1658 Heavy Conversion Unit (HCU) for 10 Squadron at R.A.F. Melbourne in Yorkshire, where he was based for almost exactly 5 months. On 9th May he was discharged "on appointment to a temporary commission" and became Pilot Officer, the commission not confirmed until 22nd May. By then, he had spent a total of 2 years and 156 days as a volunteer with the R.A.F.

HCUs fed into specific squadrons and were closely linked with those squadrons. They taught pilots to convert their skills flying twin-engined light bombers to flying four-engined heavy bombers: Short Stirlings, Avro Lancasters, Handley Page Halifaxes: the heavies they were called. 1658 HCU, originally based at RAF Ricall included 76 and 78 conversion flights, and fed into 76 Squadron at Holme and 78 Squadron at Linton. R.A.F. Melbourne became operational in late 1942 and on 23rd November 1658 HCU added 10 conversion flight, which was called D flight and based at Melbourne. [16] The base itself was functional at best. According to Sgt. Jones there were "ablutions and showers" attached to the mess but where the airmen lived, "about a mile and a half away across ploughed fields we had bucket-type toilets for the huts which were supposed to be emptied every day."[17]

The operations record book for 1658 HCU (AIR 29 613) has not yet been transferred to microform and I had the pleasure of reading the records not on a screen but on a desk and as they had been produced. The record for the day reports,

Weather cold – ground mist. Flying. Night flying carried out. No. 10 Con. Unit absorbed into No 1658. Remains detached at Melbourne. (AIR 29)

The usually spare language of the records suggests that many aircrew, particularly the pilots, were sent on ops some time before they were considered fully trained to fly heavy bombers. They flew as 2nd pilots, or dickie pilots as they sat on the dickie seat next to the pilot, and maybe did not take the controls but would certainly be active crew members; for instance on 17 January 1943, a week before Jack arrived, "5 Pupils detailed for operations as 2nd Pilot". Jack flew gardening operations, mining major sea routes, from mid-1942 but his first bombing missions overland, probably as 2nd pilot, were to the North Italian cities of Genoa, Milan and Turin. I cannot find out how often Jack flew before he officially became operational with 10 Squadron on 4 March, 1943 however there was already a general shortage of aircrew. Max Hastings writes,

> By 1942 most of the pre-war generation of regular aircrew had been killed off, promoted to non-operational posts or left languishing behind German barbed-wire. Now ... the first flower of volunteers of 1939 were reaching the Squadrons. (Hastings, p. 172-3)

The HCU training programme, for example: "Ricall. 29/11/42. Lecture on "Escaping" by F/Lt Pipkin", was interrupted frequently when all the trainers were operational flying or all the training aircraft were being used on operations as well, and sometimes when all the pupils were on operations. On 1 November 1942, for instance and again on 2 November, there was no afternoon training because "pupils standing by for ops in the afternoon, not available for flying". On 20 November there was "A good mornings flying curtailed in afternoon through lack of pupils owing to ops tonight" and on 12 December

> Weather thick today. Birds are walking. Lecture blitz in the morning, half day for flight in the afternoon. Tried to arrange cinema show on dinghy drill, but unfortunately briefing room needed for operations. No crews for night flying. (AIR 29)

Not only was there a lack of crew, trainers or aircraft but the weather also played havoc with Bomber Command training programme throughout the war, especially in the hard Yorkshire winter, when trainee aircrew were often detailed to keep the runways clear, because when ice was thick on the runways it had to be roughened to give the massive aircraft tyres purchase. New Year's Day brought "filthy" weather and a week later: "all aircrew sanding runways in preparation for ops tonight." The following night

"Runways still covered in ice preventing flying. Aircrew sanding runways. Gravel spread, which will have to be brushed after thaw to prevent tyre cuts". Occasionally it was not bad weather or a lack of aircraft, pupils, or trainers which prevented training, because on 24 January, the day before Jack arrived, it is noted sourly: "Experiencing some trouble over refuelling A/C owing to lack of petrol tankers".

On early flights, as a 2nd pilot flying over the Alps to Italy, Jack, still barely out of his teens and who had never set foot abroad or visited London, was impressed by the experience. Commenting on Freda's love of mountains, he recommends a trip over the Alps in his third letter:

> The Alps really do look beautiful on a moonlight night from the air & we always remark on this as we pass over them.

A more recent account describes the Alps as the most memorable aspect of the Italian raids. The scenery was breathtakingly romantic. "It almost seems a pity Keats and Shelley did not live to become airmen and fly with Bomber Command". I think not, but the point is made.[18]

Missions to northern Italian centres of industry took up to fourteen hours. The most dangerous aspect of these trips was unpredictable weather over the Alps. Defence over France and Italy was not as efficient as over Holland and Germany and the trips were long, so for both those reasons the North Italian raids were good training. Unfortunately Jack goes into no detail when discussing Italian ops because, he tells Freda, "This subject of war is very irksome".

The Genoa raid of 7/8 Nov. 1942 is the first time I noticed mention of Dan Brennan flying on ops. He describes this or a similar mission in *Third Time Down* (1961) when he talks of danger Jack never wrote about.

> With the fall, when the hours of darkness grew longer, came decisions from bomber command to raid Italy. It was only a gesture to frighten the Italian troops fighting in the African desert. We flew ten hour missions over France and down across the Alps over Mont Blanc, and in three raids on Milan we lost half the Squadron. Two tail gunners

were carried frozen from their turrets. (Brennan, 1953, p. 6)

I believe Brennan underestimated the effect of bombing Genoa, in particular, as this certainly delayed supplies bound for Rommel in the Desert War when he attacked El Alemein and threatened to take Cairo.

Jack's first reply to Freda, short though it is, introduces his life with 10 Squadron at R.A.F. Melbourne, a base not far from York. Melbourne, like 102 Squadron at Pocklington down the road, and 77 Squadron at Elvington, a few miles north of Melbourne, was for Handley Page Halifax heavy bombers specialising in night raids. These three squadrons became known as "42 base" or "the Clutch", and all three often flew together in formation on raids, they trained together and they shared instructors. For the three or four days after Freda's first letter arrived, Jack was probably training at Riccall or he may have been air-sea rescue training at Lissett, near Bridlington; without his log book this is a matter for conjecture.

Ten Squadron, known as The Shiny Ten, was formed in 1915 and was one of the original WW1 squadrons. In WW2 it became part of Bomber Command 4 Group, which specialised in night bombing operations until mid-1943 when they began to fly daylight ops as well. 10 was the first squadron to raid Berlin, when on 1st/2nd October 1939 they showered the city with leaflets, nickelling they called it. Bomber Command web records that "The squadron's first bombing raid of the war was on 19/20th March 1940, when eight Whitleys, each carrying mixed bomb loads of 1,500 lb, attacked the German minelaying seaplane base at Hornum on the island of Sylt."[19]

There were nineteen Halifax bombers based at Melbourne in Spring 1943, with more arriving every month. Not all went out on every raid. Folklore suggests that each crew flew only one aircraft, which they personalised with nose art. This may have been the case for some squadrons but 10 Squadron crews mixed and matched. I believe ground crew tended to care for a single aircraft but aircrew could be posted to fly in any of their Flight's aircraft. Jack flew in at least seven different aircraft but the one he flew most was ZA-X DT732 and next to that, G for George, HR696, ZA being the call sign for 10 Squadron and the letter distinguished the aircraft.

Ten Squadron's emblem was a speeding arrow pointing downwards, a reminder of the well-aimed arrows of English archers in the Middle Ages, upon whom the fate of battles often rested. Rem acu tangere = to hit the mark

Melbourne was commissioned in mid-1942 and 10 Squadron moved there on 8th August from RAF Leeming, but that autumn the runways were not fully functional and equipment not always available. Until November that year aeroplanes still had to fly over the fields to bomb-up at Pocklington. Melbourne was famous for the windmill at Seaton Ross, the stump of which is still visible from the old Control Tower. Volunteers are repairing the Control Tower and have an impressive collection of 10 Squadron photographs and memorabilia. The Operations Room has been recreated, complete with mannequin officers and WAAFs, telephones, the ops blackboard has missions chalked on it, with crews' names and their aircraft. Behind the Control Tower, the Briefing Room is still identifiable. It is filled with farm equipment now. We were not allowed into the building because birds were nesting near the raised stage where Jack's Commanding Officer once stood, maps behind him red tape stuck all over them to detail raids and routes slated to take place that night. As I leaned into the hut through a gap in the wall, a large creamy white owl flew out, over and past me.

Each aircraft had its own dispersal, or parking place. Jack's was to the west of the windmill and closer to the village of Seaton Ross than to Melbourne.[20] Aircraft lined up only for take-off and inspections. Early in WW1 it was realised that to park aircraft in neat lines close together looked impressive but made them easy targets so whenever possible they were dispersed over a large area around the aerodrome and came together only at take-off and for inspections (a precaution forgotten at Brize Norton until August 1941).

The station was surrounded by farms with Melrose and Breck Street farms at Seaton Ross, being closest to the Huts and near Jack's dispersal.

Jack's crew helped themselves to eggs probably from Breck Street farm and Brennan perhaps describes Melrose farm in this passage:

> After operational tea we piled into the bus waiting outside the mess and rolled along into the cold twilight,

passing the briefing-room, then on between two ploughed fields, passing a brick farm-house on the left side of the road; two children and a woman waved to us from a side window. They were always there when we went past on the way to flights before a raid. (Brennan 1979, p. 62)

Figure 12 Briefing room, R.A.F. Melbourne, 2010

On a crisp March afternoon in 2010 we stood in the Control Tower, Sybil, Freda's friend from school, and I. All was silent. It was very cold. We looked out towards the windmill. In the foreground, the wind sock streamed vertically in the East wind. The sock itself is new but the pole it is attached to is the original pole; there are still trees marking one end of the runway, and the concrete apron of Jack's dispersal is still visible. I drove with Sybil from the old Control Tower, past the wind sock and towards Seaton Ross, and on reaching the main runway, we turned East to face the wood, with the windmill to the right and the control tower to the left and we stopped at take-off point.

The wind whistled through the car windows and I remembered Dan Brennan's description in *Never so Young Again*.[21]

> You leaned against the starboard tail fin and looked at the airdrome. Later how well we were to learn this place! How much it became a part of our lives. The wind sock rigid in the wind, the calm still moment all over the

airdrome just before the first engine starting up somewhere would begin roaring; the windmill silhouetted against the fading sky, a line of geese trooping past from a near-by farm. (Brennan 1946, p. 97)

If a crew had flown that night, they had a good breakfast on landing and were debriefed before grabbing so sleep, sometimes falling asleep in the canteen beforehand, and then got up mid-morning or later to check the noticeboard to see if they were listed to fly that night. Photos from last night's raid would be developed by now and crews studied them to see how they had done. Most days, if not training in the air, crews attended lectures. Air-sea rescue, radar, gunnery or evasion tactics were all taught regularly. If they were flying that night then they cycled or walked over to the aircraft they'd been allotted, talked to the ground crew and flew an air test.

Figure 13 The runways at R.A.F. Melbourne, still visible. Jack's dispersal to the east of Seaton Ross © Google Maps

Briefing followed, and they were told about the target of the night's raid. All the crew were then briefed separately, according to their rôle on the raid. Once the target was known in order to keep it secret, the base was on lockdown.

The crews cycled or walked back to their huts to collect extra clothing for the flight or something to read or letters to write while waiting and if all went well, then they collected in the canteen for operational tea, a fry-up, and afterwards got back into flying gear and congregated in the mess to wait for confirmation of take-off.

Interminable waiting around before take-off: first for the Met officer to judge if the weather was suitable, then for the order to catch the bus at Flights to take them to Dispersal. Before getting tooled up, all identity tags would be checked and all personal belongings would be left in a packet or locker at base so that in case of capture, the enemy would not be able to use personal information in interrogation or be able to identify which airfield they came from, though of course if they were found close to their crashed aircraft, the identification letters might still be visible. So, although it would be comforting to think Jack had a photo of Freda in the cockpit when he was on ops, he would not.

> Buses dropped each crew off at their aircraft, "four-engined, rearing big on clean black tyres on the concrete dispersal point, with the windmill in the field behind silhouetted against a fading western sky" (Brennan, 1946, p. 138).

Once on the aircraft there was very little room so getting settled in took time. Each crew member made sure his part of the mission would run smoothly. Each gun turret was swung to check that the electrics worked properly, each wing flap was waggled, ammo stores were checked and everyone tested his own controls. The crew then had to get back down onto the concrete apron and wait for the final take off command. They chatted to the ground crew and generally kicked their heels, waiting. The go was given, normally a light from the control tower, and the crew clamboured up again, squeezing past one another to their stations. George, Jack's tail gunner, had to launch himself into his seat feet first, no easy task with all the protective gear he had to wear. Mac, a mid-upper gunner, remembers his voluble fury if there was a stand-down now.

On the back of a war report Freda cut from an unidentifiable newspaper in early June, there is an advertisement for the National Savings Committee for Wings for Victory bonds, with a line drawing of an airgunner buckling up his parachute. "Dress for the Party ..." and it says.

> We take off at 18.50 after briefing. It will be cold in the turrets – plenty of clothes – three pullovers, roll top sweater, four pairs of socks – *Mother would laugh.* Of course I wear 'em plus flying kit gloves and scarf – now details – revolver, torch, pipe – baccy – thermos, hot coffee, money, clasp knife, matches – extra scarf and gloves!!! *Yes, mother – I'll need 'em all ....* and then some! chewing gum, chocolate, barley sugar, biscuits, clean rag. I worm myself into the turret, Helmet . ... Parachute. Plug in the Intercom. Engines tested – Captain asks *'All ready?'* O.K. - We're off to another party.

Start all four engines in turn, first inners, then outers, check all gauges and test equipment again, load the machine guns, taxi out over to the runway and wait in radio silence for the green light flashing by the Control tower, the signal to go. The aircraft was heavy with a full bomb load and tanks full of fuel and habitually zig-zagged dangerously down the runway at take-off, which made it too heavy for the pilot to manage the wheel as well as the throttle, so Jack took the wheel, Derrick the throttles and Maxie watched all the gauges, ready to make adjustments. Canadian Donald Bruce says "No one speaks to the pilot, he must not be distracted, his aircraft is heavy and it takes all his concentration to get it off the ground." The tail has to be lifted first so it's necessary to break and rev up which lifts the tail and ducks the nose. Then the brakes are released and lift off is at about 110 mph. "Take-off with full petrol and bomb load is extremely dangerous" (John Sweetman, *Bomber Crew: Taking on the Reich*, p. 84). It was even more dangerous for the early Halifaxes, which were fitted with an engine they were not designed for which made them unstable and liable to turn belly-up on take-off. Nobody took any chances. After take-off, Derrick shimmied down towards the nose, past Norman and Peter while Maxie settled into the dickie seat next to Jack.

Figure 14 Member of Jack's crew. George? Wally?

Operations for the heavy bombers in early 1943 usually happened in the dark because Command learned early in the War in the Air that daylight bombing was too dangerous.[22] In 1943 only the U.S.A.A.F. and the Luftwaffe were flying bombing raids in daylight. Normally take-off was between 10 and midnight, depending on the target, the season and the number of aircraft taking part. However, Jack mentions day flying in May and although day bombing operations were resumed in mid-1943, he could just as easily be writing about flying during the short summer nights when take-off, landing and indeed some of the raids were unavoidably in daylight. On big raids, with 600 or 800 aircraft, 10, 77 and 102 Squadrons of 4

Group would rendezvous for formation and then fly together to join the main force, which could leave from Yorkshire, Lincolnshire or Norfolk.[23]

Operations lasted sometimes most of the night, for raids on Northern Italy for example, or Eastern Germany, but most of Jack's work when he knew Freda was over Happy Valley, as they called the Ruhr industrial area, so he would reckon on being in the air for about five hours and plan to return to Melbourne at 3 or 4 in the morning. The single time he flew to Frankfurt, the flight lasted over seven hours. If he was bombing Berlin, the Big City, flying time would be longer, around 9 hours. As both sides became familiar with the other's radar, routes varied and the Ruhr could be a straight in and out over Holland or it could mean circling Denmark and approaching from the North and then returning back via France.

Figure 15 Peter, radio operator

As Jack's crew walked back to debriefing, via the chicken coops no doubt, control tower staff would record the crew's safe arrival and ground crew would begin to service the aircraft engines and mend any holes in the fuselage or wings. On one occasion Jack had to take off on a sea rescue mission as soon as he had landed but this was unusual.

The Halifax II had a crew of seven under normal circumstances. Maxie, Jack's engineer, describes the seven in a letter to Freda:

> The crew consisted of Jack, pilot: myself flight-engineer: Derrick Adams, bomb-aimer: George Lawson, rear-gunner: Albert Wallis ("Wally") mid-upper gunner: Peter Grimwood wireless operator air-gunner: Norman Plenderleith, navigator. (Maxie to Freda, 9 June 1943)

Figure 16 Norman, navigator

At this stage of his tour of duty, the start of around 30 missions, Jack's responsibility as captain does not seem to have overly affected him. Apart from flying the aircraft, his job was to ensure that the crew stayed alert and on good terms so that each operation ran smoothly.

Like most pilots, he stood in awe of his navigator because, he writes, he "represents the bigger percentage of the brains of the crew, he commands a great deal of respect". In fact navigators were the captains on Luftwaffe aircraft, whereas in the RAF the pilot was the captain, whatever his rank or title or normal duty. RAF captains were frequently non-commissioned, like Jack, piloting flying officers but the captain was always obeyed, whatever rank he was.

Figure 17 Derrick, bomb aimer

Crew members relied on each other to stay alive and a pilot relied on his engineer, literally a right-hand man. The engineer checked fluid levels and mended damaged parts when he could and gave the pilot enough technical information needed to fly the aircraft to the target and to get back in one piece. So, if an engine was hit, it was Maxie who coached it back to work or who advised feathering; if the fuel tank was hit, Maxie changed to the back-up tank and when they were winged, Maxie advised Jack on the viability of the outer and inner engines of that wing. Maxie watched all the gauges and advised crew accordingly. The engineer was trained to take over from a gunner if needed but, more importantly for Jack, he could fly the aircraft in an emergency, for example if Jack was wounded. Maxie was the crew member closest to Jack both in the aircraft and on the ground.

Figure 18 Member of Jack's crew. Maxie?

Melbourne crews with time off usually caught the bus to York to see a film, drink in Betty's bar or dance at the De Grey Rooms. Though I have heard that he does not give an accurate description of Melbourne in 1942-3, Dan Brennan's novel, *Never so Young Again*, compares well with Jack's letters. Their description of dances at the De Grey Rooms are similar.[24]

Jack tells Freda that "usually I am a trifle bored at a dance but not so with you so I must have been in good company!!" while

Brennan writes "Same girls. Same line. Same faces. No thanks" (Brennan, 1944, p. 96), and later,

> The band was playing and it was crowded and hot, and now, like many dances that once were good and became no good when you went to them too often, this one might be good tonight or might not. I didn't know. Dancing bored me. (Brennan, 1944, p. 97)

The De Grey Assembly Rooms are close to the cathedral and steps nearby lead up over the Botham Bar to a narrow walkway on the old town walls. A short distance down the hill the road passes riverside gardens with ruins and a museum. The road then crosses the river by imposing warehouses and continues on up the Mount to the Knavesmire. Betty's Bar is a short walk from the De Grey Rooms, at the end of Blake Street, and opposite, in 1943, was Terry's chocolate shop.

My impression of the Assembly Rooms tallies with Brennan's: "It was a big square hotel with a ballroom on the second floor." Though not a hotel, it is indeed square and imposing. The building now houses York Information Centre and the assembly rooms upstairs were being renovated when I visited in April 2010.

The well of the staircase is lit by a skylight, which would have been blacked out in February 1943, and a small chandelier. The stairs, decorated with bunches of grapes, curve round from a wide entrance hall up to an ornate ballroom the width of the building, again lit with a large skylight and chandeliers.

At one end of the ballroom, to the left on entering, is a stage and to the right are long windows which are now a feature of the ballroom, but which would then have been hidden by black-out curtains. Towards the windows and to the right is the bar in a grand side room, where there was space to sit-out dances.

That year, dances at the De Grey Rooms lasted from 7.30 till 12. On Mondays, Wednesdays and Fridays Bert Keech and his band usually played and dances cost 2/6 but on the Friday Jack and Freda met, admission was 3/- and the band playing was The Assembly Players.

Figure 19 De Grey Assembly Rooms, York

Snowdrops were abundant and cost either 5d. or 10d. a bunch. Jack arrived early for Saturday's dance and bought Freda a large bunch. Bert Keech was playing again and the place was packed, as usual. Varying shades of airforce blue were complemented by reds, greens, yellows all encased in misty cigarette smoke. Jack chewed gum as he waited for Freda to arrive and when she did, she asked him not to. He laughed and lit a cigarette.

On Sunday Jack caught the bus into York to meet Freda and they walked round Clifford's Tower and down over the Ouse and followed the city walls to Mickelgate. Daffodils were not out yet but every tree seemed to be lit by a cone of snowdrops and every front garden scattered with yellow and purple crocuses. They walked up the Mount and over towards the Knavesmire to meet Freda's parents.

The week after Jack and Freda met, he was on ops most nights: "From 15-28th Feb, there were bombing raids on 11 nights and 7 days. Germany was bombed on ten nights and one day" (*The Aeroplane*, March 12, 1943, p. 293). Jack and Freda were not to meet again for a month.

Figure 20 The postcard of the "4 engined" which Jack sent to Freda. She attached his R.A.F. sweetheart brooch. The picture is of a 76 Squadron Halifax heavy bomber.

Chapter 3: March

TUESDAY 9TH MARCH. "I hope you won't gasp in astonishment at my swift reply" Freda writes in her next letter, and goes on to describe the week-end.

Last Saturday, Marjorie and Freda planned to go to *The Merchant of Venice*, though because Marjorie was delayed, they walked along the Embankment instead. This Saturday, they ate at a good Chinese restaurant, probably with some of the returned doctors from the China convoy, which is how they knew the food was authentic. They all crossed over to Regent's Street for coffee afterwards but unlike my mother who enjoyed socialising in the Café Royal in 1935 when 22 years old, Freda at the same age did not enjoy it in 1943.

Entertainment with close friends was more Freda's style than going to the Café Royal or the De Grey Rooms. It wasn't all tea drinking, however. Freda writes to Jack about the hostel later that month but does not mention to him the many occasions she went to the pub opposite or to the Prospect in Wapping, just as Jack rather avoids telling her about the WAAFs at Melbourne.

> Marjorie and I have asked one of two people up to our room for tea. We used to have a tea-drinking gang which we call "Healthy Friendships INC." but it's rather lapsed since most of the "shareholders" left the Section for various training courses.
> Marjorie and I are a sort of team, like you and your crew, and we like to be hospitable and ask folk in for tea, though I can't take a lot of late nights as Marjorie can, and once people get talking and spinning yarns there's no idea when the gathering will break-up. We don't have any "lights-out" or having to be in at a certain time.
> On special occasions such as birthdays, or when parties are going overseas, things sometimes get rather more noisy with a mouth-organ or accordion + singing in various keys, but otherwise these tea-drinking gatherings are very quiet and homely occasions.

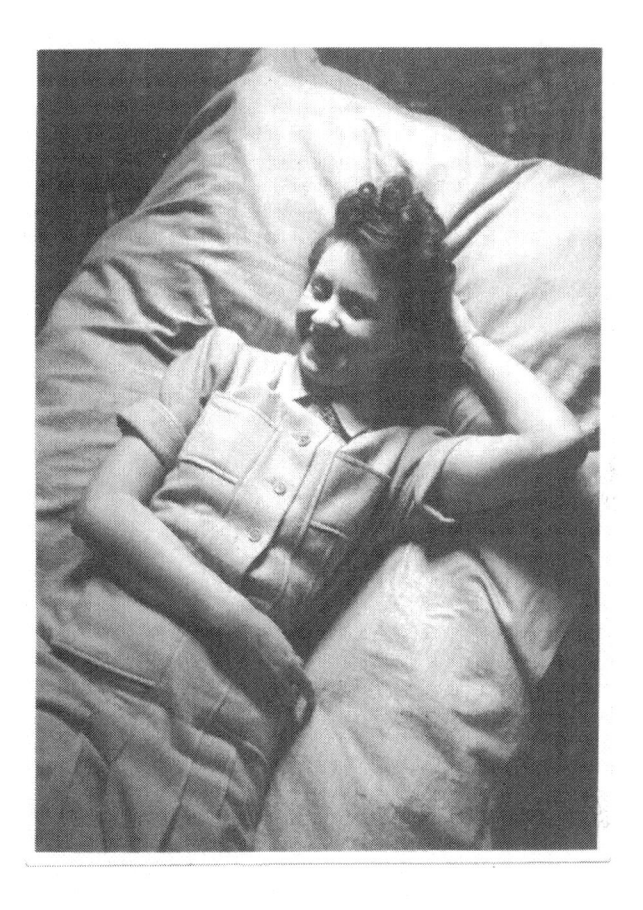

Figure 21 Freda photographed by Stephen Peet in Autumn 1942 on her sloping bed in the London Hospital Students hostel

Freda wrote in a rather different manner to an old hostel friend who was now overseas:

> Since Margaret went, Marjorie and I have reigned there in a somewhat noisy fashion. I shall be very sorry to leave the room when the hostel closes in a few weeks time.
>
> We had a party at the Prospect the other evening, when we ate a simply colossal meal, and well worth the wait we had for it. It was a bright, moonlit night and, at the foot of Pelican Stairs, the silhouettes of the

many and varied river craft stood out brightly against the sky and silence reigned, save for the occasional chug-chug of a police boat and the swish of the water as it passed.

In Melbourne, Jack tells Freda was planning to go to the cinema in York when he had finished his letter of March 5th and as Freda sees quite a number of films she replies telling him about the Troxy which is still on Commercial Road and is still gloriously kitsch. On Churchill's orders, even after Russia officially became an Ally, the Internazionale, the Red Flag, was omitted for a long time from the weekly medley of national anthems which the BBC played every Sunday and which were playing in cinemas. The Red Flag was wildly popular in the East End and welcomed it back into the regular programme. The smaller cinema Freda mentions was at the end of Philpot Street, and painted black and lime green.

> If we go to the local flicks its usually on a Saturday, we rake up a party of around 10, and ask the cooks to save some supper for us.
> Did you go to the flicks on your day off? We have quite a number round Whitechapel. There's a smelly flea-pit at the bottom of the road, but we usually go to the Troxy which is a huge place just down Commercial Rd. They have very lengthy programmes, including an organist & and a stage show of local talent which is often exceedingly funny (though not intentionally).
> The audiences in Stepney are much more lively than in an apathetic city like York. The mere mention by the News Reel Commentator of the word 'Stalin' brings forth a burst of clapping and of course Hitler is greeted in another fashion, and even the youngest seem to know "The Red Flag" so that a mere socialist like me feels very much an outsider, and I look round furtively to see if anyone has noticed my ignorance!

Freda spent many happy evenings by the water at the Prospect of Whitby, just around the bend of the river from Colonial Wharves and quite near to the Troxy. Though Scarborough was Freda's favourite seaside town, she knew Whitby well and owned a few pieces of Whitby jet, and the pub always reminded her of home. She was also fascinated by its history and decor and the steps leading down to the river, and she listened rapt, because it seemed not to have changed, when I described to her a river trip I took past the pub in 2004.

Petticoat Lane, which she frequented, was also close to the hostel. She shopped there for make-up and underwear. Freda played tennis whenever she could and when working for Rowntree's in York, had belonged to their Tennis Club. If there was a party of any description and for any reason, she always joined in and her letters to colleagues abroad are full of tales of parties to welcome people home, to see them off, or for birthdays. She enjoyed cycling and walking, and always expressed a preference for extremes of weather; rather than sit by a fire, she walked in wild wind and rain, and she bathed in burning heat when everyone else had to slope off into the shade.

The second week in March 1943 was Wings for Victory Week in London.[25] All over England cities and towns collected money and bought government bonds and saving stamps to help fund aeroplanes for the R.A.F. The previous year over £100,000,000 was raised Warship Week for the Navy but this year London deserved its Wings, as the *Times* reported on March 19th, because over £39,500,000 was raised, a staggering amount. So this Sunday was rather different from most for Freda, though it began as normal.

Freda writes two accounts of Wings for Victory week. The first is an airgraph to her friend Bertie who was, I believe, in Eritrea and the second to Jack at Melbourne.

> A couple of weeks ago London was in a decidedly continental mood. It was Wings for Victory week and crowds of people flocked from all parts to see the various R.A.F. exhibitions, and the bombers displayed in Trafalgar Square and near St. Paul's.
> It was a glorious weather, and amplifiers were fixed at street corners throughout the city from which bright and cheerful music was relayed to scurrying city workers as they made their way to their offices in the morning. It did not seem like London at all, but rather like some gay continental city, and in the sunshine the red buses shone, and the blue taxis gleamed, while high up in the sky glistened the silver

barrage balloons. If that is Wings for Victory Week, Armistice should see some celebration!

To Jack, she wrote:

> On Sunday morning I made an early start (by which I mean I got up for breakfast – sometimes I stay in bed on Sunday mornings if I'm lazy, and Marjorie scrounges round the kitchen and brings some breakfast up for me – we make sure we are on good terms with the cooks!). Anyway, I made an early start and went down Petticoat Lane (about 10 mts. walk away) in search of hairgrips and make-up. I got the hairgrips but had no luck with the other. Ah me, it's a hard life for a girl these days when she has to spend her Sunday morning in search of such vital commodities! From Petticoat Lane I went on to St. James Park for a walk before lunch. The parks are really lovely just now, with glorious beds of crocuses.
> I wandered through into Trafalgar Square which was just crowded with sightseers to see the Lancaster bomber on display there for London's "Wings for Victory" week. London is in a real holiday mood this week, as you have probably been informed by the newspapers. Flags hang from windows and music blares forth from amplifiers at street corners and the sun shines and the red buses gleam and the blue taxis glisten. There is also a Stirling on view near St. Paul's and a fighter near the Guildhall, with R.A.F. exhibitions everywhere, and everyone (except of course me and my ilk) is flocking along to buy Savings Stamps.
> Marjorie has had an old school-friend of hers here this week-end, so I went along with them to the Parks again in the afternoon. St. James really _is_ lovely in Spring.

The aeroplane at the Guildhall was a Hurricane and what a shame Freda did not investigate further, because nearby, at Dorland House, near the R.A.F. club, there was the mock-up of a Halifax. Freda thanks Jack for the postcard. "Thank you for the Halifax picture by the way. I must stick it on the wall and maybe I shall learn to know a Halifax when I see one." She may have bought an "Aircraft Recognition" card produced by the Proficiency Test department and printed by *The Aeroplane*. I have one for the Handley Page Hampden, precursor of the Halifax. On the front is a photo of the aeroplane but with no information about it and on the back is the same aircraft in black silhouette with salient features outlined in white, from underneath, head on and from the side and with details of its dimensions, weight, performance etc.

Freda gives a full picture of a typical Monday in her life. On day orderly in the kitchens, she describes her week as beginning at dawn with a bath and ending late at night with another bath. I have yet to discover when water rationing was introduced but Freda thought she deserved baths and justified what was certainly a profligate use of water. In her defence she may use bathing to mean washing at a basin.

> I don't go to Gordon Square on Mondays, when I am on orderly at the hostel. We all do one 8-hr shift of orderly each week. I am on kitchen orderly, so my Monday is spent something like this. At 5.0 a.m. I am awakened by the night orderly who presents me with a cup of tea and draws the black-out curtains. At 5.30, having donned an old pair of corduroy slacks and had a bath to waken me up – I've put that the wrong way round haven't I! -----
> To continue (after a terrific supper), at 5.30 am. I present my somewhat sleepy self in the kitchen, and from then until 2.0 p.m. my time is spent in a whirl of washing dishes, setting tables, serving at meals, scrubbing, polishing tables, peeling potatoes, cleaning vegetables and eating. We have two cooks and four orderlies on each shift.
> At 2.0'clock, somewhat shattered, I crawl up to my room on the 3rd floor. As by that time I am pretty grubby, I proceed to add a further layer of grime and clean my room, polish the floor etc. Then I soak off all my grime in a nice hot bath and emerge in time to go down to Wapping to the Play Centre, from which I return at 7.30 p.m. feeling as grubby as ever ...... So now I've told you what I do instead of going to the office on a Monday!

I'm on duty to-night so hope my sleep will not be disturbed by any alert. Crawling out of bed into the chill night air and walking down to Wapping & arriving just in time for the All Clear is not terribly amusing.

It's rather nice when we get to the Shelter, though, to be greeted by a lot of sleepy kids whispering "It's Mary" and "It's Freda" while mother or big sister ask if anything is happening outside.

One of the mothers, whose youngest boy comes to the Play Centre told us that the other day she called him off the street to get washed. Grubby, 9 year old Jackie, mischievous and somewhat-inclined-to-bad-language, told her "Yer can't jaw me – I'm one of God's Lambs";"so I sez to 'im "I don't care if yer one of God's bullocks, come in and get washed".

A Tuesday section meeting at Unit H.Q. in Gordon Square is atmospherically described as she takes up Jack's comments about darning socks.

> Here comes another interruption to this letter, though I shall probably follow your example and write on as per your "lecture-notes". I'm now at a "Section Committee". Each Section has a committee – very democratic & all that – which discusses complaints and criticisms and suggestions, etc. Anyway, the men on the committee are darning socks at the same time. Like you, they get loads of socks to darn; I think there is no more pathetic sight than a man sitting darning socks. It makes my heart bleed to watch them – almost!
>
> Actually, I quite like darning socks – it's a most soothing occupation, but if you take pity on one of the boys and offer to darn a fellow's socks the news spreads through the hostel like wildfire and I am swamped with requests to darn socks and mend sleeping bags etc. As there are about 20 girls and 90 men you can see that it just wouldn't work, so I have to harden my heart! (Snatches of conversation overheard between discussions ... "Do you know

Harry, when I washed my socks the water wouldn't run away ....."!)

On their way to Wapping in an air raid that night, Mary and Freda pass an underground shelter. Many bomb shelters were above ground, as was Colonial Wharves, which I did not realise until visiting Berlin. The bunkers of Berlin were strong enough to withstand the largest bombs but in England the safest shelters were in tube stations, the deepest of which was the Central Line at Liverpool Street.

> You know, our position at Colonial Wharves Shelter is just fantastic. We are in charge of a Medical Aid Post which contains bandages, lint, scissors, oil of cloves, bicarbonate of soda & a small bottle of disinfectant. The Borough Council have taken everything else away, so as far as First Aid is concerned we can do nothing – we haven't even an anti-septic! Of course, if raids began in earnest these necessities would be supplied, but meanwhile if anyone falls in the shelter or knocks themselves, all we can offer is a glass of water and a dry dressing!

Freda lists likes and dislikes towards the end of her letter. She likes Labradors and, sure enough, when Freda finally married my uncle and settled down she immediately bought a black Labrador she called Jet who she trained to follow shoots and later bred from him.

Dislikes include malicious girls: "catty girls like the ones who frequent the De Grey Rooms" and I wonder whether she has particular people in mind. It can't have been easy splitting away from the rest of the Rowntree workers in 1941. Most of them went into munitions or stayed on to produce fuses as well as chocolate at the factory; some joined the Forces as WAAFs or ATS or worked as Land Girls. Only a few left to do pacifist work as Conscientious Objectors. Word would have spread among the girls who went dancing in York that Freda disapproved of their work. She also dislikes "conceited little officers". Both these dislikes are described with a brutality unusual for Freda which suggests unpleasant personal experience.

Freda thought to the end of her life that relationships rather than relations were what mattered. She gives little to her mother and expects less. She was closer to her father, and treasured the perfect replica steam engine he built, which had pride of place on a large sideboard in the front room at 36 Knavesmire Crescent and which her great-nephew James now owns.

> You know, I've written all this blurb, and have yet to give you any line on my likes and dislikes, so perhaps it would be a good plan to give you a list herewith, as follows etc. etc. Where shall I begin? (I like New York in June, how about you etc. – is that the line?!) Anyway, here goes.
> I like: - London, York, and the rugged north, and of all parts of the north the best by far are the counties of Cumberland & Westmorland. My father is a Cumbrian, and I have inherited the Cumbrian's passion for the fells and lakeland.
> I like reading of most types, going to the 'flicks (if there is anything worth seeing) and the theatre (with the same proviso). In summer I like tennis and sunbathing, and at all seasons of the year I like walking, though not en masse.
> I like candle-light, firelight, moonlight, sunlight, the wind, and the rain, and the smell of dust in a country lane after a shower. And of course I like dancing, though this depends on who I am dancing with!
> I just adore dogs, with a definite accent on Labrador-retrievers. I like most things and people I suppose.
> I have some definite dislikes however: I loathe ants, spiders, relations, cinnamon & kindred spices, over-dressed women, gushing women, catty girls like the ones who frequent the De Grey Rooms, and the conceited little officers, either army, navy or Air Force, who throng the place after 10.30 p.m., aspidistras, earnest young women, complacent conchies, youth hostels, ankle socks, novels of the 3/6 & 8/6d. type.
> There's something else I don't like, but can't quite think what it is – something to do with chewing gum & dancing! ---- I wonder what it could be?!!

The reference Freda made to "How about you?" is to a song from the 1941 musical *Babes on Broadway*, starring Judy Garland and Mickey Rooney.[26] The song ends:

I'd love to see your name right beside mine.
I can see we're in harmony,
Looks like we both agree on what to do,
And I like it, how about you?

Flowers gave Freda great pleasure. Her letters are littered with references to the flowers of London squares and parks. She wrote to a colleague on 16th March, the day before Jack unexpectedly arrived in London for the first time, about the crocuses in Gordon Square.

> We are having the most wonderful Spring weather here, after our very mild winter. I hope the Summer is good. All the Spring flowers are out much earlier than usual; there's a terrific bank of crocuses in Gordon Square, purple and white.
> It's not so easy to buy flowers in town now as they are rather expensive- there has been a new law prohibiting sending flowers by rail, so that those from Cornwall and Devon which usually flood the stalls at this time cannot be sent. Small boys can earn as much as £5 over a week-end by cycling down to Brighton and such spots with trailers and returning laden with flowers for which the retailers will give a good price.

On Wednesday 10th March Freda ended her letter to Jack with a description of her afternoon and evening.

> I made a desperate search for make-up this lunchtime, cycling along Oxford Street, Bond Street, Piccadilly, Piccadilly Circus, Shaftesbury Avenue, Charing Cross Rd., The Strand, Aldwych, Kingsway and Southampton Row – in that order, and back again to the Square. My search was not in vain however, as I succeeded in tracking some down at the very last chemists I visited – phew! what a chase – "Vanity of Vanities, saith the Preacher" ----- etc!
> It's about 9.30 p.m. and I'm having a lazy evening at the moment, sitting over the fire in my

dressing gown, which is a blue one of my own design with two huge pockets with "Freda" embroidered on the one, and "Smith" on the other!

Good heavens, what a lot I've written – I do not intend to apologise – you must blame yourself for being such an easy person to write to. I find your letters delightful reading, so I do hope it will not be too long before I hear from you again, though I do appreciate your many difficulties, not least the grim threats from your crew.

It's time I went to bed I suppose; it seems so absurd to think that even as I am writing this to you (10.55 p.m.) you are probably riding the sky miles away – heigh ho, what a world!

Kind regards to Wally & George & Peter, & Maxie and the bomb-aimer & the navigator – and the Flight Sergeant – and to yourself.

All good wishes Jack,
Sincerely yours,
Freda.

P.S. When I was home on leave in York I went dancing at the De Grey rooms and met a Flt/Sgt from some god-forsaken place called Melbourne. I don't know if you know him – Denton was the name. Anyway, remember me to him will you!

Jack had not replied to Freda's first letter immediately and did not reply to this letter very fast either. The delay the first time was because he was posted to a different station for training. This time it was because he had been flying so often. Freda again expressed concern for his safety. Stoicism became the name of the game early in the war and anyone showing less than total fortitude was deemed to be weak or feeble. She wrote "You will notice that I have not as yet mentioned my P.S. written on March 3rd which crossed your letter in the post – I hardly dare, I feel so silly about it, but I do hope you will understand and not mind – I shall know better next time."

On 1/2 March, Jack and his crew raided Berlin. Theirs was one of 302 aircraft - 156 Lancasters, 86 Halifaxes, 60 Stirlings dispatched that night.

> The Pathfinders experienced difficulty in producing concentrated marking because individual parts of the extensive built-up city area of Berlin could not be distinguished on the H$_2$S screens. Bombing photographs showed that the attack was spread over more than 100 square miles ... Some bombs hit the Telefunken works at which the H$_2$S set taken from the Stirling shot down near Rotterdam was being reassembled. The set was completely destroyed in the bombing but a Halifax of 35 Squadron with an almost intact set crashed in Holland on this night and the Germans were able to resume their research in H$_2$S immediately. 17 aircraft – 7 Lancasters, 6 Halifaxes, 4 Stirlings – lost, 5.6 per cent of the force. (Bomber Command Diary © Crown copyright, 2010)

On the night of 3/4 March, they bombed Hamburg, one of 417 aeroplanes, of which 10 were lost. That night the town of Wedell was hit by mistake. Statistically, only a quarter of bombers managed to drop their bombs within 5 miles of the target. On the night of the 4/5 March, the target was Essen and one aeroplane was lost. Jack seems to have flown on all these missions even though Jack's crew officially began active duty with 10 Squadron on 4 March. 5 March was later termed the beginning of the Battle of the Ruhr, and Jack's crew, having flown the previous night, had the night off.

> Objectives in Western Germany bombed ... St. Nazaire, Berlin, Hamburg and Essen were the focal points of four heavy night raids by Bomber Command last week ... Berlin's raid (Mar. 1-2) was the heaviest yet made on the German capital. It lasted half an hour, was favoured by good weather, and the reflection of the fires left burning could be seen by returning air crews from as far away as Bremmen and Hanover ... Halfway through the Essen raid a violent explosion occurred which left a great orange cloud hanging in the sky for some minutes. (*The Aeroplane*, March 12, 1943, p. 297)

The raid on Berlin on 1/2 March was mentioned by Freda in her letter of 3rd March. It is one of the best remembered raids: remembered by Berliners as one of the most terrifying assaults on their city; remembered by Londoners, though initially hushed-up by the government, because retaliation caused the Bethnal Green tube disaster on March 3rd, when firing a new anti-aircraft gun nearby caused panic on the steps down to the platform. Freda scoffed at the official report of the disaster in her letter of 9th March. It would be reasonable to wonder whether there had indeed been a disaster from the description in *Flight* for 11th March, because while on the night of 1/2 March Berlin suffered greatly, only "some" people were killed in the reprisal raid on London.

> The name "Berlin" always acts like a charm on the men of Bomber Command, and the news of a heavy raid on the enemy's capital has an inspiriting effect on all the peoples of the United Nations. March 1st was the day, or, rather, the night. In London people were enjoying lovely weather and saying that March had come in like a lamb. Perhaps the Berliners were saying the same. By night, however, March on the banks of the Spree became a lion – for "The Lion has Wings." For a terrible half-hour the Lancasters, Halifaxes and Stirlings rained down on the guilty Capital a weight of bombs such as it had never experienced before. Among them were 4,000 lb. and 8,000 lb. monsters, besides innumerable incendiaries. … This produced the usual reprisal night raid on London on March 3rd, but the number of raiders sent over was not large. Some people were killed, but no important damage was done. (*Flight*, 11th March 1943, p. 248)

There are four stairways leading down to Bethnal Green station platform, which was used as a bomb shelter, and 172 people were crushed to death on the short run of steps, barely 20 steps and narrow, next to the Park; 62 of these were children. The accident was caused by panic, as Freda suggests to Jack, and not faulty equipment or lack of signs, as official reports claimed.

> Wasn't the Bethnal Green Tube Shelter business dreadful. "No panic" my eye! As Mary Shaw and I were going down to Wapping we passed a shelter at the bottom of Philpot Street and some 50 or 60 frantic women were fighting & screaming to get in. The shelter is underground, & if anyone had fallen there, the same thing would have happened.

The disaster made such an impression on Londoners that people I have spoken to who were children at the time, remember it vividly. News of the stampede was completely withheld for two days and has only recently been fully described and gained historical importance. At the time news of the full extent of the tragedy was embargoed partly because it could be used as propaganda by the enemy. It was believed by some that fear fed by the disaster would encourage people to live underground. Churchill and many officers in the MofI realised that by allowing the scant information released to include the phrase "no panic" only proved there was panic. "The War Cabinet's view was that an oral statement should be made rather than publishing the conclusions. The points which would be included were that there would be modifications to existing arrangements which would stop any further incidents of this kind and that there was no evidence that the disaster was due to Jewish or Fascist elements amongst the people in the shelter"(National Archives releases).[27]

The Berlin raid of 1/2 March 1943 destroyed the Herbarium, along with its Library and millions of irreplaceable specimens. The Grosse Hamburger Strasse area was also badly damaged but not the building nearby where Goebbels collected Jewish Berliners and marched them into trains to extermination camps.

One winter afternoon in late 2009, a friend and I visited the Berlin Humboltstain flak towers and bunker, and this very Berlin raid was mentioned. The bunker museum displayed a poster of a Terrorflieger, a terror flyer as bomber aircrew were called, a skeletal monster with burning eyes, riding astride his flaming bomber in the night sky, fire pouring into Berlin from his down-pointing bony fingers and we were looked at meaningfully, as a group of us, all German except for my friend and I, crammed into a small underground room.[28] We heard about Jack's work, my friend translating for me, and saw the remains of bombs, some of which were designed in Germany and delivered back, as the guide told us with a wry smile, onto Berlin. We saw warning notices about phosphorus bombs – nicknamed by the RAF flowerpots because they burst out in all directions – and we saw photographs of shattered lives.

The first mention I can find of Jack officially flying on operations for 10 Squadron in the squadron Operations Record Book (AIR 27) for 12/13 March, when he flew ZA-O. He had been flying ops from Melbourne for at least a month already as a trainee

On 12th March, Jack's was one of 12 aircraft from Melbourne joining a group of 91 Halifaxes in a total 457 aircraft, who tried to destroy the Krupps factory in Essen, one of the best protected of the Ruhr cities. 23 aircraft were lost on that mission, which was 5 per cent of the force. Although it was a short flight, from around 7.30 to midnight, it was not easy. The route was through the middle of Holland, and Essen itself was protected by banks of searchlights and Ack Ack guns. The Operations Record Books (ORB) distilled its report of the crew's work that night from the crew's debriefing:

> Bombed primary target at 2128 hrs. from 18000 ft. Visibility was good and bombs were dropped on Red and Green Target Markers. The target area appeared to be a mass of fires, these being visible from the Dutch coast. Opposition from A.A. guns was very severe and accurate and large numbers of searchlights were in action.

A photograph taken of the city on the same raid by another aircraft is described by *The Aeroplane* as "Roofless Essen, this area of Essen, adjoining the Krupp works, shows hardly a roof left after the R.A.F.'s second heavy raid on the great German armaments city on the night of March 12-13" (*The Aeroplane*, March 26, 1943, p. 350-1).

Figure 22 Roofless Essen. ©Bomber Command Diary

It had been a busy week for Jack but he does not mention, he would not dream of mentioning, the crash in Seaton Ross, just by his dispersal, when the pilot was killed. The ORB records 10th March that "Sgt Peck crashed near Seaton Ross and all crew killed."[29] Jack talks instead of "hot targets" and according to Dan Brennan these were the industrial towns of the Ruhr: Dortmund, Essen, Bremmen, Cologne, Duisburg, Dusseldorf.

> I know you are fully aware that this is the end of Wings for Victory Week – we blame this for the way we have been made to work during the last week as everyone here feels sure that Bomber Command has just been trying to put up a good show to encourage the British Public. We really have been busy during the last week- operating every night on really hot targets.
>
> I am glad to see that Wings for Victory Week has done so well for itself – such a pity they only had such low-type aircraft as the Lancaster & Stirling on view. I guess all the "Halibags" are too busy displaying themselves over Essen & Bremmen. Professional jealousy? Oh No, not me!
>
> It is now 2 p.m. & I have just risen from my beauty sleep & as there is fortunately a late take-off tonight I am grasping this precious opportunity of answering your letter to me & I do hope you will forgive me if it seems a trifle hurried but if I don't reply now there is no telling just when I will have the opportunity again.

The night of 13/14 March, the crew flew twice in one night:

> Most of the boys are still in bed but Wally is next to me at the table writing his dutiful page & a half to his wife. We have got up rather later than normal today – as a rule we rise at any time between 9 & 11 in the morning but we worked longer than usual last night.

On landing after operations we found ourselves faced with a dinghy search which meant our taking-off again to look for some of our comrades who we presumed to have landed in the sea. I am sadly afraid that the search was not successful but of course we have not given up hope by any means. We were unable to get to bed before 8 am. & so you can easily imagine how fatigued we all are after having flown the whole night through.

Things have been quite peaceful here since I have been writing this letter & I was just about to congratulate myself on it when Norman the navigator suddenly burst into a fit of snoring – I hope he will shut up soon, it is absolutely nerve racking.

The Yorkshire Evening Press for 14th March reports that the raid on Essen the previous night had been a success. "KRUPPS AGAIN HIT" – "BIG EXPLOSIONS: 23 OF OUR BOMBERS LOST"

One pilot who was making his bombing run when the second explosion occurred said that although he was flying at great height, the flames lit up the cockpit of his aircraft.

"When we arrived," the pilot of a Sterling said, "the whole of the target was lit up by fires. Suddenly there was a huge explosion. Below us a great sheet of flame shot up to about 1,000 feet."

Smoke drifted to 15,000 feet. Reports were that German defences had recently been strengthened and one pilot believed "they seemed determined that we shouldn't get through ... As we approached the town I saw three huge cones with at least 50 searchlights in each." The German communiqué declared that civilian districts suffered more than factories that night.

The night Jack bombed Essen, Luftwaffe bombers were out over England. The papers rarely identified which English cities had been attacked, though "North-East Coast towns" usually meant Hull, Newcastle and Sunderland. Hull was around 20 miles from Melbourne, and an easy target because of the confluence of the Ouse and the Trent. On 13/14 March a "mining village" was attacked. The Yorkshire Evening Press reports that

One of the enemy raiders which ventured over the North-East Coast during the night was shot down. This "terror tactic" raid was short, but on the intensive side.

Many searchlights and a strong barrage met the bombers as they flew fairly low from the sea, first to drop flares and then incendiaries and high explosives.

A mining village was rather badly hit, the Miners' Hall, Workmen's Institute, stores, shops, a public house and private houses being damaged. ... Nine people were killed in a neighbouring village, where rescue workers and demolition squads were busy throughout the night [and] a number of incendiaries fell on a town.

One of the men killed was a police sergeant who was buried by fallen masonry when a building was struck as he was running to a fire. When his body was recovered he still had hold of a stirrup pump.

He was Matthew Slack, who had served in the Force for 31 years. He leaves a widow and two sons, one in the Air Force and the other fought at Crete. Of two daughters, one is a nurse.

The same edition announces " 'plane brought down" in, I think, Hull or Sunderland: "At yet another North East Coast Town, houses were demolished." The Germans claimed to have hit Newcastle. That afternoon, Sunday 14th March, while USAAF Flying Fortresses bombed Rouen, enemy aircraft attacked the South Coast and "Defences opened up and British 'planes were seen scurrying across the sky as though in chase of the raiders."

Jack's next letter, postmarked 16th March, was written before take-off for a late raid on 15th March, which suggests a nearby target, probably gardening, sewing mines, in the Baltic. According to the Operations Record Books, there were no ops that night. It is possible that the raid was cancelled, scrubbed. [30]

In his letter, Jack counters Freda's love of rugged landscape with his love of the flat Norfolk Broads. Freda tried to interest him in tennis, and failed, though to please her he agreed to play once. [31] Her pleasure at playing tennis is answered by his at sailing and flying. He remembers that his work, though, has taken him over the highest mountains in Europe. This part of his letter reads like a Boy's Own story of heroes and villains. How many Italians had Jack met, I wonder? Were Italian POWs encamped in York? Sybil remembers an Italian POW camp on the Knavesmire. POWs worked at Melbourne but I am not sure from when. Only one or two Italians flew with the R.A.F. and not in 10 Squadron. De Grey Room girls annoy Jack, just as they annoy Freda and he discusses the whole business of slang as though a practiced career officer.

Jack was about to be given a 48 hr pass. He did not tell Freda, but he hoped to visit London for her birthday on 18th. The letter is finished in a rush, as usual with Jack but I wonder how tired he was while writing it. When he writes phrases such as a "favourite of ours for years" it is easy to forget that Jack is only 20 and the oldest of his crew is only 22. Maxie, to whom he was closest in the crew, sounds like an experienced, erudite man: Maxie was 18 at the time Jack wrote this letter.

> Are you good at tennis? – I have never attempted it. My speciality is rowing or swimming, especially on the Norfolk Broads.
>
> Have you ever toured the Broads? In peacetime I used to spend all my summer days there. They were such happy days too & I often wonder if they will hold the same attraction for me after the war. Broadlands is just about as flat as Cumberland is rugged.
>
> I am sure you would enjoy accompanying me when we fly over the Alps as we often do when we raid Turin, Milan & Genoa. The Alps really do look beautiful on a moonlight night from the air & we always remark on this as we pass over them. I bet the enemy never guesses that aircrews talk on these lines just before we go in & bomb the hell out of them.
>
> I confess to feeling quite sorry for the Italians. Those that I have met in this country do not seem to worry which way the war goes. I guess the poor Italians stand only to lose whatever happens.
>
> This subject of war is very irksome – I seem to have let my pen run away with me. I do not usually discuss it. I am not greatly interested in the details of the war – I merely believe that it is necessary for us to win & the sooner the better.

I don't suppose you know much of air-force slang since you have had so little contact with RAF personnel. Most of the De Grey Rooms girls use it very freely but this is not appreciated by most of us, as aircrew boys are inclined to be very jealous of their slang.

We use these slang terms such a lot that it is hard to curb ourselves from using them in public. I noticed that the Daily Mirror used a favourite word of ours the other day in their front page headline – something to the effect that the R.A.F. pranged Nuremburg. We all took an exceedingly poor view of this as the word "to prang" has been a great favourite of ours for years.

I was greatly impressed by your list of likes and dislikes except of course the one which referred to gum chewing – I have just realised that I am chewing gum right now – I just don't realise how deep-rooted these habits of mine are.

I am glad you like walking & outdoors. Maxie & I often go out walking & on these occasions he takes the opportunity of talking to me about Grand Opera & classics of art, literature & music etc. I don't know anything about these high-brow subjects but Maxie is very entertaining in his conversation & one could hardly be bored with him whatever subject he chose to talk about. Actually he is quite an accomplished musician, actor & artist on top of his present job, which is that of aeronautical engineer, as you know.

On the evening that I wrote you before, we went to the flicks afterwards. (Don't tell me this sounds Irish, I know!) Any way it was a rotten film & I have never been so bored for ages. It was supposed to have been the best film musical of the year but after we had seen it the general feeling was "God help the worst". It was the usual story of the boy & girl team who were trying to make their act famous in show business but the musical scores were really terrible.

After the show Maxie, Peter, Derrick & myself promised each other that we would all go to London to see a really good musical on our next 48 hour pass, just to convince ourselves that such things are still in existence. I don't know whether it was a sincere decision so far as the rest of the boys are concerned or whether it was just said in a moment of extreme disgust. If they do stick to their word I shall certainly come in with them as this will be a good opportunity to meet you, which would really be my whole idea!

Derrick has been worrying me to go to London with him for some time so that he can have the pleasure of showing me around his beloved birthplace but I think I will shake him by travelling down with him & letting you do all the showing round. Anyway, if I do come it may possibly be this fortnight although like most everything in this outfit there is nothing definite I can say about it.

Everything with which the R.A.F. is concerned is clouded with uncertainty & we are all of us wondering just how the R.A.F. manages to function at all let alone function so well.

I really must get this thing in the post right now & I hope I have not made too many mistakes. All the boys are up & fully dressed & clamouring for us to go to briefing, which I must do without further delay. So wish me luck.

The film Jack mentions is hard to identify. That week there were sixteen films showing in York, and one play (*Jupiter Laughs* by A.J.Cronin). The films ranged from *Mrs. Wiggs of the Cabbage Patch* which was showing with *Nightmare*, starring Diana Barrymore. *In Which We Serve* was followed by a concert on the organ by Austin Rayner. St. George's was showing George Formby in *Much Too Shy*. There was a different film every night at the Rialto for the 'Great M.G.M. Musical Week'. If Jack and crew craved "Excitement .. Romance .. Drama .. Comedy" they might have tried *Nine Lives are Not Enough* with Ronald Reagan. The disappointing film Jack's crew saw is more likely to have been either *Ziegfeld Girl* or *For Me and My Gal*; both starred Judy Garland.

Freda does not reply to this letter because by the time it reached her, Jack was already in London himself but her reply would have interested me. Following a very busy fortnight, the crew were indeed presented a 48 hr pass. The plan was to leave base as soon after landing and debriefing as they could so Jack, George, Wally, Derrick,

Peter and Maxie caught the bus to York on Wednesday morning, 17th March.

Wally, George, Jack and Maxie arrived at King's Cross in the evening, too late for Jack to have supper with Freda at the hostel. He may have gone straight to the Chevrons Club to drop off his bags and to phone her at the hostel on Bishopsgate 8425. At some stage, however, Freda was introduced to George, his rear gunner. She had already met Wally along with Maxie, at the De Grey Rooms. It is likely that Jack called her from York station and she stayed at work late and then they all met at King's Cross. George, who worshipped his new baby, will have wanted to rush off home and Wally was also married so he too will not have wanted to linger. Maxie had to catch a connecting train at Euston Road so they walked him there and Freda pointed out to Jack where she worked. They then set off through Bloomsbury down Southampton Row to leave his gear at the Chevrons Club, and to go in search of supper.

Jack and Freda on their own at last, arm in arm, he proudly and she rather self-consciously, as they joked and laughed. He would turn to look at her from time to time, wondering that such a charming, self-assured and beautiful woman was interested in him. Freda, flushed with happiness and pride, also wondered at her luck and hoped, but could not count on, their friendship developing into a partnership, and looked away laughing whenever their eyes met. It may have been on this first evening that they had tea in her room in the hostel, which she shared with Marjorie, who already knew Jack from the De Grey Rooms dance in February. Dennis, one of the other Friends living in the hostel, also joined them, a welcome distraction for a very nervous Freda.

If tea at the hostel was on Wednesday evening, then Jack probably caught the tube over the Whitechapel road to go back to the West End and the Chevron Club before the raids started. Although neither mention a visit to the shelter, it is likely that she took him to see Wapping, probably on Thursday, 18th March. The play centre and the shelter were a large part of her war work which, unlike Jack's, was not described in detail on a daily basis by all the newspapers. They would have followed her route from Philpot Street to Wapping High Street and she would have shown him the bombed-out shells of buildings, the wrecked synagogue on Philpot Street. When they passed girders protruding from the beer works, she probably told him how the gutters frothed and the whole place reeked of beer for days after it was it was hit.[32]

Opposite Jubilee Gardens, just beyond the shelter at Colonial Wharves, they picked their way through the wreckage of Hermitage Wharf to look out over the Thames, which until now he had seen only from the air. At low tide, ships nestled precariously in acres of mud which sank down to a busy brown stream. Barges passed within feet of each other, their sails crashing in the wind. The beach by Wapping Steps was covered with flotsam and jetsam. Ragged seagulls picked among twisted steel cables, fragments of burned wood, broken glass and shiny pebbles. Jack then spoke again about the Broads and how he used to laze in the sun, birding and fishing, the only sounds the wind in the reeds and birdsong, the cold water running between his fingers, and he told her about Norfolk's wide open skies, nowadays contrailed, crisscrossed by fighters and bombers and when he once saw, not the setting sun, but an airfcraft exploding in flames. From the Wharf in Wapping, Tower Bridge stood grey against the brown river. Freda followed Jack's gaze up past the barrage balloons into the sky. All the while they knew the misery they saw from constant shelling of docklands along the London Thames was mirrored along the Berlin Spree. As the tide came in they sat and watched the barges rise, their flapping sails flickered like flares in the late afternoon Spring sun.

They may have walked down river to sit on the steps at the Prospect of Whitby in order to meet friends, as it was Freda's birthday. She had cancelled the party to be held in her honour at the Hostel. This was Jack's first visit to London and they walked for miles and miles: "I expect I almost wore you out – I almost wore myself out I think", she writes when he has left. They visited the theatre that evening to make up for the rotten show Jack saw in York. Or maybe this was Freda's birthday treat. *Blithe Spirit* was still playing at the Duchess; it had been on for a long time so tickets were usually available and as Noel Coward was in the news all week, suffering from flu in California, they probably saw that. Constance Cummings in *The Petrified Forest* was also popular but I wonder whether *Full Swing* at the Palace with Cicely Courtneidge or Ivor Novello's *The Dancing Years* might have been more their style. *Casablanca* was on in Leicester Square but I believe they would have chosen something light and funny and not a film. Later Freda complains that Jack took the programme back up to York, and all the memories with it. The only programme I found in Freda's trunk which dates from this period is for *Bless the Bride*, a musical by A.P. Herbert, with music by Vivian Ellis Guétary at the Aldwych Theatre.

Freda met Jack at Gordon Square at lunchtime on Friday and they caught the 25B bus back from Southampton Row but got off in Kingsway to look at Astral House, part of the Air Ministry. Over the road, St Clement Danes was the RAF church and they sat a while in peace until it got too cold and off they set off again, this time along Fleet Street to a milk bar Freda knew: "so I walked as far as the Milk Bar in Fleet Street – remember? –". Afterwards they walked up the hill to St. Paul's. The fame of St Paul's, standing through the Blitz, whole among ruins, suggests that they must have walked on to see it.

They took the tube back to Westminster and walked up to Trafalgar Square past Downing Street and then down the Mall to Buckingham Palace. St James' Park was already dusty in the spring sunshine but they saw one pelican, which amazed Jack, and Freda admired the crocuses and the daffodils. The fairy tale skyline of Whitehall, the scents, the budding fig trees, the still swans on the lake brought peace and calm to them both. Back up through the long grass to the Ritz, they crossed Piccadilly to walk up through Shepherd's Market to Berkeley Square – one of the most popular hits of the early war years was *A Nightingale Sang in Berkeley Square* – and up through Mayfair to Speakers' Corner and over the road for tea in Oxford Street. Lyons corner house had been commandeered for U.S. servicemen so they may have eaten at Selfridges instead.

On Friday evening, 19th March, Jack met Freda at the Hostel and they walked by the Tower and on down Ludgate Hill to the river, to Freda's favourite London walk along the Embankment to St. James' Park. Lighting up time, or rather blackout time, was at 7.30 and when they reached the Thames, moonlight made mirrors of dark windows and flickered in the swirling water. Bankside power station was a towering dark grey mass on the other side of the river. Warehouses, some skeletal from the blitz, loomed over gun metal water and distorted voices reached out to them. He carried her gas mask and lit their way with her torch.

When they stepped from under Waterloo bridge, music from the Savoy band playing *You Made Me Care* floated down to the river and they began to dance, not the mad jitterbug of the De Grey Rooms but, a slow waltz, along the pavement by the river. Jack steered them over the wide road and into the gardens, where they came to rest by a bench and sat down, laughing. Jack became suddenly quiet and serious. Searching her large brown eyes, he asked Freda to be his wife. She demurred but knew she wanted to marry him but he was glamorous, and she was so obviously envied as she walked around London on his arm, that she did not trust her emotions. She was also scared that her desire to stand out from the crowd made her, a registered CO, fall for him, of all things, a bomber pilot. She cried with pure happiness but would still not say yes, not yet. They held each other very tight.

Later, as they walked towards Charing Cross in the gloom, liquorice-black water slapped busily against the shore reaching out for beached vessels and Big Ben struck 9. Freda pointed out the barricaded Air Ministry, gun emplacements not yet on the alert, but all she could think about was her happiness and her wonderful pilot. It was 8.15 when Jack had asked her to marry hi

They said goodbye hurriedly that Friday night at Euston Road. They fell in love the first time they met in York. The second time they met, in London, they became engaged, or rather Jack proposed to Freda, and in her letter written the very next day, Saturday 20th March, she called Jack's marriage proposal "the delayed action bombshell you dropped in the gardens along the Embankment" and asked Jack: "Would you mind very much if I told you I think of you an awful lot?" Every evening at 8.15 they can be together, though so far apart.

She had been unprepared for Jack's 48hr pass, but Ronald was a very understanding boss. Even though she describes having to catch up with work over the week-end, she goes to a show on Saturday evening.

> I suddenly remembered that a week or two ago I agreed to go dancing to-night with Marjorie and a crowd. Fortunately this was put off, but instead I was dragged in with them to a show, and I've had a simply lousy evening, and after having the supper which was saved for us here at the hostel, I've sneaked away to write this. – And what a dreadful scrawl too, is it not? but honestly, I just feel so tired and (dare I use R.A.F.

slang?!) "browned off" that I've hardly strength to hold my pen firmly!

Did you really have a pleasant leave – sorry, sir, I should say pass, shouldn't I? I expect I almost wore you out – I almost wore myself out I think. I was very tired when I got back to the hostel. It really was the nicest two days I have spent for a long, long time Jack, and believe me that for me to make such a confession is going a long way –

– that space is where I really and truly sighed this time, and not just taken a deep breath! I'm sitting in front of a cosy gas fire, and wishing you were somewhere around, and wondering where you are, and how you are etc. etc. The voices of a couple of drunks float up from the street below – a man and a woman – "Till the lights of London shine again" is their theme song:

    For a while we must part,
    But remember me sweetheart,
    Till the lights of London shine again.[33]

This is only a short letter I'm afraid, because somehow I feel rather shy of writing, and I'm rather waiting for you to write first, though I expect it will be a day or two before you find time, and I hope that you will not take time out of your sleep to write – that would never do.

Ronald spent all the morning dictating letters to me, and I shall be spending all Sunday typing them – I suppose it's time I did some work by way of a change.

I've been without stockings to-day and as a result have got my legs terribly chafed where the hem of my skirt has rubbed against my skin, and it's certainly painful.

Oh dear, what a weird letter this is – I don't know what quite to write about, and, as I've said before, feel I ought to hear from you first. I am shy sometimes, you know – don't dare laugh. I'm just so miserable I could lose my temper at the least little thing, and if you laugh I shall lose it at you too, so hurry and write me a nice letter to keep up my morale.

Arriving at King's Cross that Friday, Jack was left alone with his thoughts. Freda always hated goodbyes and this time more than usually: "I hope you did not mind my slipping off a minute or two before the train left, but I thought that perhaps it was the best way." He was soon busy shepherding George and Wally onto the train, leaning out of the window ready to shout at Maxie to get a bloody move on. He was very tired. The weather was clear, and he guessed that they would be in lectures almost as soon as they got back to base, followed by briefing and then, with any luck, airbound. "At first Maxie would insist on telling me all about the wizard time he had had whereas I with an eye to the future was trying desperately to get some shuteye." In fact, Jack was right and they were indeed slated to fly that evening. The rest of the crew were already at York station. Peter was sheltering in the canteen.

All the mainline stations Jack and Freda knew had been damaged in raids. Travelling by rail in wartime was unsafe. Though trains were blacked out, engine fires and glinting rails could not be hidden from the skies, and stations were always popular targets. York station was bombed on 29th April 1942 and one platform was rendered useless but the glass had already been removed from the roof and was not replaced until the end of the war. The old station at York is still visible in parts. Smith's is still there but the platform ticket barriers next to it which Freda knew have now gone. The station clock, which has always been a meeting place, still hangs over Smiths and tea is still drunk in the canteen where the crew met on 20th March after leave at Easter. The Tea Room, at the end of the mainline platform, with its scalloped frontage, is now a model railway club. The revolving door has gone but the cobbled road leading to the goods platform still winds past it and is still called Tea Room Square, though unofficially. Norwich Thorpe, Jack's local mainline station, was bombed badly in 1940 and 1941. King's Cross was so badly hit that it was almost unrecognizable with the canteen, ticket office, lost luggage offices relocated.

Jack was moody his first day back at base and having the first night scrubbed did not help matters. After a few hours in the air on Sunday, he felt better and wrote to Freda.

> When I arrived at York I had to be wakened
> roughly whereat I staggered out into the cold night air,

half-asleep & allowed myself to be steered into the canteen where we met Peter as he was about to attack his 15th cup of tea – he had already been on the station 3 hours. There was very little room to sit in the canteen but the 3 of us managed to wriggle into the corner where we managed to keep each other awake & in fairly good spirits by talking & imbibing tea until 7.15 when we caught the bus for Melbourne.

Hardly any of us had had any sleep worthy of mention but we all managed to get through the morning without falling asleep although most of the time was spent enduring lectures. In the afternoon I was again wakened roughly, having scrounged an hour's sleep between lunch-time & briefing. From then on we went through all the usual procedures until we finally took off in pretty filthy weather. However, we didn't get half way to the target before we were recalled to base owing to bad weather closing in. We got back at about 11.30 & you can imagine how relieved we were to get to bed & restore ourselves to our usual high standard of fitness!

I still think of you very often & make a special point of this at 8.15 each evening. On the two preceding evenings I have been flying in at 8.15 but I have been lucky on each occasion in that there has been silence over the intercom at that time.

I regret to announce that it is now necessary for me to investigate the needs of my profession – in fact I shall have to pedal like hell to get to this briefing racket in time so please forgive this short letter. I will surely write a longer one as soon as the opportunity arises.

    Sincere good wishes & Love
    Jack

On reading through this letter it really does seem an awful mess but I hope you will forgive me as it has been a terrific rush.

    Friends Ambulance Unit,
    4 Gordon Square.
    London. W.C.1.

March 24th 1943

My dear Jack,

I was hoping I would hear from you to-day, on account of I wanted to wash my hair this evening and thought it would be a good opportunity to write to you at the same time.

So here I am (reminds me of "There was I, upside down"!), anyway, here I am,[34] having washed my hair, drying it over the fire and all ready to pop into bed just as soon as it is dry (my hair I mean, of course), and where you are as I write goodness only knows, but I expect its somewhere en route for your target, or is the weather still bad?

I thought of you when I was in the library at 8.15 this evening, as I sat with my eyes glued to the grey and green pattern on the carpet, and pictured you flying east over the north sea. Not that that's the only time I think of you by any means. Would you mind very much if I told you I think of you an awful lot?

Incidentally, I've had no small amount of teasing from my cheese since last week, and also incidentally, I hope it won't make your head grow too large for your helmet if I mention that one or two individuals here rather feel that you have upset their plans!

Someone yesterday read out to me very pointedly an article in some magazine or other as to why the R.A.F. is so popular among the fair sex.

I hope you are not expecting this letter to be a newsy one, because I thought that by way of a change perhaps I might write more of a chatty one instead – sort of wishful thinking that if you cannot be sitting here talking to me this is the next best thing, and anyway there are one or two things I should rather like to say if I can pluck up the courage to do so.

I'm glad you managed to survive your first day without falling asleep, that would have been dreadful. I also hope, much as I hate to think of you flying, that you did not find it necessary to go and get drunk on Monday night in order to drown your sorrows, and anyway, what sorrows?

Flight Sergeant Denton J.B. I beg to report that your insinuation that I don't work in my "pen pushing" job hurts me deeply, especially when I think how I slogged away all day Sunday and ever since. Anyway, I don't push a pen (except when writing these letters to you, when it's a pleasure) but rather pound a type-writer! A fine thing it is to have you dismiss all my efforts to keep the unit going as a mere nothing, while I toil away sending cables and airgraphs to the uttermost ends of the earth with now and then a letter to the War Office thrown in! If you think I ought to be doing something else tell me, and I'll give your suggestions every consideration etc etc!

When are you due for leave, by the way, and will you be able to get to London for at any rate a week-end of it? It would be nice if you could, and my leave (due somewhere about May 7th) seems such miles and miles away. If I knew anyone going to York, I might think of hitch-hiking up one week-end, though I suppose even if I did you would probably be flying.

By the way, a point that has been much on my mind since Friday is that you've returned north with my favourite photograph and a theatre programme (if you've still got it) as a souvenir and yours very truly is left with not a thing. Can anything be done about it? I'm sure it's about time you sent your mother a photograph of yourself in uniform, and you might find you had one or two extra which you might care to send to a good home! Seriously though, it would be nice to have some little memento, if only an improvement on the Halifax which is stuck in my photo-frame.

Do you still think of me in the same way as you did on Friday night? I've been wondering a lot since then as to just what you do think, and whether it is still the same. I do hope you do not think my hesitation was due to wondering what people would think – I have never been one to worry about such a point; but I did feel that I ought to be quite sure that I was not being influenced in anyway by the "glamour" of a uniform. Does this sound very absurd to you Jack? If it does just roll it up into a cigarette paper, but I was too shy to say all this to you then, and now I feel that I must let you know that whether I like it or not the fact remains that I miss you rather terribly.

I could wrap all this up in all manner of nice compliments about your ability to hit your target in matters not merely aeronautical, and about the delayed action bombshell you dropped in the gardens along the Embankment, but I won't. Instead I will just say that I miss you more than somewhat and am looking forward very much to seeing you some time in the not too distant future.

Goodnight, Jack, and all the luck in the world.
Freda.

Jack's reply to Freda was delayed for a couple of days. Relaxed and comic to begin with, it shows signs of fatigue. Three raids from Melbourne in quick succession were scrubbed because of bad weather, then a group of 36 aircraft from The Clutch joined the Duisburg raid on 26th March; Jack thinks the weather is still too bad to fly but 455 bombers flew that night, 114 of them Halifaxes. "It was a cloudy night and, for once," Bomber Command Diary records, "accurate Oboe sky-marking was lacking because 5 Oboe Mosquitoes were forced to return early with technical difficulties and a sixth was lost. The result was a widely scattered raid."

The following night, Jack's crew was one of 12 from Melbourne who joined 384 planes, including 124 Halifaxes, which set off to attack Berlin. *The Aeroplane* commentary on the week's bombing operations explains that what is now called area bombing was necessary. "The duty of the British and American bomber forces based in Great Britain is to present the enemy in the Reich with a continuous task of defence and repair." The report continues under the subheading "Berlin's Heaviest"

> Bomber Command made three heavy raids last week after the lull caused by unfavourable weather. The first was against St. Nazaire; in the second Duisburg was the principal target; the third gave Berlin its second heaviest raid on the War.
>
> Crews making for the Ruhr to bomb Duisburg had to fly through thick cloud. Between them they carried a great weight of bombs to this largest of Germany's inland ports.

Clouds partly obscured the target, and hindered the searchlights, but three large explosions, each of about 10 seconds' duration, were observed by one pilot.

In the raid on Berlin on the night of Mar. 27-28, more than 900 tons of bombs were dropped, most of them in the half hour between 23.00 and 23.30 hrs. They included a proportion of 8,000-pounders and many 4,000-lb. bombs. (*The Aeroplane*, "The 186th week of The War In The Air" April 2, 1943)

Crews were certainly worked hard, Squadron Leader Thompson "insisted on a very high standard of flying from his pilots" (Rapier, *Melbourne Ten* p. 6), and they appear to have been dog tired much of the time. Wendy Bishop recalls being a WAAF at Grantown, a base in Scotland: "We gave the crew Benzedrine; it is called speed now, to ... keep them awake" (*Their Past*, p. 69). An RAF doctor quoted in *Tail-End Charlies* noticed that crews rapidly became tired and listless, lacking the enthusiasm they had when they first began operations (Nichol and Rennell, p. 127). He said they began to look old.

The weather was still foul on 27th, and Melbourne records "a rough north westerly" even though *The Aeroplane* for that week recorded that the weather had cleared, and "heavy raiding was resumed". There was a lot of 8 mm flak from Berlin that night, according to Rapier (Rapier, p. 34) and over Bremen Jack's aircraft was hit. George, the tail gunner and Derrick, the bomb-aimer, had a close escape when they were flying low, maybe to get a better look at the target, maybe to evade coning, and this seems to be rather a turning point for Jack. A Wellington rear gunner from Grantown said in interview that tail gunners were the most exposed and most often killed of all crew, although on one occasion he was the only survivor in a crash. Wendy Bishop, on the same Scottish base, agreed. "Rear gunners were the most vulnerable, and were usually shot away from the plane, or were dead on landing." Bomb aimers must have felt unprotected too because they were often flat on their bellies as they calculated when to call "Release bombs, Skip," with nothing between them and the flak but Perspex and a narrow sheet of metal for them to lie along as they took aim. (*Their Past*, p. 20, p. 69)

The debriefing report for the Berlin raid on 27th March says that they bombed on Target Markers which were believed to be in the centre of Berlin. Weather was fair and many fires were seen. Flak was moderate at target, but south of BREMEN aircraft was hit in the starboard mainplane at 15000 ft. None of the crew were injured.

The Aeroplane called this raid "one of the most successful and least costly assaults of the R.A.F. of Berlin" but it was apparently poorly marked and therefore off-target. The comment made by the crew in debriefing that the markers were "believed to be" accurate implies to me that Derrick was uncertain that they were, and he was correct. According to Rapier (p. 34) the Pathfinder's yellow target markers were indeed off target. Bomber Command Diary calls this a "failed raid on Berlin". Pathfinders marked areas which were not even in the city. In fact "no bombing photographs were plotted within 5 miles of the aiming point at the centre of Berlin."

The Operations Record Book says that Jack flew ZA-X on all three raids at the end of March however, Jack says he flew S for Sugar to Berlin on 27th, when it was hit, implying that this is his usual kite and that he was having to fly the unfamiliar X on 29th while S was being repaired. Although the discrepancy is minor, unless details are the same in Jack's letters as well as the ORB then they cannot be certain. In this case Jack has no reason at all to tell Freda which aircraft he was flying so it is probably an ORB mistake. Rapier reports that ZA-E's bomb aimer was hit but he does not mention ZA-S or ZA-X.

Two nights later and Jack was again at Berlin: "Monday, March 29 NIGHT .. Main target: Berlin. One Ju88 night fighter shot down by bomber. Twenty-one bombers lost" (*The Aeroplane*, Diary of the Week, April 9, 1943, p. 413). Again Bomber Command Diary calls this a failed raid:[35]

> "Berlin attacked unsuccessfully by 329 aircraft. ... Weather conditions were difficult, with icing and inaccurately forecast winds causing most of the bombs to fall in open countryside 6 miles south east of Berlin."

This Berlin raid, the third in four nights, was a bomb and nickel raid. 30 raiders from The Clutch took part. Visibility would have been poor that night because it was "pouring with rain with cloud up to 16,000 feet" according to the R.A.F. Pocklington web. Jack flew ZA-X, as one of ten aircraft from Melbourne, and was in the air for almost eight hours. Four of the Melbourne bombers came home early because of icing (Rapier, p. 34). 6.4 per cent of the force was lost: 21 aircraft: 11 Lancasters, 7 Halifaxes, 3 Stirlings. Jack's crew reported that they

> Bombed primary target at 01.08 hrs. from 18000 ft. on Target Markers dropped by P.F.F. Built up area was seen and a good number of fires observed. Flak was severe over BERLIN and a large number of searchlights encountered.

The weather boys, or met boys as the meteorologists on base were called, did a bad job at predicting the weather that night. According to Harold Swain two bombs fell on the Anhalter railway station and hit trains loaded with soldiers but most bombs were at least 5 miles off target.[36] The Anhalter station was used by Hitler, being the station nearest to the Chancellery, and it was also close to one of Berlin's largest flak towers, which was also an air raid shelter. The flak tower is now a night club, in a cul-de-sac off the main road from the Anhalter to the river Spree. The railway station ruins are impressive but disconcerting, standing like a triumphal arch to nowhere.[37] Apparently a quarter of the bombs dropped on that raid were duds. As a Luftwaffe stores facility at Teltow outside Berlin was hit badly, the Germans decided that this had been the target.

The U.S.A.A.F. realised at about this period that with such unpredictable weather it made sense for fighters, they normally sent Mustangs, to reconnoitre targets before bombers were launched. Equipped with lightweight extra fuel tanks the fighters could, for the first time, accompany bombers on their raids to Eastern Europe. With the extra fuel, Mustang pilots could scout out the target, describe the weather and visibility accurately and stay on to help protect the bombers as they raided. Once this procedure was functioning, US daylight raiders' efficiency increased. However, the R.A.F. bombers in 1943 had no luck using Mosquitoes as forward fighters and relied on the Met boys before take-off and once at the target, they followed Pathfinder flares.

Losses which were not reported to the general public included the crash of one of Pocklington's Halifaxes as it took-off and crossed the path of a Halifax from either Melbourne or Elvington – the holding pattern for the flight paths of the three stations crossed. Pocklington's G for George took evasive action, stalled, flipped over and crashed. The other unidentified aircraft crew survived. According to Andrew Sefton's web, the weather was too bad to fly that night but the met boys believed it would clear.[38] "The late Raymond Slaughter, the chief firefighter in 1943, holds the fire service report relating to the Halifax crash. The report reveals that the aircraft was fully loaded with high explosives, phosphorus bombs, and incendiary devices." Flying too low for them to escape, they made sure the aircraft crashed away from Pocklington village houses in the full knowledge that none of the crew would survive.

A pilot's task in bad flak or under attack from night fighters was physically exhausting. There are many accounts of 2nd pilots or engineers taking over from tired pilots or helping them hold the controls to keep the aircraft on course. Ted Stocker, an engineer in the Pathfinders 35 Squadron, describes his pilot evading heavy flak in a damaged aircraft after the earlier Berlin raid of $1/2^{nd}$ March:

> The raid seemed to last forever, especially that second time we were caught in the flak. I remember just sitting there, fully illuminated, watching our skipper sweating at the controls, with all hell breaking out around us. ... The journey home was incredibly hard on the pilot.

Tom Wingham of Pocklington, 102 Squadron writes eloquently about the Berlin raid of 29/30 March, 1943.[39] Pilots from the two bases often became acquainted during training on the ground and met again, as they achieved formation in the air before reaching the Channel over Flamborough or Southwold. His description is in chapter 13 of *Bombs Away* (Bowman) and, along with Ted Stocker's account, is also a major part of the December 2009 volume of *Flypast*: 'War of the Roses: Lancaster or Halifax?' His article in *Flypast* is titled 'Canadian Halifax 'Ace': Pathfinding to Berlin'; the chapter in *Bombs Away* is called 'It Just Couldn't Have Happened'. He writes of the closeness of his crew: "Like most crews who managed to survive, we were very close-knit, very rarely being off the station unless we were all together" (Bowman, p. 160). Of the night of 29th March, he recalls that "The weather forecast at briefing was ghastly and our station Met officers unofficially predicted a certain "scrub" so they ended up flying blind, because the windscreen was iced up. They unloaded and turned back before reaching Berlin, with both inner engines damaged" (Bowman, p. 160-1). If Jack was flying blind on the Big City raid of 27th March, that would explain why he was low when hit at 15,000 feet.

On both 27th and 29th Berlin raids, Jack was flying for over seven hours without a break, much of it hard work. Evasive tactics, which being hit would have forced on him, like those described by Tom Wingham, were exhausting. From this stage, less than a month since Jack began operational flying as captain, he became progressively more conscious of the heavy responsibility he had for his men. Jack managed to write to Freda just before the Duisburg raid.[40]

> Fl/Sgt Denton J.B.
> Sergeants Mess.
> RAF. Melbourne.
> E. Yorks.
> March 26th 1942.
>
> My Dear Freda,
> I was so happy to hear from you this morning. It certainly brightened me up a great deal since I have been feeling decidedly "cheesed off" (modernised form of "browned off") for the past 2 or 3 days. The weather has been bad & although we have been working pretty hard all this time, there has been little flying – hence the "cheesed off" feeling.
> It is raining outside now & I don't expect there will be a great deal cooking tonight although I expect we shall go through all the usual preparatory actions. However, so much for the shop talk!
> On second thoughts whilst on the subject of work I feel I must apologise for the wise-cracks against pen-pushers – but since you are a typewriter basher instead I think we can dismiss the whole issue as inapplicable. I hope that by now you have pulled up on all your neglected work – it will be too bad if you haven't by the time I come on leave again. This should be in the next 3 weeks sometime but as I happen to be in the R.A.F. believe it or not one cannot place a high degree of reliability on this estimate. Being one of the lucky

types, I usually have about 3 cancellations, advancements or postponements before it eventually materialises, but if all goes well 3 weeks should prove a fairly accurate guess.

You asked me if I still think of you as I did on the famous Friday night & my answer is "Of course I do." I am thinking of you almost constantly & I don't think I shall ever be able to forget you. I could feel myself getting more & more in love with you each moment I spent with you & some inner thought suggested that this was no temporary infatuation.

I feel a trifle guilty for having put forward my proposal so suddenly as this must have taken you by surprise our having known each other for such a short time. But I did feel that I knew what I was doing & time has since confirmed in my mind that I did not make any mistake as far as my own desires are concerned. When I asked you to become engaged I rather anticipated that your answer would not be a direct "yes" – I guess it is a necessity for you to be the type who likes to think things over thoroughly unlike my type which is always quickly decided! Then again I was not very, shall I say diplomatic, as I did not leave a great deal of time to discuss matters.

Apart from the fact that I love you deeply & feel that I always shall I guess we should have mentioned that ghastly word money. I have always been the extravagant type & I guess I am not entirely cured of this vice (?) & as a consequence I am afraid I have not saved nearly as much as I could have done but who could ever foresee me falling in love?

However if I am given reason to try, there is no reason why I should not save quite fast & add to the moderate hoard that I have. This sort of talk is painfully practical & in all probability very premature but I guess it will give you some idea of our future situation & will give you something to consider in your spare "sticking around" moments.

Then again, I guess I should have talked about many other things, to do the whole thing properly, but to me they all seem to be such secondary considerations. In the meantime I will certainly attend to your desire for a photo – I will get organised on it the next time I go into York, whenever that is. Mind you this will be a loathsome task for me but as it is for you I will endure it as bravely as I can.

By the way, at this stage of the war I did not realise that there was still such a thing as the "glamour of a uniform" so this remark of yours has shaken me to the core. But, Freda, if ever you decide you are not just being influenced by this glamour you may rest assured that I am still asking & and just waiting for you to give up merely sticking around.

Here I regret to say there has been a pause of no less than 48 hours duration.

I started writing this letter on Friday & I wish I had had sufficient time to round it off then but we operated on Friday night and last night as well, when we did a long trip to the capital of the Fatherland.

In a short while I shall have to do an air-test on a different machine as poor old "S for sugar" had a rough time last night & this time it was George & Derrick who had narrow escapes. I am afraid this air test will mean that I shall have to close this letter & get it into the post before there are any more delays.

I had intended you to have this letter yesterday but no one can tell you when you will get it now as today is Sunday & everybody just dies in Melbourne on a Sunday – but I will post it right away & then pray for a quick deliverance. I trust you will pardon the delay of my reply & also this very patchy letter – I am hoping to have a day-off in a couple of days time when I will endeavour to write a really decent letter to you.

I seem always to be excusing myself like this but I am convinced the pace will slacken off soon when I shall be able to give you much more of my time. Until then I'll just keep you in my thoughts & not let you leave them any more than I can help.

And so, Freda Darling,
Cheerio for a little while.
Jack.

Jack was to fly to Berlin again the following night; one night off between very heavy raids.

In London, the Students' Hostel was being redeveloped and most F.A.U. members based there were moving to other lodgings. The atmosphere at the hostel was soon to change and it became a quieter place to live but at the end of March Freda was still sharing a room with Marjorie and working at Gordon Square in the day, at the Sugar Loaf many evenings and on air raid duty every night and the hostel was still full of friendly faces.

>
> FRIENDS' AMBULANCE UNIT
> 4 GORDON SQUARE
> LONDON, W.C.1.
> MUSeum 5986/7/8
> Tuesday 28. 4.0 p.m
>
> My dear Jack,
> Very many thanks for your letter which I found waiting for me when I arrived here this morning. Don't think for one moment that this is meant to be anything like a reply, or even an apology for one. I shall probably curl myself up in front of the fire tomorrow evening to write you properly – I can't this evening, but I thought I would just turn aside and let my typewriter cool down for a moment in order to drop you this thank-you for your very nice letter.
> Actually, I've just heard about last night's raid, in which you were probably occupied, and so I'm feeling rather sick and writing all this with my fingers crossed for you, and it seems such a long time until tomorrow when I really can write to you. I hope you'll overlook the official note-paper, in view of the circs.
> I'm afraid I get rather tongue-tied, or should I say nib-crossed, when I feel rather deeply about things, but I do hope you will understand, and not feel my "reserve" is lack of feeling, but I hope you won't forget ever that I'm keeping my fingers crossed for you all the time, dear, so take care of yourself.
> Freda.

Freda's next letter of 30th March, 1943 was returned to her. The Postmaster had failed in his task for once. It is sad Jack never read this letter because it is optimistic and happy; exactly what he craved. The return date is 13th Sept. 1943.

Figure 23 The letter which never arrived at Melbourne

Friends' Ambulance Unit
4 Gordon Square,
March 30th 1943

My dear Jack,
At 11.15 pm. (which is now) I find myself able to write to you after all. The room is rather untidy and I've just up-tipped an ash-tray onto the floor (accidentally of course) but as Marjorie is gossiping downstairs and will probably continue to gossip for another hour at least I ought to be able to get something down on paper before she returns.
Why I thought I should not be able to write to-night was because Ronald (my cheese) and I invited

105

round the five doctors who are going to Ethiopia, and so I've been sort of hostess up here. Marjorie came too. The doctors are a good crowd with a fund of amusing yarns, and they all seem to have enjoyed themselves.

I have continued to be pretty busy over the weekend, but as I've been having a string of early nights I'm not feeling tired – much! I was on orderly on Sunday this week as I wanted to get some work done at the Square on Monday. Sunday was a simply glorious day, and looking from the window over the scarred roofs of Whitechapel I wished very much that I were out of London and miles away up in Westmorland walking along the edge of Esthwaite lake or cycling down Red Bank in Grasmere – heavenly dream.

On Sunday afternoon four of us went along to St. James and Hyde Park. We had tea at a weird café just off the Strand called the "Kurb". We must go there when you are on leave. Mary Shaw knocked a pile of plates over, but fortunately only one was broken, and by some miracle the others survived.

We are having our big party here on Thursday, to celebrate, or rather mourn, the closing of the hostel. There will be games and dancing etc. until about 2.0 a.m. I hope everything goes off well. There should be about 160 people here, and then afterwards we shall be changing rooms etc. I shall be moving across to the other wing of the hostel. All the rooms there are single rooms. I hope Marjorie is next door to me or opposite.

So much for my activities. I dare say you have not exactly been sitting around kicking your heels over these past few days. I'm sorry you have had to change planes, but very glad to know that no-one suffered any damage. It was very nice to get your letter this morning, and such a nice letter at that. It's good to know that you will be able to come along again fairly shortly. I took my dress to be cleaned this morning, and my jacket, so I hope that by the time you do come I shall be all spick & span. I have warned Ronald that I hope to be wanting more time off, and I am preparing for this by working week-ends etc & not having any more time away from Gordon Square than I can help. It's sweet of you to have your photograph taken at the request of your humble servant, and I assure you I do appreciate your great sacrifice on my behalf – I hate photographers myself.

Honestly Jack, your letter is so sweet and thoughtful, that I just don't know how to reply to it, and almost feel that it is best not to try. I'm not so really very practical myself, and I'm fearfully extravagant you know – at the moment (my sole surviving five quid excepted) I've got 1 ¼ d. Fortunately it's the new month on Thursday so I can start afresh on my 25/-, though I shall probably finish up again with a penny in my pocket.[1] I once found myself with a week to go before the end of the month and one farthing to carry me through, though I must say I'm rather proud of the fact that what is more, I made it, and got through the 7 days without spending even the ¼ d! So you see, I'm not exactly beyond the extravagant mark myself!

The wind is roaring outside in true March tradition, and whistling along the corridors and under the doors – how nice it would be to be out in it, (you probably are, but I mean walking, not flying). I adore a wild and windy day, with the grey rain clouds scurrying across the sky – though not as seen from Whitechapel!

Were you in this recent Berlin raid, or is this one of the things one does not ask. I felt very sick when I heard the news. My feelings are twisted and torn between thoughts for you and for the people of Berlin – I suppose you will think that rather ridiculous, but believe me darling it's a bit of a strain, though I can (I hope) take it. The fellows here might well tell me I'm very subdued these days!

---

[1] 1 ¼ d. was called 'a penny farthing'. 25/- was called 'twenty-five shillings'.

I too am looking forward very much indeed to your next leave. As you say, there will be so much for us to talk about – we'll have a terrific time I'm sure, though you must tell me some of the things you want to do this time, and not let me drag you from one end of London to the other and all over the place.

Heavens, doesn't this letter seem stiff. I do hope you will recognise that its due to shyness and a northerner's reserve. When you come on leave you must shake me and shake me & make me relax – will you?

12.30 a.m. and I really must turn in. I'm too tired to have a bath, & anyway I had one before supper, so I will say a very good-night to you my dear, wherever you are.

Au Revoir,
Freda.

Chapter 4: April

THE HOSTEL AT THE LONDON HOSPITAL closed on 2nd April to be redecorated before nursing students moved back in. The F.A.U. needed to find new quarters. Freda writes to Stephen Peet in the Near East that it is now "well and truly closed". After a goodbye party, people drifted over to the Sam for another party, to console themselves.

> This morning the hostel seems horribly flat and empty, with old packing cases about, and most of the floors closed, and smelling foully of new distemper – it's terribly desolate and depressing.
> The hostel has, for me personally, delightful associations. I have made many new and good friends there, and its gradual change of atmosphere has been very painful to watch. This time last year the end was, so to speak, beginning, but there were so many of you all here still. I wonder whether we shall all meet again, après la guerre. Will it be on some European field on the Post War Reconstruction ticket? I've been thinking rather a lot recently about after the war, and wondering what I shall be doing. I've come to the conclusion that on the whole thinking about it is a bad thing and I think in future I shall just live day to day and see what sort of mess I get into!
> The Hadfield-Spears boys arrived back last week – all very fit and brown – what a day it will be when everyone comes back. I wonder if I shall be here for that occasion. I expect I shall.

The closing of the hostel coincided with not hearing from Jack for a week and Freda's mood plummets. The strain of reading of raids but not hearing from him shows in her letter of 6th April, which, for Freda, is very short. She may have read the press report after the Essen raid on 3/4 April from R.A.F. Linton, the other side of York from Melbourne. The bombers returned and a crew interviewed was subdued: "... Sgt Hoover's bleary-eyed crew quietly related their two runs on the target and the coning by searchlights both times." Jack's letter is overdue. She knows he's been busy, and she probably knows that she would not be told if he were missing or killed because their engagement has not been formally announced, indeed Freda has not yet agreed to marry Jack. The letter sounds agitated, too full of future plans. Resist as she might, all she can think of is the future; après la guerre she calls it, having been with the Anglo-French Hadfield Spears hospital boys during the week. In her next, longer letter, she's sometimes subdued, an unusual state for her, and it sounds as though she is keeping as occupied as possible. She wrote to a friend that she's "keeping her powder dry". It is a shame for her that the hostel at this time was becoming emptier and quieter.

The fact that 12 bombers did not return from the Kiel raid of 4th April was common knowledge by Monday 5th in London evening papers and, as far away as New Zealand, but Freda still had not heard from Jack[41]. She wrote to him on 7th April, begging for news.

> Friends Ambulance Unit.
> 4 Gordon Square.
> Tuesday 6th April 1943
>
> My dear Jack,
> A week has passed without any communiqué from you, from which I am assuming that you have been just terrifically busy, as indeed the newspapers and news bulletins confirm.
> I had hoped to be able to write you this evening, and still hope to do so, but as I have been roped in for orderly duty from 6.0 p.m. onwards I'm taking no chances and getting this short line in first. If I finish my floor scrubbing early, however, I shall dash upstairs to a nice hot bath and then toast myself over the gas-fire while writing to you a real letter – this at the moment is my favourite evening occupation, and I should be able to find lots of news to write about, having had such a busy week last week.
> It's a simply glorious day again. I do hope it's like this when you come on leave – it will be terrific – how I am looking forward to it – we must go to Kew Gardens for a picnic one day – would you like that? I keep planning all kinds of things, but you may have

other ideas. How many days will you be able to spare from home?

We shall be busy changing rooms at the hostel this week. The one I am going to is not by any means as nice as the one I am in with Marjorie, but I hope to be able to make something of it over the week-end, we must have tea there one day when you come.

Please drop me a line just as soon as you can to let me know that you are safe and sound – please Jack.

I hope you can sort out this letter. I seem to have folded everything the wrong way.

Au revoir, darling, and take care of yourself.
Freda.

Friends Ambulance Unit,
4 Gordon Square.
Wed. 7th April

Darling,

Tonight I've begun very early. It must only be about 8.0 p.m. and I'm glowing pleasantly from a nice warm bath and am all ready to begin this weekly diary, which is rather like having a date with you except that you are not here to answer back, so I can just talk and talk and talk, and breathe a prayer to the Post Master General that he will deliver me some news from you in the morning.

Now, what have I been a-doing of since I last wrote. On Thursday we had the dance at the hostel to celebrate it closing. There were about 160 people altogether, and it was quite the most successful dance we have ever had. I quite enjoyed the evening myself, though often found myself wondering what you were doing, and where you were. The party did not finish until 2.0 am Friday, when, after helping to clear everything away, I crawled up to bed.

On Friday the cooks and quartermaster gave a farewell supper for everyone, and a very good supper too, though somehow feeling rather depressed on Friday, I was rather a wet-blanket I'm afraid.

On Saturday I was busy pounding my typewriter at Gordon Square all day – not but what I did not pound just as heartily all the rest of the week. Sunday was a day for taking things easy. I washed my hair in the morning and then sat on the roof to let it dry in the sun. Marjorie roped me in to make a four for tennis in the afternoon, we play on some courts belonging to the hostel about 100 yards away.

I went to bed very early on Sunday, and also Monday and Tuesday, and shall probably be fairly early again – you will observe that I am busy storing up energy for this leave of yours!

The hostel is very strange now that most of the old brigade have left, and it's practically deserted and smelling foully of distemper as most of it is being redecorated. The girls are going to live on the 3rd floor corridor, and as the rooms vary greatly in size and furnishings we decided to draw lots for them. Marjorie has been lucky and got one of the nicer rooms. I'm afraid I have not done so well either for room or furniture, and when you come again in a week or two I shall not be able to give you tea in quite such a nice room.

Monday was gloriously warm, and if it's as warm when you come it will be terrific. To-day has been pretty chilly, however, and there is a marvellous wind blowing through the streets and whistling through the gaunt skeletons of what were once synagogues, factories and homes in this district.

I love being out in a really good gale, with lots of heavy rain, with an old mackintosh on. It's not quite so good in the city then, though it's fun to go along Tower Bridge or the Embankment and watch the motor launches and barges and other river craft bobbing up & down on the water.

Talk of the Embankment brings back very delightful memories of one Friday evening a few weeks ago. I have not been along since then, and the next time I go I hope it will be in the same delightful company saying the same delightful things.

I wonder if you are flying to-night. I wonder every night and a great deal of the day. I expect you will think me utterly stupid about this my dear, in which case I hope to goodness you will tell me so in no uncertain terms, but when a week passes without hearing from you – you always seem to write before Tuesday – it's so difficult to know just what to think, and I may as well confess that I get very worried. I suppose it's one of those things I shall have to get used to ---- "A weary lot is thine, fair maid, a weary lot is thine ------" seems fairly appropriate in some ways!

It occurs to me that this is the fourth time I have written to you since last Tuesday, which is rather shocking – my reserve must be being gradually worn down! – but I know I have more time on my hands than you, and expect that it will all help to keep up your morale & all that! Does it?!

I seem to devote a great deal of time to keeping up people's morale in some way or another. Do you realise quite what you're wanting to take on in wanting to spend your life keeping up my morale?!

I would like to go on writing this far into the night as somehow I don't think I'm going to sleep so good, but perhaps I had better wait until I hear from you – or I may run out of ink!

Good night my dear, & Good Luck,
& Love.
Freda.

"A weary lot is thine, fair maid, a weary lot is thine!" comes from a ballad by Walter Scott called *The Rover's Adieu*.[42] That Freda thinks it apt shows her constant worry that she would never see Jack again because the Rover is a soldier with "A lightsome eye, a soldier's mein, A feather of the blue". He leaves for battle saying,

> 'This morn is merry June, I trow,
> The rose is budding fain;
> But she shall bloom in winter snow
> Ere we two meet again.'

Freda writes on 7th April that "talk of the Embankment brings back very delightful memories of one Friday evening a few weeks ago." She and Jack and often think of each other at 8.15. At the end of March Jack writes "I still think of you very often & make a special point of this at 8.15 each evening" and Freda replies "I thought of you when I was in the library at 8.15 this evening ... and pictured you flying over the north sea". At the end of April Jack wonders "what you are doing now. I thought the same thing at 8.15 this evening when we were in the briefing room." On the last day of April, Freda wonders "if you are sitting in the briefing room, as you were on Wednesday?" She does not know th Jack is flying towards Essen. "It was almost dark when I got out at Whitechapel, though the sky was very cloudy, and there was just one solitary star. I wondered if you were just about to take-off, and looked at the stars and wished you good-luck, as I did at 8.15, pausing for a moment during my blitz on the typewriter."

Freda's fear of losing Jack grows in April but it is from the end of March that Jack also shows signs of strain. Land and air crew were given enormous responsibility for winning the war. Churchill's 1940 statement shows just how much the whole country relied on Bomber Command:

> The Navy can lose us the war, but only the RAF can win it. Therefore our supreme effort must be to gain overwhelming mastery of the air. The fighters are our salvation but the bombers alone provide the means of victory (Winston Churchill, 3rd September, 1940)[43]

Reminiscences of Larry Donnelly in 10 Squadron Association newsletter no. 32[44] express well the strain bomber crews were under. His initial courage turned out to be based on ignorance but with knowledge came fear:

> That courage promoted by ignorance and curiosity resulted in high morale for the first 5 trips, but after that it could possibly descend to a 'crack-up' point by the 11th or 12th trip.
> That 'crack-up' signs were the adoption of a brutalising, callous attitude about the deaths of friends and a possible change in demeanour – the noisy ones became quiet and the shy ones became clamorous.
> That the relief of surviving the traditionally 'unlucky 13th' boosted morale which remained fairly constant until about the 22nd trip when it diminished. This was the time when the legacy of ulcers and other stress-induced diseases would follow survivors through their later years.

By 26th March Jack had completed 12 raids as pilot. His log book was burned in the 60s with all other unclaimed logbooks (the archives were running out of shelf space) so it is not possible to work out accurately the number of operations he flew. The record books for Jack's Heavy Conversion Unit (AIR 29) rarely names the trainee pilots who flew on ops though they were named in the squadron record books. Scrubs, which might or might not be recorded in the record books for the squadron (AIR 27) often counted as operations. Maxie tells Freda later that he and Jack flew to Cologne before Freda met him. Jack flew to Italy at least once, probably as 2nd pilot. With all the times I can find him mentioned, this could therefore be his 19th operation. He planned to finish active duty in July and he had flown ops for two or even three months by the beginning of April, some of this as a 2nd pilot, which implies that he had only another 10 or 12 ops to go before completing his tour of duty. This is simply guesswork but we know of 12 operations he had flown as pilot by the end of March when he flew to Berlin and his aircraft was hit.

The first lucky escape had been the week before, when they had flown three difficult missions in four days. On Friday 26th March the target was Duisburg and on 27th it was Berlin, both times in the same aircraft. On the 27th his aircraft was hit in the mainframe. This was the first time an aircraft Jack flew sustained severe injury, and the whole crew must have been terrified but on 29th March they flew again to the Big City which is what they called Berlin. After Essen on 3rd April and the second time they were hit, Jack tells Freda, "times have been very shaky for all concerned".

Dan Brennan uses the same word, "shaky", in *One of Our Bombers is Missing* to describe different ways aircrew reacted to losing friends. Mack goes "whoring around and drinking" to dull the sense of loss and the fear of death. Others find religion. Others smoke non-stop. Mack sees signs of strain in the crew and unsuccessfully asks his Flight Commander for leave.

> 'It's not that we're nervous,' I lied. 'It's just that we're fed-up, you know. We've seen so many fellows killed and missing that we hate flying. If we could get away for a while –'

> 'It would only relieve you temporarily, then as soon as you had another shaky trip you would be the same again. It's best to stay on. I know'. (Brennan, 1979, p. 105)

During the battle of the Ruhr from March to June 1943, crews had less than a one in three chance of returning unscathed. By the Spring of 1943, everyone knew that it was unusual for crews to finish a tour of thirty ops unharmed. Camaraderie on the base suffered as a result of this, as crews stuck closely together and rarely bothered to make friends with other crews. Your crew alone was what was important and examples of single crew members surviving a raid and then collapsing under the strain of survivors' guilt are not unknown. According to Max Hastings, such men would be considered, at least at the start of the war, as "lacking moral fibre": LMF, it appears in record books.[45]

Freda described Jack, in a letter to friends at the end of April, as not intellectual but "– as he says, he obviously would not be in the R.A.F. if he thought, but that's not what they're paid to do –". From his letters, it sounds as though, clever as he was, he tried hard not to philosophise but to enjoy his work when possible and forget about it whenever he could. Hastings exaggerates but not much when he writes that "The men who fared best were those who did not allow themselves to think at all" (Hastings, 2010).

Mike Rossiter records the words of George Laing, a 76 Squadron pilot:

> There was always a reason not to be affected by the deaths announced on the green sheets of paper pinned up on the notice board: "You had only met him briefly, or he came from a different town, or they must just have had bad luck." It was a way of keeping those black thoughts at bay. (Rossiter, p. 209)

In the same book, squadron life is described as "a sick society."

> You ignored the new guys in case they would not be around for long ... You were friendly with guys in your hut, but it was your crew that was important, you all went together". (Rossiter, p. 219)

Tailgunner John Stuart said,

> I just kept going. Just luck I suppose. We just did not worry about anything. We did not make any friends ... there was little point because they weren't there very long. (*Their Past*, p. 20)

An air ambulance WAAF, recalls that on operations nights, "all medical staff on duty for that night used to sit playing cards and smoking endless cigarettes waiting for the return of planes."

> It was always a very tense time, especially when planes were late, or in trouble trying to land. Then the casualties on board ... Almost every morning there were several planes missing. They had been seen on fire by other crews, or else they men in them had been seen ejecting over occupied countries. We were never given any counselling, so we had to just get on with it. (*Their Past*, p. 69)

John Stuart, from the same station, describes a crash early in the war in a twin-engined Wellington. They lost one engine to flak over Holland but managed to limp back over the North Sea. They were refused permission to land back at base for one reason or another. Their second engine then failed so they crashed. This is when he says, chillingly, "I was the only survivor. There was none of them actually killed outright" (*Their Past*, p. 69). Nichol and Rennell include two shocking photographs in *Tail-End Charlies* of damaged aircraft which illustrate the precarious nature of flying a bomber. One aircraft made it home with a missing nose section. The other disappeared but the photograph shows the tail actually being shot off by flak and dropping away from the mainframe (Nichol and Rennell, illustrations 9 and 16). Crew saw sights like this most nights.

Freydis Sharland, one of very few women who flew during WW2, also describes the sense of foreboding she felt as she watched aircraft flying off on operations.[46] She was not allowed to fly on missions but delivered Spitfires and Hurricanes for the Air Transport Auxiliary.

> You were just sad when people got killed, as they often did. ...When they all went out in the evening, and

there was a great roar as they went away, it was quite difficult that, really, to cope, but you had to go on and not worry about it (*Shooting the War*, 2010).

A mid-upper-gunner who joined the Shiny Ten in 1944 says that it was Squadron legend that the boys who flew in the Spring of 1943 had it hardest of all. Night after night of flying on terrifying operations, taking off one after the other with only two minute gaps, flying in a formation which would not last out the night because aircraft were shot down, then returning at first light, and waiting, at times in vain, for friends on the same raid to return, sleeping inadequately, attending lectures and briefings, and then starting all over again. Even the most optimistic and enthusiastic fliers became strained. Dan Brennan writes that the unpredictable dangers of the job affected crew morale: "Returning we expected anything; being lost, attack by night fighters, engine failure. There was always these troubles" (Brennan 1979, p. 58). He also writes "Somehow in the beginning there was a magic in all of it. But later, in the end, we only grew to hate it". (Brennan 1946, p 97)

Crew losses in the Spring of 1943 appear to have affected most of R.A.F. Melbourne and Brennan writes

> You remembered before the worry, before the squadron began to lose crews. When it seemed impossible for anyone to be missing and it was all a rather pleasant, exciting adventure. (Brennan, 1946, p. 110)

A brief glance at any of the lists of lost aircraft shows that often more than one aircraft from the same squadron went down on the same night. On 24th May, for instance, the list of crashes in Holland includes 20 aircraft, one of which is a Junkers 88. All the others are R.A.F. bombers and of those 19 bombers, 2 came from 57 Squadron, 2 from 78 and 3 from 166; the last two squadrons had close links with 10 Squadron. That night 3 out of the 21 bombers which took off from Melbourne that night were lost: one crashed in Holland but two others crashed in Germany, though overall the odds were better that night than usual. In almost every raid airmen would know, maybe not well, but certainly be acquainted with somebody who they would never see again. After particularly heavy squadron losses, crews were normally given a 48hr pass.

So far as Jack and the other pilots were concerned they may have fraternised with their own crews almost exclusively once they became captains but they all knew two or three other crews very well. Jack knew at least three other crews because he had flown with them as a second pilot. On St Valentine's Day 1943 he was 2nd pilot in ZA-S, one of only two bombers from 10 to fly to Cologne that night. The other aircraft "failed to return" so on that raid 10 Squadron losses were 50% and the eight men of Pilot Officer Cobb's crew, which included Jack, sat alone in the canteen and sat alone for debriefing. Jack was 2nd pilot with P/O Allan on two occasions, one of which was a long flight to Turin and the other would also have been to Turin but the raid was abandoned because the undercarriage malfunctioned. He must have known this crew rather well. Sgt. Harrison who stood in for Maxie on occasion, normally flew with F/O Wann. Eddie Curtis, a bomb aimer whose wife Freda would meet, also flew with F/O Wann though his usual captain was W/O Price; Price was posted in from 1658 H.C.U. with his crew the same month as Jack and his crew and they all trained together. So although crews stuck together, their unit was not detached from the other aircrew on the base.

Jack's crew had second-hand experience of crashes, prangs. They almost certainly saw Sgt. Peck's aircraft destroyed on 10th March or saw it soon afterwards. He crashed close to Jack's dispersal during training exercises and the aircraft burned. Training accidents happened so often that special gear had been invented to pull airmen from burning wreckage.

Slowly, the strain was beginning to wear down Jack, as it began to wear down Dan Brennan. At the same period in 1943 that Jack was writing to Freda, Brennan muses before a flight:

> And the nights when someone did not come back you remember, and how at first it bothered you, and how the smoking wreckage of a crash bothered you. Not many, but you had seen enough aircraft running smoothly and fast along runways and you had seen them rise and something happen, a wing go down, a stall, a propeller dropping off, and then explosion and smoke and flame, and running across the field and stopping beside the wreckage while they pulled scorched, crumbling bodies out on long hooks attached to poles. (Brennan, 1946, p. 117)

The letter of 7th April, and the envelope likewise, is written in a new hand, a large sprawling hand, which Jack never uses again. This may have been one way anxiety affected him. It is in this letter that Jack expresses his fear that the number of missing crews may reach a critical point, meaning that if there were too few trained pilots available for ops all leave would be cancelled. He tells Freda he expects leave to go as planned "unless squadron losses are high". Jack is not demoralised, because he loves flying, "I am not a bit unhappy about this topsy-turvy life", but he is shaken and the tone of this letter is different from his last, where he mentions, in a typically cavalier fashion, flying a damaged S for Sugar and how George and Derrick almost 'bought it'. To marry while he is still on ops, would be reckless; better to wait until he is training new pilots after his tour of duty: "for reasons which are obvious." He did not know, as we now do, that one in four pilots were killed during training, and that in the first year of the war, more died in training than on operational flying.

Anxiety among aircrew is relieved by writing letters home, gambling, singing in the mess, dances on the base and evening passes to York, along with the occasional 48 hr pass. The ORB mentions days when there are "No ops. Crews resting". Sometimes air crew went a bit crazy on nights off in York but the escapade Jack's crew initiate at an airbase in Scotland, where, in the general hilarity of having survived the Kiel raid by the skin of their teeth, the boisterous crew cut off their hosts' ties, seems out of character. The crew must have been pretty close to exhaustion.

Though shaking inside, crews all knew the unwritten rules about stiff upper lips and staying cheerful at all times so instead of complaining, Jack writes on 28th about other people's nerves before operations:

> This letter has seemed tragic so far – I seem to have related all my troubles to you – actually they are not troubles to me ... However these things don't worry me as much as they used to & it gives me quite a sense of superiority to sit here calmly writing letters while the newer boys are all huddled together & talking so earnestly.

On 3ʳᵈ April a Fokker Wolfe 190 Luftwaffe bomber attacked Eastbourne in daylight and strafed streets full of shoppers.[2] The same evening Jack's crew flew ZA-X DT732, one of thirteen Halifax heavies from Melbourne to join a further 338 aircraft on their way to Essen.

Figure 24 An aircraft like Jack's

All aircraft tend to wobble on take-off but the heavies had a habit of swerving violently when fully loaded and it took all Jack's strength to hold the wheel. Derrick wedged himself beside Jack and worked the throttles while Maxie checked the gauges. Everyone was silent.

After take-off, and once the trees at the end of the runway had been cleared and while Norman plotted their course, Derrick eased himself to the nose of the aircraft. He was lookout and gunner until they reached the target, and then he'd be flat on his stomach in the nose cone, watching for the target markers. Norman gave terse instructions, Jack relaxed back into his seat and gave a thumbs up to

---

[2] The word strafe comes from the WW1 German greeting: "Gott strafe England" = God punish England.

the pilot nearest to him in the formation. Peter sent his co-ordinates back to Melbourne control tower and exchanged information with other wireless operators in the flight. George and Wally chatted about the sky, the weather, other aircraft they recognised from The Clutch. Engine noise was deafening and their voices sputtered through the intercom, which was distracting so, over the Channel and before the coast of Holland appeared, Jack ordered them to "Put a sock in it you two and test your guns." "Right-o, Skip."

Soon the Amsterdam searchlights began to appear. "It was dark below coming up to the Dutch coast and then the long beams of searchlights south of us sabred the sky suddenly and began moving and probing." (Brennan, 1953, p. 25.) Jack warned his crew he was about to weave, even though this happened on every mission. This manœuvre, called jinking, was to be expected but that did not make it any the less tiring, especially for the pilot who had to keep in formation on the way to the target city while avoiding searchlights and Ack Ack in a deadly game of hide and seek. If the aircraft was caught in a cone of searchlights the pilot could try to make a run for it but often the only escape was to dive perilously low, down to where the cone broke, which made their con trail wide and white, therefore their route predictable, as well as making them temporarily an easy target because they had to break formation to do the manœuvre. A stream of explosions from flak was now added to the constant roar of the bomber's four large engines.

There was usually a flak barrage between the powerful Amsterdam light and Rotterdam, which continued on and off through central Holland, over Nijmegen and Kleve and on along the Rhine into Happy Valley. By the time Essen was reached, Jack had been flying for around two hours taking evasive action all the time, and over the target he still had to keep in formation while avoiding nightfighters, searchlights and ack ack: stooging around, they called it. On Jack's first raid as the captain of his crew, the crew of W spent 20 minutes over Essen trying to evade two cones: "Essen was always a hell of a place." (Brennan, 1946, p. 110) Jack's crew were in the air for four and a half hours, most of the time spent evading searchlights, flak and nightfighters.

12 Halifaxes were lost on the raid and two more crashed back in England, trying to land. According to the Operations Record Book ZA-X sustained what is termed "minor" damage – two of the hits

could have compromised a safe landing, however, and the third could have turned them into a fireball. The crew reported:

> Flak was severe and three minor hits were sustained, one on the starboard flap, another in the port undercarriage and the 3rd under No. 2 Tank in the starboard mainplane. None of the crew were injured. (AIR 27)

One flap being hit probably made it impossible to keep the aircraft on an even keel, and Derrick came back to help Jack tug on the right handle of the wheel and control the throttles to keep the aircraft steady. Maxie was working flat out to maintain fuel feeds to the engines because he had to maintain maximum engine power, his task complicated by the damaged flap. If the port undercarriage damage caused hanging metal there would be extra drag on the aircraft. This was the second time they were hit in the starboard mainframe, the first being exactly a week before. Sometimes the flight path was routed to the south or to the north of the Ruhr but on this occasion they flew straight in and straight out again. Occasionally there would be stretches known to be peaceful then sometimes Jack handed over his controls to the engineer or 2nd pilot on the way home, or to George the auto pilot but on this raid that was impossible.

Peter radioed in a damage report to the Control Tower to make sure fire engines and medical orderlies would be ready by the main runway for X to arrive. Deciphering the record book brings the raids into focus and I imagine these knights of the air arrive safely back at base elated, probably delirious with relief, and climb down from the bomber, gripped by their sticky sweaty clothes, stiff from the cold. Air crew hand over the bird to its ground crew who are glad to see it safely on land and are ready to patch up and mend injuries. They all discuss the damage briefly and then the night riders make their way slowly back to debriefing and the mess. Jack's crew had waived off congratulations as though nothing out of the ordinary had happened on landing. Passing smiling erks whose attention was now fixed on the next of Melbourne's raiders to land, Derrick gives the camera to a WAAF, then to the canteen. They are exhausted, and from time to time look around to see who's back, who's still expected back. Then in the canteen they loll about on chairs or lean against a table, drink strong sweet tea or chew gum, or both, cadge cigs off one another while they wait to go in to tell the sergeant and WAAFs in debriefing what happened that night and by now the excitement has worn off and all they can think of is sleep.

Figure 25 At debriefing, Norman with his back to the photographer

The damage that night but have been surface or relatively easy to repair because the next night Jack flew ZA-X again. Kiel was the target for 4th April. For the second time, they were one of thirteen aircraft which took off from Melbourne, this time to join a force of 577 aiming for the Deutsche Werke, the boatyards and railway terminals of Kiel. Apart from the Thousand Bomber raids, this was so far the biggest raid of the war. Pathfinders were buffeted in the winds and the bombers who followed them were misled by decoy fires. Jack and his crew took off just before nine at night and it was a long flight of six hours. Their part in the raid is described by ORB after debriefing:

> Bombed primary target at 23.22 hrs. from 18000 ft. over 10/10th cloud on Target Markers. Visibility was poor but the glow of fires was observed below the clouds. Fairly severe flak was encountered over the target. (AIR 27)

There was total cloud cover on this Kiel raid. Of the 12 aircraft which went down, 2 were from 10 Squadron. Some of the aircraft on the raid had to fly perilously low when trying to get their bearings and when Jack and his crew flew over Kiel, clouds were so thick that Derrick found it hard to make out targets. With no accurate marking possible it appears that very few target buildings were hit on the raid. There was thick flak and night fighters, depending on which reports you read, but of the 116 Halifaxes which reached Kiel, four were lost. Fewer people died in Kiel that night than airmen who attacked it.

For whatever reason, whether unable or unwilling to disclose the amount of resistance or whether debriefing reports from Melbourne were not made public by the Air Ministry, *The Aeroplane* does not mention the severe flak 10 Squadron crews reported at debriefing. The Kiel raid is described as "A Weighty Bomber Offensive" in winter weather over northern Europe, in the section called "The 188th week of the war in the air":

> Shipyards at Kiel and industrial targets in the Ruhr and South-Western Germany were bombed by the R.A.F. Thick clouds extending to great heights, and icing conditions, were encountered by the raiding crews. ... At Kiel the anti-aircraft fire was not heavy, but many fighters were about. A Halifax shot down a Ju88. (*The Aeroplane*, April 16)

ZA-M crash-landed at Thornaby and ZA-J went down with all crew killed: both aircraft were lost trying to make emergency landings.[47] Bad weather forced Jack to make an emergency landing somewhere near Edinburgh, at what he terms a non-operational base, when the crew, still dressed in their operational sheepskins and heavy boots, arrived uninvited but welcomed at a formal gathering. I cannot find any mention of his forced landing in the ORB, and I cannot find out which base Jack's crew disrupted. There is no reason to doubt Jack's tale – he had witnesses Freda knew, after all. Aircraft landed wherever they could in an emergency and this is often not mentioned in Squadron records.

The wintry weather that night, especially the high winds, would certainly have made landing difficult and could well have blown Jack off course. Ice, in particular, was a major problem during this week and at R.A.F. stations across England there were briefings, only to be followed by stand downs, or at best scrubs, as weather failed to clear. There were no ops from Melbourne for the next three days because of the bad weather. A few days after the Kiel raid, "The captain of a Lancaster said that he had never had a bumpier trip. The weight of ice broke an aerial on a Halifax, and chunks of ice from the airscrews hit the wings and fuselage with the noise of pistol shots" (*The Aeroplane* April 16). Icing also caused equipment to malfunction and guns to freeze solid. Most seriously, freezing air could prevent oxygen reaching crew, who then became light-headed and could lose consciousness. For all these reasons, icing conditions frequently caused crashes, often into the sea, or emergency landings. Ice and wind together were exceptionally dangerous.

The weather was never predictable. Freda writes on 6th April that it is "glorious" in London, but in Yorkshire a cold wind is blowing a storm. Whether he can fly or not determines Jack's view of the weather, so he has what appears to be an unusual reason for a holiday-maker to cut short a trip to Edinburgh: "unfortunately we could not stay long as the weather was fast clearing up". On the other hand, at base, he kicks his heels in frustration when it is stormy and he can't fly. Not only did he love flying but the more operations he completed, the sooner he would be off ops and able to get married.

By Wednesday 7th April, London was unnaturally cold and windy. Freda's love of wild weather makes her see bomb damage as a backdrop to display the weather at its best: "there is a marvellous wind blowing through the streets and whistling through the gaunt skeletons of what were once synagogues, factories and homes in this district."

Jack says Melbourne is like a desert in a cold sandstorm. By Friday 9th, however, the weather is "glorious" again both in York and in London. Thick cloud blankets Yorkshire a few days later but by then Jack is on leave.

In fine weather, Jack flew and was therefore given leave but if in bad weather he was grounded, he was not given time off to visit Freda. Freda was confused between not wanting Jack to fly, so wanting the weather to be cloudy and dull, but also wanting him to have 48hr passes. It was certainly, as Jack says, a "topsy-turvy life".

        Sergeant's Mess
        R.A.F. Melbourne
        7th April 1943

        My Dearest Freda,
    Since I last wrote life has been very full for me & this of course largely accounts for your not having

heard from me for so long. I (being one of these types that are always full of good intentions) intended to write to you 2 days ago when I should have had a day off.

However after the Kiel raid I landed in Scotland & did not get back to Melbourne until last night – so much for my day-off.

The weather is atrocious today – we are having very high winds which are blowing the surface dust off the neighbouring ploughed fields into one continuous dust-storm. Some witty person must have thought Melbourne very reminiscent of the Sahara because I found the following notice posted on the Sergeants' Mess board.

"All senior N.C.O's to parade outside the oasis with camels at Sundown"

The long & short of this detailed summary of the weather situation is that owing to its intensity we do not fly tonight & so I am grabbing a few moments to write this epistle whatever happens. It really has been a tremendous lapse of time since I last wrote to you but I am glad you did not think I had forsaken you – what a break for me that our activities are of so much interest to the news-hounds – it keeps such a good tag on us.

You have no idea how much we have been messed around recently by the weather & the office-desk strategists, but of course you know there has been plenty doing for the hot targets lately & times have been very shaky for all concerned. Most of my activities have been confined to service matters during the last week & so there really is very little to write about in that respect, & I guess these wouldn't interest you any way. I do feel awfully guilty for letting you write 2 letters in succession – I had intended to write an improvement on my last letter since it was written so hurriedly but all my time has been pretty fully occupied. I have quite a stack of mail to reply to but I guess most of this will now have to wait until my leave comes around.

My mother has written me a very haughty letter today requesting to know the reason why I have "ceased to correspond with her" & so after this I shall have to get cracking on a few excuses to her for not having written for so long. Unfortunately it is not possible for me to tell her the real reason as she is not aware that I am on operations – I shall have to tell her that I have cut my right hand or that there isn't a scrap of paper on the camp or something!

Actually apart from the fact that I have not been able to write to you often enough I am not a bit unhappy about this topsy-turvy life I am living in fact I get quite a kick out of it. I had to say this because this letter has seemed tragic so far – I seem to have related all my troubles to you – actually they are not troubles to me – I merely offer them to you as some measure of excuse for not writing for so long.

Anyway I did have a break from the general sum of things the night before last when the crew went to a dance in the Sgts. Mess at the camp at which I was staying in Scotland. This was a non-operational camp & so everyone was very properly behaved so I am afraid we caused quite a sensation. We were clad in flying gear & really did look a scruffy gang. At first we were very cordially received until some irresponsible members of my crew took upon themselves the task of livening the joint up. This they achieved by cutting off everyone's tie just beneath the knot causing other irresponsible people in attendance to follow suit.

In all there were some 30-40 people walking around the dance floor minus neckties so thereafter we were treated with the gravest suspicion.

The following morning Maxie & I rose early & journeyed to Edinburgh & spent our time buying books & other things but unfortunately we could not stay long as the weather was fast clearing up & we knew that we should soon have to be on our way to Melbourne.

We took off at dusk & within a fairly short space of time found ourselves once more installed in bed.

Today has been spent very profitably attending lectures etc. right up to tea-time & now, here I am after tea, wondering just what I am going to write about next!

Well so far the date of my leave has remained at the 12th April & unless squadron losses are high before the week is out this should prove to be the goods. My leave starts after duty hours the 12th which means that if there is flying on the night of the 12th I shall not get away until 13th. I expect to get away with about 10 days leave which means I should be able to spend 3 or 4 days or perhaps more with you, depending on how much opposition Mother puts up but I think I know to how get around her by now.

Do you think your boss will take a poor view when you ask him for time off – I must be already deeply in his bad books for robbing him of his star typist during my 48 hours pass – anyway I'll hope for the best.

I do so want to talk to you again.

By the way what is all this about the busy week you have had – has the Sugar Loaf been working overtime? And how is that gallant concern getting on now – I trust all the little ones are attending regularly!

I am afraid I really must pack up now in favour of the arduous letter I shall have to write to Mother. I will give you further gen on my leave situation as soon as I can.

All my Love, Darling.
Write soon.
Jack.

F.A.U. 4 Gordon Square.
Friday April 9th

My dear Jack,

A fine nerve you've got! Here I am running around tearing my hair, so to speak, wondering what's happened and then you write asking me to write soon – pshaw! I suppose I had better drop you a line now though, as otherwise nothing will reach you until after the week-end, which is cutting things rather short before your leave.

I do hope you manage to smooth things out with your mother. Even if she doesn't know you're on ops she will still worry, you know, and it was very thoughtless of you not to manage to slip in a post card or something to her – what are you going to say when you go on leave and cut a few days off to come down here?

Sorry. I haven't time for more just now, but you must admit you've had a good ration this week!
Don't forget to let me know as soon as you get things planned out so that I can make my arrangements at this end.

Kind regards please, to all the boys, and my love to yourself.

Au Revoir.

Freda.

P.S. I don't like your change of handwriting – i.e. the huge scrawl on the envelope – but probably you don't like this scrawl either, so we're quits!

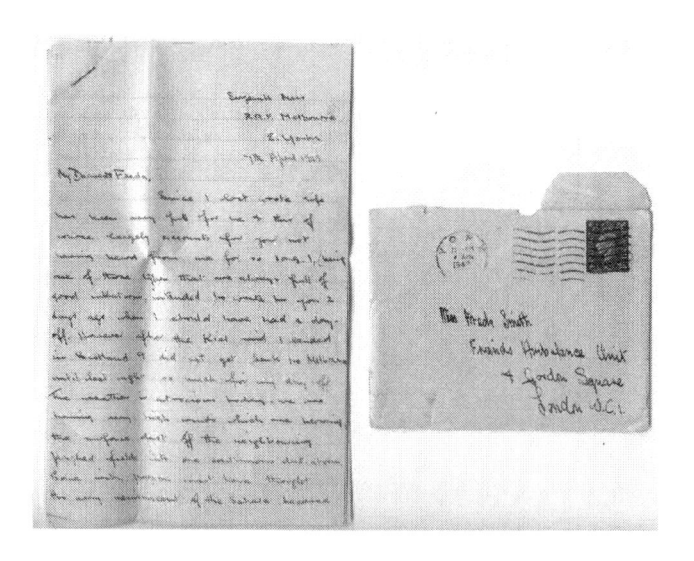

Figure 26 Jack's new handwriting

Sergeants Mess
R.A.F. Melbourne
9-4-1943

My Dearest Freda,

I am writing this in the crew room since I happen to have some note-paper handy & also some spare time (I also have your latest letter which I received this a.m.) It is only 2 days since I last wrote to you I hope I am improving – I don't mean the letters themselves but the rate at which you receive them. I had intended to spend quite a lot of time on the last letter I wrote to you but unfortunately something cropped up & I had to dash it through just as fast as I usually do.

It is about 4 p.m. now & as usual I am scrounging time off from my proper work to write this letter. This afternoon I did a spot of flying in "X" (our latest kite) just to see if she is on her best behaviour & as she was, I cut the trip short to give myself time to write this small letter to you. This is a great sacrifice for a man who loves flying as much as I do especially as we are having such glorious weather at the moment. But since I am doing it for you, it is no trouble to me whatever.

I hope you don't really consider it shocking for you to have written 4 times since last Tuesday – any way if this implies that your reserve is cracking up this is just too wonderful. On Tuesday the 31st you wrote that you would probably send a longer letter the following evening – if I know your long letters it is probably coming by parcel post & so I guess that would take longer!

Such a pity you are losing your little room & also many thanks for invitation to tea but whose rations will I be pinching? You can leave some of the scrubbing for me if you like – I wish to get some practice in case I have to earn my living this way after the war.

There is to be a C.O.'s inspection of the camp tomorrow so I guess we shall all be doing some scrubbing then to keep up the good name of our hut! The boys do not know this yet so I guess there will be much moaning & groaning when they find out. These super clean-ups present the most amazing scenes when in the process of fulfilment – there is more activity in the hut than in a beehive & what with the noise & dust & other objects flying around the whole spectacle is about 10-times more impressive than Dante's *Inferno* would ever have been.

  The reason why we shall have time to do this tomorrow morning is that we are not flying tonight & so after I have completed this letter I shall have a spot of tea & go to York on the 6 o'c. bus with the complete gang. Actually I would prefer to go in later so that I may spend a little longer on this letter but the crew will not hear of this as they are scared that I will back out altogether. However I have been writing this letter at such a speed that I am quite convinced that my hand will pack up soon with paralysis or worse – you know what an awful writer I am.

  I must ask you to pardon this choice of notepaper as it is the only sort the NAAFI has in stock at the moment & what the NAAFI hasn't got is unobtainable as far as I am concerned. At this place we have to rely on the NAAFI for all our shopping & the great trouble is that the institution has a habit of running out of stocks at the most awkward moment.

  And so, Dearest, for a short while this must be the end of our "date". I hope I shall be able to keep another one with you in a day or two's time. As there is quite a good chance that I shall not hear from you any more at Melbourne (at least in reply to this particular letter) I will give you my home address. i.e. 44. Hillary Avenue. NORWICH, NORFOLK.

  Jack.

After inspection the following day, the crew piled into ZA-X DT752, one of eleven bombers from Melbourne to attack Frankfurt. The flight was long at 9 hours; the load included 2 1000lb bombs. 10 Squadron joined the other raiders at Colne Point and left land at Dungeness. Frankfurt was bombed at around 3 am on Sunday 11th April. The raid was disastrous with 10/10 cloud making the city invisible to the bombers, according to the Bomber Command records and to the crews' own debriefing reports:

  502 aircraft - 144 Wellingtons, 136 Lancasters, 124 Halifaxes, 98 Stirlings - raided Frankfurt. Complete cloud

cover in the target area again led to a failure. The bombing photographs of every aircraft showed nothing but cloud and Bomber Command had no idea where bombs had fallen. Frankfurt reports only a few in the suburbs of the city south of the River Main. 21 aircraft - 8 Wellingtons, 5 Lancasters, 5 Stirlings, 3 Halifaxes - lost, 4.2 per cent of the force. (Bomber Command Diary)

Jack and the crew returned to base at 6.50 on Sunday morning but were not allowed on leave until Monday when they rushed through breakfast and ran for the bus and leave at last. He never describes catching the bus at Melbourne and the train at York to go on leave but it went something like this:

> And you thought of those mornings of going on leave, of the crew walking out along the road to the bus, everybody gay and a little mad with happiness, suitcases piled in the bus, and then the train steaming plumes of smoke in the winter-afternoon air under the glassless roof of York station. "So long, fellows! See you, chaps! Have a good leave!" And a wonderful feeling of relief with the spires of York Minster fading across the afternoon sky ... (Brennan, 1946, p.111)

> Friends Ambulance Unit.
> 4 Gordon Square.
> Monday [12th] 3.30 p.m
>
> My, my, what sacrifices we're making. First you sacrifice some of your precious flying to drop me a line – for which I'm truly grateful by the way, and now it looks as though I shall be sacrificing one of my nice hot baths to write this, having just come off orderly at the hostel.
> I rang up Gordon Square to see if there was a letter for me from York with the handwriting sloping backwards and asked them to send it round with the next person coming to the hostel in case it wanted an early reply. I expect by now you will be more or less waiting for the word "go". I hope you all enjoyed your domestic activities and scrubbed as energetically as you fly, and that your room – sorry hut – passed

muster for the inspection. We are supposed to have room inspection twice a week but during this present higgledy-piggledy time things have rather lapsed, which is a good thing as I don't feel like cleaning out a room when I shall be leaving it in a day or two.

Marjorie has already deserted me & taken up residence in her new room, though of course it would not be Marj if she did not leave quite a few of her possessions behind!

I was at Gordon Square yesterday morning, and I'm afraid I just lazed around at the hostel for the rest of the day, doing odd jobs of sewing & darning. One of our fellows landed last Saturday from China – it only took him 5 weeks to come from India, which is pretty good going. We learned to-day that the girl who used to share this room has now arrived in India, after being torpedoed or something – what a way to go to India: via New York, Panama & New Zealand!

I would have phoned my cheese to-day to see what time he could spare me at the weekend, but he is always busy on Mondays at a Committee Meeting. I see in the Bradshaw there are lots of trains from Norwich, and on Friday there is one that leaves there at some time after 10.0 & gets to London about 2.0 p.m. (which would enable you to get fixed up at the Chevron Club etc & meet me at about 5.0 p.m.), and there's another train leaving Norwich after 2 which gets in about 5.0). However I'll leave it to you to decide what will suit you best and then you can let me know. How about coming round to the hostel for supper which is at 6.0 p.m.?

I hope you have found your family well & in good spirits. What does your mother say to this idea of coming down to London – I don't suppose she will be too pleased, and I must say I feel rather guilty about it. Have you told her about your being on "ops" yet?

We're not having very good weather at the moment – I hope it improves before the week-end, but we won't let that prevent us from enjoying ourselves

This letter is frightfully practical & business-like I'm afraid, but there's not much time for anything else at the moment, and I've just time to fit in a bath before the Play Centre – I shall require another by the time I get back, so it's rather extravagant on water, but I deaden my conscience by the thought that the number of baths I have make up for all those that citizens of Stepney don't ever have.

Meanwhile I hope you are having a good time in the bosom of your family, so to speak – its only 3 or 4 weeks to my leave, I've just realised. Mary Shaw – my co-Sugar Loafer – is on leave. I think Marjorie will be coming down with me to-night – I hope there are not too many kids there.

It looks as though one of my letters has gone astray – you will note that I'm ignoring your sarcastic comments on its probable method of delivery by parcel post. I warn you that the sarcasm of my own tongue takes some beating if I let it run along lines, so your comments will probably be returned a thousand-fold, so to speak!

Oh dear, this won't get me to the bathroom, so I'm afraid I must close down, and say au revoir, darling, until Friday, unless I have occasion to write before then.

Freda.

44 Hilary Avenue
Norwich
14.4.1943
[written on RAF notepaper]

My Dearest Freda,
    Your letter beat me home by a few hours & caused me much joy to have it waiting for me when I got home. It also served another good purpose by warning my mother that I would possibly be home sometime that day.

I left Melbourne latish on the 12th & arrived at Norwich about midday the 13th. The journey was reasonably pleasant as wartime journeys go – I always have company when I come home on leave these days since Peter my wireless-operator lives on Broadlands about 7 miles from here. Since I have been home I have spent most of my leave sleeping & am feeling much fitter already – this is undoubtedly a good thing as I am sure I shall need all my strength when we start hiking around London together.

According to people who have been around to see me since I have been on leave things seem to be pretty desolate around here in the way of entertainments. It seems that the bombs which have dropped here since the last time I was home have sorted out all the best spots. However I don't think a nice restful leave will do me any harm at all.

By the way I have broken the news that I am intending to spend a few days in London & Mama didn't seem to mind in the least – so everything is O.K in this respect.

Since I last wrote I spent my time in the usual uninteresting way whilst in camp. My journey down here was uneventful as I said & since I have been here I have been either sleeping or doing commando raids on the pantry in quest of delicate grub. Tonight I expect to go to the flicks with my sister & that will be another job done!

Au Revoir until Friday.
Jack.

Jack was on leave in Norwich from 12th – 23rd April and he spent a long weekend, from Friday to Monday, in London. On Monday 19th, their third meeting, Freda agreed to marry him.

On 20th April, as soon as she was on her own again, Freda wrote happily to her friend Stephen Peet, who was working with the Hadfield-Spears Mobile Hospital in the Western Desert. She uses Jack's RAF slang, "gen". Yellow airmail paper was all they had in the office and all they were allowed for personal use.[48]

The day Jack leaves, Freda writes to him. She calls the letter a Feathered World bulletin and all I can think is that the idea came from Handley Page Halifax advertisements. A whole series called "Feathered Flight" were reproduced in all the papers and magazines of the period.[49]

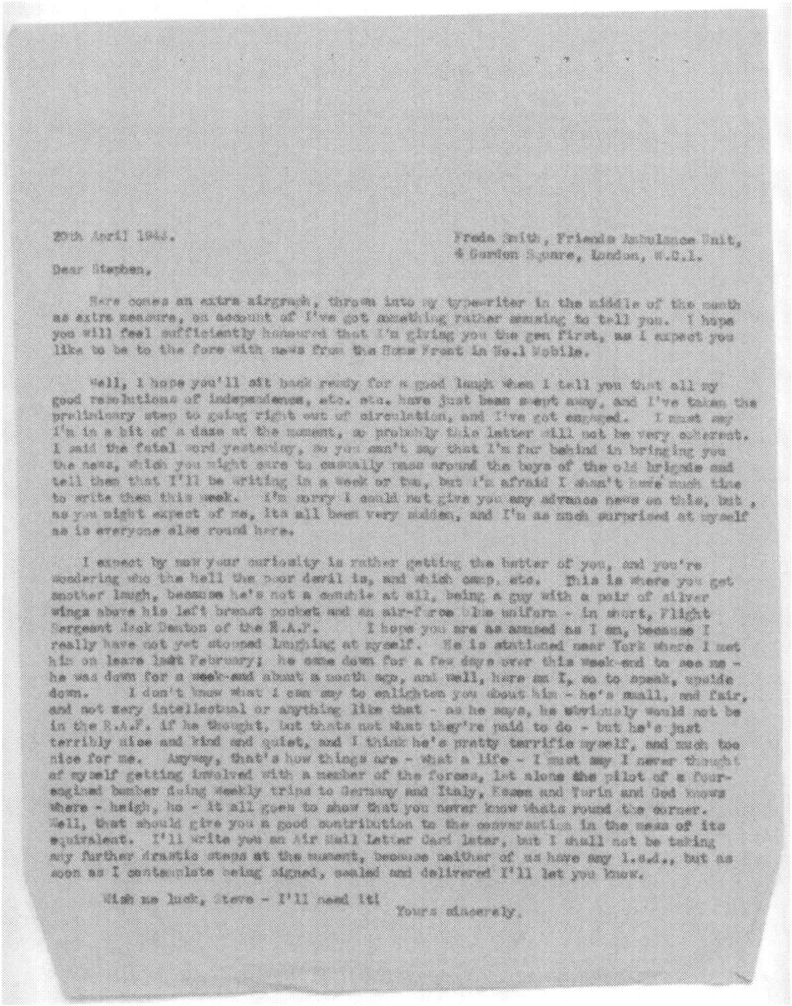

Figure 27 Freda to Stephen Peet about her engagement

F.A.U. 4 Gordon Square.
Wednesday. April 21st

Hello Darling,
Good afternoon to you if you've just tuned in, as is more than likely you lazy blighter. This is the latest

edition of the "Feathered World" and this is your favourite bird-in-hand writing it. Remember me?!

I'm longing to hear the reaction from your homefront, not to mention my own, and am hoping that tomorrow morning's post will satisfy my curiosity in both respects. I hope you were not too hungry by the time you did get back, though I expect you were terribly thirsty.

I'm slowly settling into work again, making lots of mistakes on my typewriter. Fortunately this week seems rather less busy than usual, which is a good thing because I'm on orderly on Friday morning; and on Saturday I shall be scrubbing at Gordon Square when we are changing offices so I hope you will spare me a thought as you laze in bed of a morning. What a super char woman I shall make after the war, shan't I!?!

I had a letter to-day from the girl whose coupons I lost. She has been given 15 to replace the 20, so that really means I shall have to give her 5 of mine at which I could weep. Her wedding will now have cost me 13 coupons, as I gave her 4 and lent her 4 when she was getting married, and now I suppose I shall have to part with another 5 and say good-bye to any thought of a new summer dress.

I'm writing this in my room, having just returned from the Sugar Loaf. When we got there this evening we found the floor absolutely strewn with jig-saw puzzles, all mixed up, and the asbestos twiggly bits in the gas fire were all broken – somebody seems to have been in having a fine time over the weekend.

I am glad I've introduced you to my present abode, darling. The room seems much more pleasant, and somehow I feel as if you are part and parcel of it, which is rather a clumsy way of expressing things. But you know what I mean; I feel that it's your room as well as mine, and hope that you think of it in the same way.

The news of my going off the market, so to speak, is slowly seeping through the sections. Everyone is terribly nice about it, bless them. I hope mother is as nice, not that I should take any notice if she were not!

I don't quite know what to say in this epistle, Jack, as I'm rather waiting to hear from you, and so perhaps if I just say that, well, that I'm gloriously happy, and hope you will let it go at that.

Would you like me to stay on in the Unit during the war? It seems the most sensible thing to do in more ways than two, and I do hope you think so too; and, apart from practical considerations, just as next to your flying you put me above all else (or I hope you do), so, next to loving you, my loyalty to the Unit comes in second.

I had thought of posting this by the midnight post but don't know that it would reach you any more speedily, but I'll write again when I hear from you. I hope the wretched siren doesn't go to-night – it went last night and although I was not on duty, someone was away, so I went. We got within 50 yards of Colonial Shelter when the All Clear went, and I lost no time in getting back to the hostel and to bed!

It's almost 10.30 p.m. and perhaps it might be an idea to join the queue for the bath. I suppose you will be back at Melbourne by the time my next letter reaches you. Give my kind regards to everyone, Jack, and I hope they all had nice leaves, and that George is not too cross with you. With meeting George & Wally & Maxie I feel that I really know you all. Please, darling, try and write at any rate once each week – if you're frightfully busy just send me a Post Card or anything. I do try not to worry, but it's not very easy; honestly though, I will try.

I was trying hard over the week-end to think of --- well, what I was wanting to say when I was so anxious to know just why you like me so much on Monday was, ----- God-damn-it, Jack, how can I say it – I think Elizabeth Browning could express it better than I ever can when she wrote:
If thou must love me, let it be for naught
Except for love's sake only. Do not say,
"I love her for her smile – her look – her way
Of speaking gently, - for a trick of thought

That falls in well with mine, and certes brought
A sense of pleasant ease on such a day" –
For these things in themselves, Belovèd, may
Be changed, or change or thee – and love, so wrought,
May be unwrought so. Neither love me for
Thine own dear pity's wiping my cheeks dry:
A creature might forget to weep, who bore
Thy comfort long, and lose thy love thereby!
But love me for love's sake, that evermore
Thou may'st love on, through love's eternity.

    Good-night, my darling, and good luck, and all my love, Freda.

[Postmarked Norfolk, 9.45 am, 23rd April]
    44 Hilary Avenue
    Norwich
    21.4:1943

    My Darling,
    Since I have not been able to get you out of my mind for a single moment since I have been back I feel that I might get a small measure of relief by writing to you in spite of the fact that I do not have anything to say apart from the usual things.
    I have missed you so terribly that I keep thinking there is a pair of brown eyes looking at me & I am fast becoming convinced that the spirit of the Schmidts is haunting me.
    I regret that I did not say goodbye to you very nicely on the station but goodbyes are my weak point, especially in the daytime. I had to stand in the corridor as far as Ipswich but this did not prove to be very unpleasant.
    The train was quite fast & I had a pretty continuous conversation the whole way with the guardsman who stood next to me. He was a hellish line-shooter but it did make the time pass more quickly. I arrived home at 5.30, had tea afterwards, & retired to bed at about 9.o'c. not to rise again until 11.30 today.

I am still enjoying brilliant weather & life here is very sunny & peaceful. In spite of this I confess to feeling a trifle sad that you are not with me. This must be a selfish sort of sadness – I guess I must be very happy at heart now that we are so close. I also feel ridiculously in love – in fact I am scared people will notice it before long but no one seems to find any difference in me. When I broke the gladsome news to the folks at home very little comment was made.

My mother didn't believe I was serious but when I reassured her, she did not seem disturbed. My sister was thrilled when I told her but she scolded me severely because I did not time things better so that I might have bought you a ring. Anyway choosing a ring is much too much of a job for an inartistic person like myself to take on by my lonesome, & so we have no alternative but to wait until your leave.

Talking of leave I more or less consider mine finished now & am quite looking forward to going back to the Melbourne Wilderness to do a spot of toil. I usually do get fed up with leave before it is finished – everything is much too quiet at home & with the reaction after my happy time with you, I am now quite bored.

It is hard to prophesy how quiet things will be in an hour's time as it is Sylvia's 5th birthday & she is having 3 or 4 of her pals to tea – woe is me! She is taking a very active interest in the preparations for tea. In fact she was responsible for getting me out of bed at 11.30 to pick wild-flowers from the neighbouring fields in order to decorate the joint.

This afternoon before commencing this epistle I became very conscientious about the paper shortage, & salvaged some of paper and card that I used during my short career as a part-time poster-writer. This was all stuff which I hadn't looked at since I joined the R.A.F. & it was a great surprise to find what a lot of junk I possessed. I have been diving through drawing boards, T squares, pots of colour & Indian Ink, drawing paper used & unused & every conceivable odd & end you could imagine. However I did a great job & I am sure the war effort will benefit by it.

This seems to be the extent of my actions since I have been back & I can find little else to talk of in a constructive sort of way but I shall write again tomorrow & try then. In any case the kids are rolling up now & so I shall soon be forced to pack up.

And so, Brown Eyes

My very dearest Love to you Darling,

Jack.

Figure 28 Jack, mid 1943

That same day, before he left for York, one of Jack's friends took a photo of him. The film was not developed for some time (most films held only 12 pictures and people did not take many photos) and Jack forgot about it.

On 22nd April Freda wrote again about her Jack and the letter positively bursts with excitement about their engagement. This letter was to Percy, working in clinics in the Near East.

> I don't know what I can say to enlighten you about him – he's small and fair, and not very intellectual or anything like that – as he says, he obviously would not be in the R.A.F. if he thought, but that's not what they're paid to do – but he's terribly nice and kind and quiet and I THINK HE'S PRETTY TERRIFIC MYSELF, AND MUCH TOO NICE FOR ME. So there you are – what a life – I must say I never thought of myself, as conscientious an objector as ever was, getting involved with a member of the forces, let alone the pilot of a four-engined bomber doing weekly trips to Germany and Italy, Essen and Turin and God knows where – heigh, ho - it all goes to show that you never know what's round the corner.
>
> I've not heard from my mama yet, and am wondering how she will take it –I expect she will think me even crazier than usual – she's probably right, but well, I'm fully aware of what I'm letting myself in for – I suppose in many ways I might as well be engaged to a land-mine as someone in Bomber Command, but other girls can take it, and I don't intend to be any exception, however nerve-wracking a business it may be. I hope you will both wish me luck – I'm going to need it!

Once back at Melbourne Jack tells Freda: "I don't feel a bit normal and it's all your fault too." Crewmen forming serious romantic attachments, whether on the base with a WAAF or not, was frowned upon. It was recognised that any distraction could spell disaster. A pilot of 57 Squadron wrote of an airman that "Getting married was an unnecessary distraction, and having a wife was bound to affect his concentration." (*Bomber Flight Berlin*, p. 278.) Max Hastings goes further and writes that pilots who formed emotional attachments were actually feared by other aircrew. "When a pilot was seen brooding over a girl in the mess, he was widely regarded as a candidate for 'the chop list'."(*Bomber Command*, p. 250.) Jack's crew seem not to have believed this at all. Freda kept Jack concentrated on the future and the end of his tour and though all shook up by her, at least she helped distract him from that more dangerous emotion: fear: Fear was sometimes called the eighth member of a crew.

Sergeants Mess
R.A.F. Melbourne
York. [Friday 23rd April]

Darling Freda,
This is my first evening at Melbourne & to make a good start there is no flying to be done so I take this golden opportunity to answer the "feathered world bulletin".

We arrived here at about midnight last night and as everyone was together at the time I took the opportunity of breaking the news of our engagement to the crew. I am glad to report that this venture proved a very happy one – I was simply overwhelmed with congratulations – George being the first one in the rush, (& he didn't condemn me as a wastrel either). Any way the short & the long of it is that everyone here is overjoyed at my success & the boys just cannot forget about it. I must say I hardly expected it to cause such a sensation. There have been all manner of prophesies of likely dates & such wise & everyone is trying to find out all our plans & just refuse to believe me when I say we haven't made any as yet. This will give us something to discuss next time we meet in person.

Apart from all this nattering to me very little else has occurred in the great city of Melbourne. This afternoon we did a spot of local flying just to assure ourselves that we are all still capable of performing our respective duties. Well, since we all found that we were, this trip does not afford much to write about.

Any way this is about 8 in the evening & the day has ended for us. Everyone in the crew is writing letters & most unfortunately I was not lucky enough to get a seat at the one & only table in the room – I therefore find myself stretched out on my bed leaning on one elbow as I write this to you & I assure you it is not a very comfortable position at that. I only hope that George & Wally write letters to their wives of the usual length then I know I shall not have to wait long.

Shall I be able to get away with such short letters in time to come? I really think I shall still be much too much in love to pass you over so lightly. By the way are you still making hoards of mistakes in your typing – I sincerely hope not for the sake of the unit which you love so much.

Talking of the Unit I thought it was an understood thing that you were to stay & I am quite sure I would not wish you to do anything else, especially anything which does not coincide with your ideals. In any case you seem so wonderfully happy, I should be exceedingly wary to do anything to upset the balance of things as they are.

Your letter was indeed of a serious nature & I took all your comments deeply to heart & agree with them 100% but find it very hard to comment on them in the noisy atmosphere which prevails at the moment.

I am sure we are both happy to have been matched with this hour "whilst we are young" & though we are attacking these problems in different ways, I am quite sure that neither of us is narrow-minded enough not to respect the opposite point of view. I certainly respect your views & I am sure that after the war our views will be very much the same about the practical side of post-war reconstruction, especially the social side of the reconstruction – it is my belief that social reconstruction is very nearly the solution to everything.

This is undoubtedly very vague especially for a person who claims to work on a practical basis. To be practical one should do first things first & I cannot be sure that I have done this always. For instance we have not done much in the way of discussing a plan for the most wonderful wedding in the world. Since I left you my mind has been so full of sweet memories of you that I have not done much practical thinking.

I must not let my love for you run away with me altogether for if I did, I know I should want to run away & marry you tomorrow.

However I do not in any case wish to marry whilst I am engaged on operational flying for reasons which are obvious. This of course will not worry us a great deal since I shall be off ops in another three months approx. But then we shall not have a great deal of money in the pool in 3 months time, & I don't think it a good plan to do these things with insufficient financial backing. As you know I am not particularly well off at the moment although the income will be steady in the future.

What I should like to do is get married & still have £100 to £150 in the background as a sort of capital. I do not think it will take me too long to achieve this if I try really hard, but time will tell. If I am still in the R.A.F. at the time, as I almost certainly shall be, our income will increase quite considerably after our marriage & so as a consequence the rate of saving will be faster & our position much more healthy. But do please tell me how you feel about all this, Darling, as I am relying a terrific amount on the suggestions etc which I hope to receive from you.

Here there has been a pause of about 1 hour to enable me to go for supper – this was necessary since we were flying at tea-time today & therefore did not partake of this meal. The pause has made it rather difficult for me to get back to my original trend of thought & as it is now long after "lights out" I think I will abandon same & go onto different topics.

I must say how sorry I was to hear of your coupons entailing the loss of your summer dress. This is something I just cannot help you with, unfortunately.

I am so sorry, my Darling, but there is such an argument going on amongst the boys that it is almost impossible for me to do justice to this letter. I have been writing the whole of it now on my bed because when the boys finished their dutiful letters they began a game of pontoon & so the table has not been within my grasp all evening. I have just read what I have written & a sorry mess it is indeed – but I dare not scrap it as we are sure to be getting back to normal tomorrow & then opportunities of corresponding with you will be even more limited. All I can do is promise to write to you just as soon as I possibly can

& hope to make a better job of it then. Until I do write you may rest assured that I am thinking of you & loving you the whole time.

Goodbye for a little while Darling.

I love you dearly.

Jack.

F.A.U. 4 Gordon Square.
April 23rd 1943

Greetings, Herr Flight Sergeant! This is Fraulein Schmidt, the Spy with the Twisted Finger, or la dame aux yeux brun (pardon my French), or just simply me, darling.

How's Melbourne and the rest of the crew? It seems difficult to imagine you back up in Melbourne again. I hope George & Wally etc. had as happy a time as we had.

I was on orderly here (the hostel) this morning, but phoned the Square to see if there were any letters for me, then dashed over this afternoon to collect yours & a letter from my mother informing me that it's no use her saying anything to me because I wouldn't take any notice of her if she did, but she hopes I won't do anything rash, and anyway she doesn't believe I'm serious! I seem to disturb my mother about as much as you disturb yours, but I never bother about parents anyway.

We had a hectic time at Gordon Square this afternoon moving offices from No. 4 to No. 3. We passed all the furniture, files etc. over the balcony on the first floor from one building to another in the pouring rain in record speed – it was very funny I must say. Ronald thoroughly enjoyed himself because it gave him an opportunity to change into his old tropical kit so that he would not dirty his suit.

I hope your sister had a nice party, and that you did your duty by her and rendered the necessary assistance at the tea-table etc, as befits a big brother!

I came over from the Square early to-day, and wish that I had not done so, as its terribly quiet here and I miss you a lot, but I suppose that's something I shall have to get used to. It's good to think that it's only two weeks to-day before I go on leave – I do hope you're not busy that week – if you are I shall have to slip out to Melbourne to see you, or Pocklington or somewhere, though I hope you will be able to come into York for one day anyhow.

I suppose I shall have to drag you round to meet my very ordinary working-class family. Will you mind terribly? We're a very ordinary crowd – not that there's anyone but mother & father & David (who is 27) and I.

Father is a foreman at the motor-fitting shops on the L.N.E.R, so you see we're just ordinary, but mother often gets annoyed with me because she says I have big ideas, which I suppose is only natural. She has appalling taste in most things, and we don't get on too well, but she's very generous & good to me really, and I suppose I'm none too helpful a daughter really. Father is very quiet and has little interest outside cars, about which there is little he does not know, and most nights he stays in & smokes his pipe and twiddles around with the radio, & perhaps goes for a walk. He's not what you could call a person who mixes with people. He's a bit exasperating at times but he means well. I get on with him better than mother, who of course rather leans more to David, who's a very bright & cheerful person – David gets very home-sick, but I'm afraid homesickness is something I've never suffered from.

So there you have a bit of gen on my home. I hope it won't make you feel obliged to give me any on yours, darling. You seem a bit of a mis-fit, like me, & you said of course that you didn't hit it off too well with your father, but, anyway, it's you I'm marrying, not your parents.

You know Jack, I think we're going to get a terrific kick from forging ahead on nothing at all, don't you. I don't mean forging ahead in a materialistic sense, but, well, building up a life of all the things the way we ourselves would like them to be, if you see what I mean.

It won't be very easy to buy a ring in York dear. Pat (my friend) had a terrific job, though, as I say, I would rather have a good antique ring really – and that's NOT just because I want to be different! However, when I come home we'll make a great tour of all the antique shops in Stonegate, shall we? But much as I adore good things I don't think you ought to spend a lot of money on one – we could do so many other things with the cash. I do feel dreadful about not being able to save anything but it does just seem impossible here – still, I wish I could feel I were doing something.

What a disgustingly practical epistle this is turning out to be. I did not begin with that intention. I merely meant to say how-de-do to set you off on your daily round once again, though I suppose we shall have to get down to being practical at sometime or other.

Please don't feel that you did not give me a sufficiently adequate good-bye at the Station, Jack. I hate Station goodbyes myself, and the real one I count as the evening before at Whitechapel, darling

I think it might be a good idea for me to have an early night to-night – I scrubbed out five bathrooms this morning, and was latish going to bed last night. Fortunately there's been no Play Centre on account of it being Good Friday, and the Priest would not have liked it if we had opened up as usual – Wapping is very Catholic. We shall be closed on Monday too, though of course I shall be at Gordon Square.

It's a glorious evening, with a wide expanse of blue sky, save where, to the west, grey clouds, tipped with red & gold, hover across the setting sun ......and I do miss you.

Do you think I might trip round to the Air Ministry & vamp them into sending you down to Oxford when you've finished your "tour"?! It will be too sickening if you have to go up to Lossiemouth again.

Well, I think that just about brings me up to date with my doings. I shall probably drop you odd lines mid-week now & then, but I shan't expect replies to them – they will merely be in an effort to keep up your morale & all that – or to keep up my own – I'm not sure which!

Perhaps if there's a midnight post from here I can get this away so that it's waiting for you when you get to Melbourne on Saturday. I think I'll try it, so au revoir from now darling, and happy landings.

All my love,
Freda.

P.S. My home address, by the way, is:- 36 Knavesmire Crescent, The Mount, YORK

P.P.S. The most terrific wind has just blown up, and a terrific black cloud has crossed the sky, bringing with it a heavy shower – its glorious – I love this sort of weather – I could get drunk on it!

Room 323.
London Hospital Students Hostel,
Philpot Street.
London. E.1.
Tuesday. April 27th. 10.45 p.m

Darling,

I'm sitting up in bed to write half of this letter, and will probably finish it from the same spot tomorrow night. It seems so silly putting the Gordon Square address on top of these letters, when I always write them from here, but I hope you will continue to write to me at Gordon Square – it's nice to have a letter from you on the desk when I arrive.

I'm so glad that George & Wally and co. were not cross with you. I hope I might meet Peter & Derrick & Norman sometime & then I shall know everyone.

I've just been having a tea-party of the old crowd in here – Marjorie felt that the occasion demanded it. I've not heard from mother again yet – she'll be writing some time this week I expect. Everyone around here, just bombards me with questions, and probably thinks, like the crew, that I'm holding out on them. As you say, we did not do much practical discussion, but then, time seemed so short and well, I suppose we were both far too dreamy to think of such things.

Meanwhile, you raise one or two points in your letter on which I might perhaps comment. Let me see, what are they. Oh, yes, this business about not getting married while you're on ops – I think that's crazy, darling. Don't ever get any idea that I should not want to marry you while you were on ops. When I said "Yes", I didn't make a lot of mental provisos and conditions – and I refuse to see any difference that might be made.

However, as you say you will be off ops in 3 months, and I suppose that is when we shall have to review the situation. And here, darling, I shall throw myself entirely at your mercy, so to speak.

You see Jack, I'm afraid that beyond my solitary £5.0.0d. left in the bank and my Unit clothing allowance, I haven't a penny, having long ago used up what small capital I had. I can't guarantee on mother being too helpful, because I haven't been exactly a model daughter and stayed at home as a thoughtful girl should, and in any case I doubt if my pride would let me, so that's how things are from my side.

Just what your position is, you know best, but it's you I'm in love with and not your capital-to-be, so to speak, and I really don't see why we should not be able to make it on less, darling. I'm willing to try it if you are, and I expect lots of other people do. Those are just my ideas on things, Jack, and whatever you say goes, of course, - you're the pilot on this trip, but it will give you another line of thought and will, I hope, get across the idea that I love you, if it does nothing else!

It's queer to think that this has been Easter weekend. On Saturday afternoon I went up to see our new hostel in Hampstead, very close to the Heath. Afterwards Mary Shaw and I walked back across the heath and caught the tube to Whitechapel. I went to bed very early, about 8.30 p.m., but had to get up at about 12.30 when the siren went. Fortunately the All Clear sounded before I got out of the hostel, but as I did not feel tired some of us adjourned to the kitchen to make tea.

I stayed in bed all Sunday morning, which was shockingly lazy, but very pleasant.

A friend of Marjorie's arrived unexpectedly for the week-end.

She is in the Land Army and brought lots of flowers. Marjorie passed some on to me, and I've got a glorious jar of lilac, pink tulips, and irises in the room – they're terrific.

On Sunday afternoon we went along the embankment and into St. James' Park. The Park has the most glorious display of tulips I have ever seen – they are just wonderful – splashes of almost every colour one can think of, with lots of other colours one did not know existed: red, pinks, yellow, gold, bronze, mauve, purple; just bed upon bed of brilliant colour; and withal a blue sky and white clouds, and a bright sun, and just sufficient breeze to ripple the water on the lake and sway the laburnum trees with their heavy laden branches of golden blossom. I wish you could have been here.

I was on orderly again on Monday morning, but it did not seem a very busy shift. Afterwards, in the afternoon, I walked slowly through the city to Gordon Square, meandering just wherever my fancy lead me, along past Liverpool Street & London Wall, Moorgate & Aldersgate – vast areas of desolation, legacies from 1940, heaps of rubble and ruin and decay.

It's 11.45 p.m. and I really ought perhaps to close for to-day, which I forthwith proceed to do, with a murmured "Good-night" darling, wherever you are.

Wednesday. 7.45 p.m.

I've just returned from the Sugar Loaf where a fairly quiet evening has been spent – thank heaven! We've just got a new supply of paints, so everyone is kept more or less happy daubing paint all over the place and trying to swipe the old Christmas Cards which they are using to copy from.

The office is in a chaotic state at the moment because Works Squad are knocking a hole in the pantry wall between Nos. 3 & 4, and brick dust is flying all over the place & and settling everywhere, and I was glad to get away early to come to the Play Centre. I managed to get a lift back on one of the Unit lorries, so came back in record time, in company with a sack of potatoes and goodness knows what else.

Only ten more days before I come on leave, my sweet. I do hope you're not busy that week, because there's so much for us to talk about, and we really must get down to it this time. I do hope mother is helpful Jack, it will make such a difference if she is. Not that there is any reason why she should be otherwise, but I never know quite how I'm going to find her! This will be making her sound rather an ogre, but she's not in the least really – just inclined to be awkward!

It's just not fair that money should be such a stumbling block to people who could be so happy, and I'm dashed if I'm going to let it stand in our way.

(Here there's been a break of about 2hrs while I attended a Section Meeting called for the purpose of advising our representative to Staff Meeting next Saturday which nominations he should support for the Executive Committee, which is the Unit Committee, so to speak which decides Unit policy & work etc; we elect our own officers. However its now 10.0 p.m. & I've lost no time in coming up to bed, from whence I am contriving this epistle. I hope I can pick up the threads fairly quickly)

Oh yes, darling, about this wretched business of money, I'm sure it need not bother us unnecessarily, but as I've already said, you're the pilot on this series of ops. For a hitherto cautious person like me this seems rank heresy, but all goes to prove the devastating effects of the R.A.F. when it hits its target!

What a pity I'm not living in York now; we could see one another so much more often, though I suppose many people are much further apart that we are. Will there ever be a possibility of you going overseas – that would be pretty grim, would it not.

Actually, in many ways I'm glad I'm not in York. The slow and heavy drone of planes, flying eastward out of the sunset in the evening sky has always depressed me, and my present personal interest in Bomber Command would not exactly detract from my gloom, so I'm glad we don't often hear planes flying over London en route. What a coward I am, darling – I ought not to have written all this rot. Don't take any notice of it, and I promise it won't ever occur again – sorry, sir!

David (my brother) was going home for Easter. I wrote to him last week, so I expect I shall be hearing from him eventually, though he does not usually write to me except on my birthday & at Christmas, when he sends some cash. David is 27 and works at Vickers-Armstrong at Barrow-in-Furness, as I expect I already told you.

11.0 p.m. and perhaps it's time I got some sleep. Did Maxie manage to straighten out his mix-ups while he was on leave? Did Wally manage to make his peace with his wife re the epistles! I warn you I shall not be so easily soothed!

(Knock on the door & in comes Marjorie to see if I've got some sugar – she's having tea in her room but I made my excuses and apologies & did not go on account of I'd got this date with you – aren't you lucky!)

Within a week or two I hope I shall be having a real date with you – I was going to show you round York – remember?

So until we write again, darling, all my love, and all the happiness I would like to bring to you.

Freda.

Freda writes also about Easter Sunday to Stephen Peet but adds to him that after walking in St. James',

I wandered through Aldersgate and the blitzed acres of the city. I looked across a vast stretch of rubble and ruin, one long stretch of grey, and right at the end, some 300 yards away, was a cluster of irises

– my hat, this sounds like Beverley Nichols at his worst – sorry – excuse please.

I also went to Hampstead Heath on Friday night, and looked in on the fair which is flourishing there this Easter, complete with darts, merry-go-rounds of all descriptions, rolling pennies, rifle ranges, but alas no coconut shies. So you see, London continues to enjoy itself in its own sweet way – what a place.

Melbourne

My Darling,
I cannot guarantee how long this letter will be – we are waiting for X to be made serviceable so that we can fly her on an air-test. I am actually writing this on the navigator's table in the aircraft – thrilling isn't it!

As you will have guessed by the interval between my last letter & this one, we have been doing a spot of flying since I last wrote: i.e last night & Monday night. These have been not too eventful but as is usually the case they have taken up about 100% of my time.

By the way Miss Schmidt I received your Aryan (?) greetings last Sunday & as a morale-keeper-upper they fulfilled their duties excellently. I am so happy that your chère Mama did not take a strong view of her daughter's actions – what does she mean by "Don't do anything rash."? However I guess we shall find out what this all implies when you "drag" me round to see her when you come to York.

So sorry to hear that rings are difficult to obtain in York – still that will be something else we shall find out about when the time comes – by the way much as I like to try to agree with you on most everything I do think you should have a nice engagement ring regardless of cost (within reason – ahem). I do really think we should start right even if only as a symbolic gesture. However stop me if I am wrong because I usually am & and in some respects I have rather deep-set wooden-headed ideas – only you are capable of shifting them! How so ever, let's fight this out when you come back to the family fold & we do our tour of Stonegate – incidentally I have not the slightest idea where Stonegate is. I still do not know my way around York – in fact had it not been for Peter I am sure I should never have found my way from the station to the bus stop the last time I was in York.

Since we have been back at camp life has been quite busy for us as usual. We are due to fly tonight but are all hoping that the weather will save us – it is pouring with rain outside at the moment & the mechanics & other gen men seem to be having quite a rough time of it. The rain is beating on the air-frame & creating the most disturbing din – however this will not disturb me much longer since I have just been informed that she will be O.K to fly in about 5 minutes time.

It is about 3 ½ hours since the last sentences were written since which time I had a quick air-test, darted back to have a late tea, proceeded to briefing which was, after much delay, postponed, played a quick game of table-tennis with Norman and had my pre-take-off shower. It is now 9 p.m. & as yet we have not been briefed so it looks as though take-off will be very late indeed. This is one of those occasions when the weather plays funny tricks with us & everyone sits jittering in the mess as they are now, waiting for the phone to ring telling us whether we shall fly tonight or not. I guess it is hard for you to imagine how tense everyone seems to be on these occasions. However these things don't worry me as much as they used to & it gives me quite a sense of superiority to sit here calmly writing letters while the newer boys are all huddled together & talking so earnestly.

As you would gather from this I am in the mess now. Maxie is at the moment playing marches on the piano – such lovely stirring music! George & Wally are playing draughts & cursing each other quite freely, when they fall into traps. However all this is getting a long way away from us – so far I seem to have given you a running commentary on the passing show & that's all.

I wonder what you are doing now. I thought the same thing at 8.15 this evening when we were in the briefing room. I do wish you were here & talking to me, but not with all these folks around.

I had thought that perhaps when I had been on the squadron for a week I might find myself getting back to normal – well my actions are still very much the same as before but I don't feel a bit normal and it is all your fault too. I just feel so wonderfully contented about everything & nothing seems to affect this happy feeling at all. This is what it feels like for me, to be in love for the first time & I hope it lasts for ever – I am sure it will.

By the way, Darling, you did not say just what date you expected to get home. I would like to know in advance since we are hoping to do a spot of wangling when the time comes with regard to scrounging time-off. When I say we I mean the whole crew because, faithful as ever, they have pledged themselves to co-operate with the scrounging when the time comes.

We are due to be briefed in about 15 minutes time so I don't think I will embark on any more paragraphs. I have been feeling pretty certain of a "scrub" all evening & it now seems we shall be going after all. I make the usual plea for forgiveness for such a ramshackle and irrelevant letter but conditions for letter writing have been bad tonight.

Wish me luck, Darling.
Jack.

On Sunday 25th, Jack's second night back in Melbourne, there were test flights, often called circuits and bumps, but no operational flying.

On 26th Jack flew ZA-X again but with an altered crew. Crew changes may have been necessary to test radar because at this time new radar, such as H2S, and navigational aids, such as AI (Airborne Interception), were being added to aircraft. More likely the test flight was made to accustom new crew to the aircraft. Norman Plenderlieth, the navigator, was on leave in Belfast so not flying that night and P/O Taylor, A.G. took his place, while Sgt. Wright, L.A. flew as 2nd Pilot.

Jack, Derrick, Peter, Maxie, Wally and George completed the crew. Take off was at midnight and they returned at 5 a.m., in broad daylight. The debriefing note in the ORB says "Bombs were observed to burst in a built up area. The whole of DUISBURG appeared to be a mass of Incendiaries and smoke ..."

The raid was "a partial failure," according to Bomber Command Diary. Pathfinders claimed to have marked accurately but did not. "However, Duisburg had more than 300 buildings destroyed and a death toll of between 130 and 207 (reports vary)." That same night bombs hit 6 other towns in the Ruhr.

On Tuesday 27th, 6 aircraft go gardening (Freda guessed wrongly that they bombed Wilhelmshaven that night, the raid discussed in all the papers) and Jack's in X and with the usual crew again. As he guesses in his letter, it is another late take-off, this time at 01.50 and they land at 04:59. He carries 4 mark V mines and the other five aircraft carry 2 mark IV mines. They fly out in formation over Hornsea and return via Flamborough. "Visibility was very poor with rain and position was determined by a gee fix [radio]. No opposition was encountered." It was the biggest minelaying operation of the war; the Bay of Biscay, the Channel ports of Brittany and the Frisian Islands were all sown that night.

Wednesday 28th and Jack has been flight testing ZA-X so maybe this was one of the aircraft which, according to ORB, had "hang-ups" on take-off that night. The problem was fixed and Jack sounds sure he will have to fly. ORB says that on 28th, 9 aircraft from Melbourne were out gardening in the bad weather, but Jack's crew are not mentioned. Testing is mentioned however, though crews doing test flights are not listed. The weather was so bad that take-off was clearly touch and go so the crew would have eaten operational tea and then waited while Jack, and the other pilots, took turns to phone the control tower to ask what the met boys were predicting, to find out whether the flight was on, with everyone expecting to stand down.

The following day, Thursday 29th April, the weather was worse and there were no ops.

The weather had cleared a bit by the 30th April and Jack and crew set off in a new kite, ZA-E HR698. They rode out just after midnight, raided Essen at 2.30 and returned shortly after 5 a.m. on 1st May. Debriefing from Jack's crew says that "Flak was heavy but few searchlights were in action." The crew did not get to bed before 7 a.m.

    4 GORDON SQUARE
    Friday. 30th April 1943

    Sorry to be using official notepaper, darling, but I've just received your epistle and wanted to make sure that you got a fairly early though decidedly inadequate reply, because you said you wanted to know as early as possible when I was due to hit the old hometown once again. I shall be travelling down to York on Friday 7th There's a train leaving here at 3.50 or 2.50 or something, which gets me into York at about 7.30 or 8.0.

    If you by any chance have the evening off on Friday, I shall look out for you under the station clock. I hope to be in York for about 10 days – say until Sunday the 16th, when I shall probably return by the mid-night train.

    I'll write you a long epistle over the weekend to reach you on Monday, and will crave forgiveness for the brevity of this, which is written at my desk, which is not half so thrilling as your navigator's table, I'm afraid, though I hope you will feel sufficiently honoured by the knowledge that right now I ought to be typing a letter to the Archbishop of Canterbury, but have given you No. 1 Priority and am scribbling this first! I take it Wilhelmshaven was your target on Tuesday – I hope you all had a good trip, darling, and flew through the air with as great an ease as ever.

    All my love, darling,
    Yours ever.
    Freda.

    London Hospital Students Hostel,
    Friday. April 30th. Approx. 8.15 pm!

    Darling Jack,
    So now you know what I'm doing at 8.15 p.m. this evening! I wonder if you are sitting in the

briefing room, as you were on Wednesday. If so I hope you are listening attentively to all that is being said to you – remember 10.30 Euston Square?! Anyway if you are about to go off, I'm wishing you good luck, all the time dear.

It's been a horribly wet day. I've just returned from the Play Centre and my legs are very dirty and rain-splashed. We had a crazy last half-hour of musical chairs, musical flop, Here we come gathering Nuts in May & The Grand Old Duke of York. – such stirring tunes! – ye gods!

At 10.0'clock this evening I'm going to have tea with Dennis (whom you met) and Alan Jones, as they are leaving the hostel to-morrow and going to live at Mile End Hospital Section about a mile away. Dennis returned from leave on Monday and was terrifically pleased when I told him the news about us.

If you do find that you are not flying & can get into York next Friday it would be nice to see you somewhere outside the Barrier near Smiths (no relation) Bookstall at the Station.

I can see that we are going to have a slight argument next week – what fun! I wonder who will get the last word on this ring question.

It is nice of George & Wally & Co to co-operate in trying to scrounge time off, and I certainly do hope you will be able to wrangle it.

Thank goodness it's the first of the month tomorrow. I must remember to use up my sweet-coupons. I think it might be a good idea to take some home to mother (sweets I mean) as I gather they are rather scarce in York.

By the way, I hope you don't mind being in print in the F.A.U. Chronicle which comes out tomorrow. The Editor usually prints a list of all the engagements etc. he has sniffed out, and at the bottom of the list of congratulations they've put me and you.

I'm terribly drowsy, and do wish I were not due to drink tea in a few minutes time, but I can't let the side down, & all that, so I'll adjourn until tomorrow evening.

Saturday. 11.15 p.m.

I've just come to bed via my usual route – i.e. the bath, after the most delightfully busy day I've had for some time. George Mallory, who usually copies out official airgraphs as they come in from overseas, is away this week-end and so I've been doing the copying instead. He certainly chose the right week-end. Yesterday we got a 10 p. airgraph report from the Middle East and to-day a 20 p. one from Ethiopia.

Fortunately Ronald has been away to-day at various meetings, so I've been able to get down to the job without being disturbed, and typed almost continuously since about 9.30 this evening, but I must say I've thoroughly enjoyed the day. I moved into Ronald's office which is smaller than ours & has a gas fire, and I've just plodded steadily on – of course when typed on ordinary paper the reports were much longer than on airgraph forms.

It's been raining most of to-day, but it was quite dry when I left Gordon Square, and fairly light, so I walked as far as the Milk Bar in Fleet Street – remember? – and had some coffee & a sandwich before walking on in the gathering dusk to catch the tube at Blackfriars.

It was almost dark when I got out at Whitechapel, though the sky was very cloudy, and there was just one solitary star. I wondered if you were just about to take-off, and looked at the star and wished you good-luck, as I did at 8.15, pausing for a moment during my blitz on the typewriter.

How marvellous it would be if you were somewhere around – I always think that when I'm tired – not that I don't think it most of the rest of the day! I'm so glad I can make you happy, darling,- it's my post war reconstruction aim from now on.

Big Ben is just striking twelve and if I'm not careful I shall be falling asleep with the pen in my hand, so Goodnight darling, and an advance Goodmorning for when this reaches you.

Au Revoir.
Freda.

So, Freda finished her last letter of April on Saturday 1st May. It rained for much of that first day in May 1943 but by evening a warm setting sun shone through the clean air. Earlier that same evening, Jack had just got up after returning late from a raid to Essen.

Jack flew ZA-E HR698 for the Essen raid of 30/1 May. They took off just after midnight and did not return to base until 5 am, which means they flew back at dawn over the banks of anti-aircraft guns in Holland, continually climbing and diving to avoid night fighters flying in wait, difficult because until they reached relative safety over the East Coast, they were silhouetted by the rising sun. The record book reports that "Flak was heavy" but the entry for the raid is hard to decipher.

The whole Ruhr was a dangerous target but Essen seems to have been one of its better-protected cities. "Essen ... When you were scheduled to go there and the trip was scrubbed the crews rejoiced, and when it was not scrubbed very few were gay and smiling at briefing." (Brennan, 1946, p. 110.) Returning safely from Essen was always to be celebrated but the celebration was usually tempered by sadness as crews waited in the mess for debriefing and other crews did not appear to wait with them. That day the crew split up; they had the afternoon free but they did not spend it together.

Congratulations to Freda Smith on her engagement to Flight Sergeant J. B. Denton.
(F.A.U. Chronicle no 47, 30 April 1943)

Chapter 5: May

FREDA WORRIED she'd run out of funds. She was generous but always thought carefully about where her generosity should be bestowed. Her plans for marriage bucked the trend. She wanted to get married and would probably have done so in York registry office the week she was on leave, if Jack had agreed. He was more conservative where marriage was concerned but less so in the rest of his life on base. He gambled, for instance. To Freda, a Quaker, this was anathema but even if the moral code she lived by had allowed gambling, she would not have been so reckless.

Both realised that the war afforded them financial luxury which they would maybe otherwise not have had. Thanks to the R.A.F., Jack's income was secure, and although Freda could earn a good wage in the armaments industry, her unpaid but supplemented work with the F.A.U. was equally secure. At the end of April Freda was frustrated that they might have to wait to get married "when we could be so happy it seems too infuriating to think of delaying everything because of l.s.d." but she agreed to wait until he was off ops in July. Jack wrote on receipt of this letter that "much as I do not wish to trade on the war, I cannot foresee an end to it for a year or two & I am sure we will be quite O.K for the duration."

Freda was on leave in York from 7th May for ten days, and after Jack's letter of 11th there's a gap until 17th when Freda writes to him again from London. It was very cold at the start of May and few missions were flown but by 12 May, 1943 the good weather began to break through and the record book states that "The weather at base was cloudy with occasional drizzle. Wind was South to South Westerly." Full moon would not be until 19th May but the skies were clear enough.

Jack hoped he could get a day or two off to come into York before Freda had to return to London. They appear to have met over the week-end of 8th May, but I doubt Jack met Freda at Smith's in roofless York station on Friday night to celebrate the thirteenth week since they met, as she had hoped. "I'm wondering whether you will be in York tonight." Air Marshal Harris was lecturing at Melbourne that night and although Jack makes no mention of this, it is unlikely that he missed the lecture because Harris travelled infrequently. All crews would have been expected to attend, in any case because Harris had been Air Commodore 4 Group before his promotion so there were no operations that night. His nickname was variously Bomber, Butcher or Butch (i.e. he butchered RAF crew).[50]

Jack and Freda managed to meet five times during the week. Details of their meetings are unclear. On one occasion they played tennis in the courts at the foot of the city walls. Jack probably joined Freda on one of her favourite walks: either over the Knavesmire, through the woods and to the river and back through the town, or across the Knavesmire, through the white metal fence which still separates the race course from the road, and past one of the Rowntree mansions and onto Hob Moor. Sybil, who knew Freda all her life and lived a block away from her, told me that her father came home and had seen Freda with Jack on one of these occasions and described him as "very smart".

> Sergeants Mess
> RAF. Melbourne
> E. Yorks. 1.5.1943
>
> My dearest Freda,
> The condition of my morale has improved greatly since the arrival here of no less than 2 of your letters & great has been the rejoicing thereof.
> Tonight there is to be a social evening in the mess in celebration of some of the squadron's recent victories since there will not be any flying tonight. However I doubt whether I shall turn up until pretty near the end since I have pledged myself to abstinence from wine, women & song. Perhaps a little song will have no harmful effects.
> Last night we did a spot more flying as you probably will have read by this time. I have only just risen from the sleep of the just at 6 pm having been in bed since 7 a.m. What a way to spend a day off.
> By the way it gives me great pleasure to be able to report that you were wrong about Wilhelmshaven – actually it was mine-laying so there! There goes another official secret. Good job there are still some

things an airman can say which are not censored such as – I'll leave you to guess.

By the by, Maxie is still in the same old muddle with his females, but he did succeed in avoiding a show-down. Wally also managed to smooth over all his marital troubles & is at present getting ready to take a W.A.A.F. to the do in the mess. George has brought back a set of photos of his baby & has taken great pride in displaying them to one & all. Norman & Peter have gone to York to play tennis & this leaves Derrick who is writing a letter alongside me. So ends the bulletin on the activities of the crew of X.

George is in quite a miserable mood since he has lost most of his wages playing cards with Wally & a few more gunners. I have heroically given up gambling since I have been back & on the whole I think I am better off financially although whether it has done anything for my morale is a very moot point. Anyway so much for the shop talk.

I really was happy, when I read your letter this morning. I do think you were sweet & sporting re your remarks about the financial side of this proposition of ours. Of course, my darling, I do not want any more delay than necessary & it would take quite a few months to achieve what I had set out. But since receiving your letter I find that you feel largely the same way as myself about the whole thing, & I dare say we can modify those plans quite a bit. However for the time being I suggest that we both sleep on the problem.

In fact we will lay out a complete plan of campaign – bring your pencil & note-book & you can make notes in shorthand. The short & the long of it is that I do not want to start quite from scratch. In the event of the war ending more quickly that we expect we have no guarantee that things will be as secure. However, much as I do not wish to trade on the war, I cannot foresee an end to it for a year or two & I am sure we will be quite O.K for the duration. After that of course we shall just have to take our chance with millions of others – but I am sure you understand all this.

I have noted all your remarks re estimated time of arrival of your train & if humanly possible I will surely meet same. I hope the pace slackens off a bit before then. Since I have been back from leave I have not had more than a couple of opportunities of getting into York but I can only hope for the best for the period of your leave. I am so glad that it will be a period of 10 days – I understood it was to have been 7 days. Is this an example of F.A.U. wangling very much akin to the R.A.F. species?

Since I have not as yet had anything to eat for about 20 hours I think I must go & appease the pangs of hunger. You see I do get hungry sometimes! I will surely write you again before your leave but, Darling, most of the things I could write about I much prefer to leave until I see you.

Goodbye for a little while, Darling.
Jack.

Friends Ambulance Unit.
4 Gordon Square.
Tuesday. May 4th. 11.15 p.m.

Hello Darling,
I hope the next time I address you in this way it will be verbally and not in writing. I rang up Gordon Square yesterday morning to see if there was any post, and on hearing that there was I dashed round in record time to collect it in the afternoon when I had finished doing orderly here. I had a short note from mother today, she seems quite cheerful, which is a good thing.

I went to Gordon Square on Sunday, though not until 11.30 a.m. and I did not stay very long, as it was so cold. I took some sandwiches over for lunch, and shortly afterwards I packed up and made my way back to the hostel on foot, as I did not see much point in getting back too early in the afternoon.

I strolled along, gazing in what few shop-windows one finds in the city. It's quite amazing how quiet and deserted the City can be on a Sunday, and I was both amused and horrified when, while gazing in the window of a shoe-shop, I was approached by a New Zealand sailor who said Hello would I like to go for a walk! To which of course I replied with my coldest stare, went a little red in the face and hurriedly walked on – that put an end to my shop window gazing until I reached the crowded streets near Petticoat Lane & Aldgate, which is just thick with people and gay flower stalls and very active indeed.

Orderly went off quite well yesterday. I learn that in future everyone has to do one shift on night orderly per month. I'm quite dreading mine because I shall be terrified of being, so to speak, the sole person alive in the hostel at night. One keeps hearing all kinds of creakings & noises off – I hate it, and shall be scared to death. The work itself is not so bad, mainly scrubbing & polishing floors & attending to the boiler.

This evening I've been up to the Hampstead Hostel to hear one of the chaps speak on China. He returned about a month ago after being there 2 yrs, and had of course lots of interesting things to relate about driving on the Burma Road & life in China generally.

So I was wrong about Wilhelmshaven! Ah well, now I've wormed another secret from you to send to my führer. I'm sure he'll pay me well for it. What an easy way of getting money spying is!

Again, and this time most seriously, I don't mind your drinking, within limits; and cheer up the girls by all means – I can even take that, but gambling is one thing that I really hate, and if you really are giving that up I, well, I'm so pleased I don't know what to say. Anyway, it would surely be an insult to any fellow's fiancée to hint that his life was so devoid of thrills that he had to turn to gambling for them!

It's almost midnight & perhaps time I was asleep. Unless you can post anything to reach Gordon Square on Friday morning it will be best to send anything you write to 36 Knavesmire Crescent.

Au revoir, darling. I'm very much looking forward to seeing you in a very short while.

All my love.

Freda.

As Freda was writing her letter on 4th May, Jack was on route for the Krupps factories in Dortmund, flying ZA-E HR698 again. Dan Brennan's crew was flying ZA-X that night.[51]

Sgt. Narden joined Jack as 2nd (trainee) pilot for this raid. Looking through the records, it appears that from 26th April, when Jack flew his usual ZA-X with Sgt. L.A. Wright as 2nd pilot, the crew normally included a 2nd pilot. This must mean that Jack and his crew were now trusted old hands, professionals at staying alive against the odds.

12 bombers took off from Melbourne. 11 hit the target and one bombed "off target". Jack left shortly before 11 pm and returned just after 3.30 am. The records state that his crew had an uneventful journey. Jack's crew normally reported a successful raid succinctly and this raid was no exception:

> Bombed primary target at 01.05 hrs, from 17500 ft. on RED-GREEN target markers. Visibility was good and bombing well concentrated, with good fires and many incendiaries visible. Intense heavy Flak was encountered and numerous search lights were operating.

There is no hint in this record of the fog which hit most crews as they flew home to Melbourne that morning but it was so bad that at least one aircraft was lost. JD105 was unable to land at Melbourne and was diverted to R.A.F. Leeming but crashed into Hood Hill, and most of the crew died. The story is recorded in the station record books.

> The navigator [Sgt Cox] was taken ill so the captain [Geddes] reduced height. On reaching England, aircraft was diverted to Leeming owing to unsuitable weather at Base and aircraft struck some high ground at Hood Range and all crew [Sgt.s Cox, Ward, Way, Taylor and Hill] were killed with the exception of the captain, Flight Engineer and Tail Gunner .. the aircraft was completely wrecked.

Later in the war Melbourne was the first airfield in 4 group to install fog-busting FIDO: petrol was set alight from installations along the main runway to burn off the fog.

For the next couple of nights, there was training and no operational flying with Harris' lecture on Friday. Probably on Saturday and certainly on Sunday, Jack was in York.

>As from: 36 Knavesmire Crescent.
>The Mount.
>York.
>7th May. 1943
>
>Dear Jack,
>I thought I might be hearing from you again this week, but expect that you have been pretty busy. Anyway I thought I would post you this little note before I left London for the wild north – bless it! By the time you read this I shall be up in York, what a lot of water has flown under the bridge since last time I was in York darling, hasn't it!
>
>I'm wondering whether you will be in York tonight, or whether there will be a letter awaiting me when I arrive home. What a barrage of questions I'm going to have to face from my dear mama – phew!
>
>I'm at the office this morning, but have been working hard all week to get things through by this lunch time, and I've succeeded pretty well.
>
>This is a terrible note, isn't it – I don't know what to say in it – probably I'm excited or something, probably I'm scared, probably anything!
>
>Pending further news, I shall be around home in the evening if you find you can get into York, so you had better know how to make your way to my home from Piccadilly (York I mean!) You should catch a No. 4 bus from Nessgate. It goes from Fulford via Nessgate TO SOUTHBANK, and you get off the bus at the South Bank Terminus and walk straight down towards the Knavesmire for about 50 yards & you will come to 36 Knavesmire Crescent – it's about the second house down as you may remember!
>
>So, until I see you again I will say goodbye darling, and I hope the weather keeps bad.
>All my love.
>Freda.

36 Knavesmire Crescent.
Monday afternoon

Hello darling,
I'm hoping that with the weather as it is, maybe I shall be seeing you later in the day, but we seem to have made such a good beginning I suppose it's too much to expect. Anyway, if you don't arrive by about 3.30 I am going out to tea with Gwendy Knight who is a doctor in York. She used to be in the Unit until about a year ago.

I went for a marvellous walk yesterday afternoon along by the river as far as Bishopthorpe and then back across the Knavesmire. It was very windy, and a terrific change from London. It made me wonder what I ever see in places like St. James Park. I did wish you could have been with me.

I stayed in until about 8.0'clock and then went round to see Pat for an hour. I managed to get on a bus just before it began raining and when I left her house at about 10.0 p.m. it was dry again.

I do hope you didn't mind going round to see her, Jack. Actually I would rather have stayed in and put a fire in the room at the front so that we could have a good talk, but probably in that case we might not have done much talking, so perhaps it's as well we went out and really got quite a lot planned out!

I told mother this morning that we were thinking of next October or thereabouts, and once she got used to the idea it seemed all right, though she chattered a bit at first saying that I ought to be getting a paid job and saving some money. She seems to think that the Unit surveys me as a bit of cheap labour, and just can't understand that it's a voluntary service on my part, and it's no use trying to explain why I couldn't do as all the girls around here seem to be doing and making a packet on munitions, so like Tar-Baby, I just lie low and say nothin'.

It's about 2.0 p.m. I suppose it hardly likely that you will be catching the early bus, but I'm just spending the week sitting around and hoping. I don't suppose there was any flying last night – what a nuisance – it will set us back a day but I suppose it can't be helped. By the way – Wednesday is York's early closing day, so don't have Wednesday for your afternoon off if it can be arranged any other way, though naturally I would rather you came on Wednesday than not at all. If it's going to rain like this all week you might as well pack up at Melbourne and come here for a few days instead!

You know, darling, the way you and I fit in together like pieces in a jig-saw puzzle seems almost uncanny, don't you think! I keep wondering where the catch is, & what we are likely to quarrel about, and I just can't find anything!
Au revoir, darling,
All my love.
Freda.

Freda could not predict when Jack might arrive. Twice she walked round the corner to Albemarle Road and called the sergeant's mess from the phonebox next to the post-office, and then went home to write to him. Between letters, Freda alters from wanting bad to wanting good weather, as though she has only just begun to understand that good weather means raids and therefore time off and bad weather probably means training which is not rewarded with leave. Jack writes on Tuesday 11th May "I have done nothing useful since I last saw you & I fear that this must be due to your prayers for bad weather." The weather was cloudy, windy and wet on 8th and 9th May and on 10th flight plans were scrubbed and because of the weather, crew names rubbed off the blackboard in the control room. However, this probably means Jack was able to leave the station those evenings and when he could get away, they met after tea and walked.

Meanwhile, waiting for him, Freda visited old friends such as Gwendy Knight, who had trained her up at Barmoor when she first joined the F.A.U. She walked on the moors and by the river every day. Recently the town council had elected to release another 50 acres of the Knavesmire for allotments. Cattle were always grazed on the part of the common over the road from Freda's home but an Italian P.O.W. camp had been erected near the Grandstand, on the road to Terry's factory, and there was a German camp slap in the middle of the race course, on the way to the woods, in the middle of the meadow.[52] It was not the empty place Freda grew up with and which we now know.

> 36 Knavesmire Crescent.
> The Mount.
> Tuesday. 10.15 p.m.
>
> Darling,
> This is to confirm what my unlucky telephone calls will probably have hinted to you – that I miss you an awful lot! As you probably have been informed, I phoned you yesterday and this evening to have a chat about nothing in particular, but my luck was out. This "so near & yet so far" business is not so good, is it?! I say to myself – am I woman or mouse – and then I say to myself - woman obviously, a mouse wouldn't be so in love with its fiancé, if mice have fiancés – I wouldn't know!
> I went for a walk on the Knavesmire this afternoon. There were quite a few planes flying around – were you by any chance among those present – I wondered if you were. I went into town this morning & spent most of this evening sewing until about 9.o'clock when I went for a stroll & then phoned you. I think I might try phoning you every night this week at about 9.30 p.m. – there's no harm in trying I suppose.
> I do miss you darling – you sort of grow on me you know. I keep thinking I couldn't possibly love you any more than I do but every time you come around you're just twice as nice as before, but I can never pluck up the courage to tell you so – except from a distance like now.
> The light is getting bad, so excuse please if this writing is not up to the usual. What a nuisance your having to go to Bridlington yesterday – hasn't your C.O. any heart! You're sure to be able to get in again this week though (I hope!). By the way – I don't intend going back until the midnight train on Sunday

– just in case there's a chance of you coming in on that day.

I haven't any news or anything, darling. I'm sort of writing to you to make up for not being able to speak to you on the phone to-night, & because I thought it might be nice for me to swell your masculine conceit – I don't suppose you're any exception to the "men are so conceited" rule! – by saying, or trying to, just how much I miss you, and adore you, and am looking forward to next October or whenever you say.

All my love darling,
Freda.

P.S. Sorry the envelope is so grubby
but it's the only one I can
find to match the notepaper.

Melbourne.

My Darling,
  Since it seems rather unlikely that I shall be able to get in to York to see you today [Wednesday, 12th May] I feel I ought to let you know that I am still around. After a roaring start it seems that all our hopes for scrounging time off have been dashed to the ground. In actual fact I have done nothing useful since I last saw you & I fear that this must be due to your prayers for bad weather. If only a couple of fine days would come along then I should be sure of the following day free, but as things now stand I still have a couple of days to fill in.

On Monday there was a scrub but I did not have the good fortune to get time off, which Maxie explained to you over the phone I believe. Most of the pilots were sent to Bridlington for an air-sea rescue course of one day's duration – I had hoped to be able to entrain to York from Bridlington but the dammed course was not completed in time. If you remember it was such a lovely day to spend at the seaside too!

However I still entertain hopes of seeing you for a few more times before you leave for London again. I have been working out an extremely rough calculation & I believe now that you are due to leave round about Sunday or Monday so I feel pretty confident of wangling something by then. But for Gawd's sake don't hang around for me too much – it shakes me to think that you might be wasting your time for something that isn't going to turn up. If I come in & you happen to be out then I am sure I can stick around until you turn up – O.K.?

As usual I am in great haste since all the usual routine is now being put into operation so I shall just have to ring-off.

Hoping to see you very soon.
Lots of Love.
Jack.

Station records note that the weather was clear enough for operations 12th May 1943.

> Thirteen crews detailed to attack Duisburg. Two crews were cancelled owing to their aircraft being unserviceable. Three crews abandoned due to icing, Sgt Beveridge had an encounter with enemy fighters and had to jettison his bomb load. seven crews Bombed the primary target reporting a successful attack. Weather at Base was cloudy with occasional drizzle. Wind was South to South Westerly. (AIR 27)

Jack flew ZA-D HR695 with trainee Sgt Pinkerton as 2nd pilot. The aircraft took off for Hornsea at shortly before midnight and returned via Flamborough 5 hours later on what was a difficult raid.[53] On the same night Acting Squadron Leader James Swift was observing in an 83 (Pathfinder) Squadron Lancaster. His grandson writes

> ...at one minute before midnight on 12 May he lifted off again as observer with the same crew. This time the Lancaster 4904 dropped green target indicators at three minutes past two, over the town centre of Duisburg, and half an hour later when the main force passed over there

were fires across forty-eight acres. The reconnaissance report the next day noted 'very considerable damage' to the town ... (Swift, p. 172-3)

Debriefing records for Jack's crew state that they bombed Duisburg just after 2 a.m. from 18000ft, "on RED Target markers and visual identification of target features." "Several powerful concentrations of Searchlights were in action." The target was visible but most of the fires which Jack's crew saw were, however, not on target and were seen mainly to the south east of the aiming point. When a target was pinpointed, the pilot had to fly straight and steady for a very long time so that heavy bombs and lighter incendiaries could reach the same place at the same time and then a photo be taken of the damage caused. The photo was then analysed to assess damage. According to the reconnaissance report Swift quotes, the damage that night included "four factories, an oil refinery, and the docks" as well as "over 2,000 houses or other buildings" (Swift, p. 173). If the target was not visible by Gee fix (radar) or visually the first time around but when there was hope of the target becoming visible then it was circled, the queue of bombers joined again and the whole procedure endured again. If the target was obscured, and no alternate target available, the raid would be abandoned. Occasionally bombers chose another target, as happened on 13th May when two pilots from Melbourne could not bomb Bochum, the main target, so they chose to bomb Dortmund and Düsseldorf instead.

All this time, while in line to bomb the city, searchlights attempted to find each aircraft and fairly accurate flak blasted into the sky. Unlucky aircraft were ensnared in a searchlight and passed from one light to another until the bomber was held in a cone of light, like an ice cream in a cornet and then anti-aircraft gunners rarely failed to reach their target. At these times the whole aircraft was lit, inside and out and night blindness became a real danger. Experienced crew might break formation and dive to get out of a cone, then swoop back up, knowing the searchlights merged at around 4,000ft, but this manœuvre was extremely dangerous and used only as a last resort. Some pilots tried to outfly the cones but usually with little luck. One occasion over Essen, Dan Brennan's crew flew back and forth over the target for twenty minutes trying and succeeding to escape two cones.

> And that night at Essen the aircraft was held twenty minutes in the searchlights on the third trip there, and the flak came up more quickly and with greater accuracy than you had ever seen. And crouching in the turret it did not look as if you could escape. Harry yelling, "Weave! For F- sake, weave! The stuff's right behind us! For f- sake! Weave!" (Brennan, 1946, p.110)

Sgt. Beveridge in ZA-L JB974 had one of many escapes – Sgt. Beveridge appears to have had at least nine lives.

> At 0200 hrs. at position 20 miles East – North East of ARNHEM this aircraft was attacked by an ME110 and hits were sustained in the tail unit, bomb doors and Numbers 2, 3 and 4 Tanks were holed. The Rear Gunner returned the fire and observed hits in the belly and nose of the enemy aircraft which reared up and dived away and was claimed as probably destroyed. During this engagement the bomb load was jettisoned. At 0230 hrs. 15 miles East by North of THE HAGUE an ME109 was seen by the rear gunner on the port quarter. The E/A [enemy aircraft] closed to 200 yards and Rear Gunner instructed the captain to turn to port and E/A overshot and was lost to sight. Aircraft returned to Base safely. (AIR 27)

Some aircraft became 'scarecrows'. Rumour in RAF mess huts was that the Germans had invented a bomb to scare RAF intruders, which looked like an exploding aircraft. It later turned out that these 'scarecrow' bombs were in fact bombers exploding but Command did nothing to correct the misapprehension. Schräge Musik, an innovative use of cannon by the Luftwaffe, was devastating. Fighters manœuvred underneath enemy raiders, totally invisible to any of the crew, and then they fired up into the belly of the bomber. The bomber exploded almost every time. The only problem was that it took Luftwaffe pilots some time to realise that when a bomber exploded right above them, it was most likely that they would also explode.

All Dutch radar stations went on the alert again once the bomber stream turned back for base, and fighters were sent out to stalk them and attack when possible. Once the bombs were dropped, Derrick concentrated on scanning the skies, his machine gun in the nose at the ready. The way home from Berlin and the Ruhr was through heavily defended industrial areas, which meant either searchlights and flak or night fighters. If the flak stopped and the sky darkened and all seemed at peace bar the thrumming engines, Jack told the boys to keep their eyes skinned because this was the time when night fighters, the "goggle-goblins", appeared as if from nowhere. Unless a fighter was spotted, only occasional laconic directions came from Norman giving Jack co-ordinates to follow or from Peter reporting their co-ordinates to base, or Maxie telling fuel levels or from Jack to each of the crew, checking to make sure all was well. Goblins, Schräge Musik, scarecrows: picturesque jargon.

Radio silence in the aircraft was maintained for the most part so that German control radio could not pick it up and pass on their position to night fighters. This was no protection against Freya radar which was also supposed to be able to identify aircraft but this function never worked. Freya could hear signals from single aircraft and from formations from the coast of England and combined with Würzburg radar, nightfighters could be given extremely accurate information. Würzburg dishes fixed on a gun mounting, were effective up to 30 kilometres and provided accurate flak. Usually in pairs, one would follow a nightfighter and one an enemy bomber and they were the nightfighter's eyes. It is surprising that any RAF bombers returned to base.

Peter's view of the sky was not good so he had to leave his cubby hole and join Derrick in the nose or perch near Jack to watch the skies. Norman, sitting directly under Jack, was curtained off from the rest of the crew, his window blacked out so he could keep his light on and would not get blinded by searchlights. He kept his eyes on his charts, plotted and measured and recorded it all in his book. George was the main look-out for nightfighters because most of them came from behind. He was alone way back in his turret, and swung it back and forth as he peered into sky, blinking to keep focus sharp and only closing his eyes to avoid being blinded by searchlights. If he saw another aircraft he immediately told the crew and then worked out in a split second whether it was friend or foe.

Monica, their radar warning system, only worked once a fighter was close enough to fire so rear gunners got no rest and had to be alert throughout the operation. If George thought a fighter was flying low he screamed "Skipper! Dive!" or "Corkscrew! Left Left". His main dread, though, was icing so he kept his turret moving to keep the oil warm and fluid; that and being temporarily blinded by searchlights would make him a useless crew member. Wally, the mid-upper gunner, scanned the skies from his position on the spine of the aircraft for a telltale sheen of metal or a shadow dark against the clouds in the moonlight or which momentarily blocked the morning sun. Unlike George, Wally was not locked into a turret and he and his equipment were in less danger of freezing. George or Wally were the most likely to suffer or lose consciousness from the cold or lack of oxygen, so if they saw a fighter but kept silent and Derrick or Peter saw the same fighter, they got on the intercom straight away and berated the gunners for not announcing it, fearing as they did so that they were hurt. One of the gunners would erupt with expletives about whose job was what and Jack would have to bring them all to order. "Glad to hear you're all awake, chaps. Now pipe down."

Maxie was normally busy keeping an eye on gauges and trying to maintain oil pressure and when they were hit, he did running repairs, and shouted advice to Jack. Following his crew's observations and warnings, Jack dived away, sometimes screaming for the ground in a corkscrew and back up again. The Halifax aircraft Jack flew from March 1943, the Mark II, series I (Special), had been streamlined in a number of ways, most noticeably by flattening the mid upper gun turret, to make evasive manœuvres easier and with less risk of the aircraft flipping onto its back. Jinking, zig-zagging, across the skies, and diving, was extremely hard work for the pilot. In emergencies, when controlling the aircraft took all his strength, Jack called on Maxie or the 2nd pilot to help on the wheel or throttle. If an intruder was busy over Yorkshire, the crew kept an eye out for it returning, planes passing in the night, but if it was quiet over the North Sea, the 2nd pilot and Maxie took over the controls, Jack swung off his seat to make way for them and then squeezed back into the rest area behind Peter and Wally to grab a bite to eat or to use the Elsan or have a quick cup of tea from his thermos: strong, sweet and with lashings of condensed milk.

Once back over the sea, any bombs not released would be jettisoned and then home to the Yorkshire coast, with luck. When fog-bound, black-out made runways invisible and an alternate landing had to be found in a hurry.[54] All along the coast were temporary emergency landing strips, like the one at Carnaby, close to Bridlington, but they too had to be found. Black-out was literally all hours which were not full daylight so in mid May 1943 blackout ran from 22.56 p.m. until 05.10 a.m. with the full moon on 19th May. The navigator's skill and his knowledge of the landscape was beyond price, especially where the rivers flowed and the hills rose; he could save the lives of a crew by finding an alternate landing.

On 13th May Bochum was attacked.

> It was drenched with bombs for 45 minutes and at the end of the raid a thick blanket of smoke lay over it with columns rising many thousands of feet. Such was the congestion over the target that a Stirling brought back the tails of three incendiary bombs from another bomber embedded in its wings. (*The Aeroplane*, "The 193rd week of THE WAR IN THE AIR", May 21, 1943, p. 582-4)

Jack took off shortly before midnight in G for George, serial number HR696, and he returned at dawn: "Up 23.54 Back 04.58" That night Jack captained a crew of eight with Sgt Ayres as 2nd pilot, and Sgt Harrison in Maxie's place as Flight Engineer. No novice, Maurice Harrison was a highly experienced engineer having flown operations for almost a year. Later, Jack called him the Engineer Leader.

The route was: "Out via Southwold, back via Flamborough" which means they approached the Ruhr from the South West. The debriefing report suggests a straightforward run in, with no mention of nightfighters. Jack in ZA-G and Sgt Mills in ZA-X took off within minutes of each other, so probably reached the target at about the same time. Jack's debriefing reports that they

> Bombed target at 02.27 hrs. from 17500 ft. Visibility was good and target was identified on RED-GREEN Markers. A good number of fires were seen in target area and a large column of black smoke was rising from the North West area of target. Moderate Flak was experienced but a large number of Searchlights were in action (AIR 27).

Ten Squadron's report for the night's raid implies difficulty, confusion and danger both from Flak and nightfighters.

Thirteen Crews detailed to bomb BOCHUM. Ten crews bombed primary target, reporting moderate Flak and Searchlight opposition but considerable night fighter activity. Sgt Beveridge bombed an alternative target between DUSSELDORF and HAMM, his aircraft was caught by Searchlights and during violent evasive action the mid gunner Sgt. McCoy baled out. Subsequently the aircraft was engaged by enemy night fighters and received considerable damage. WO Fennell bombed the DORTMUND area as his aircraft was coned by Searchlights for seven minutes. The crew of FSgt. Mills failed to return from the operation. Weather at Base was cloudy with drizzle and a south to south westerly wind. (AIR 27)

Sgt. Beveridge had another interesting raid. The station report is the longest I have seen. They were caught in searchlights and "during violent evasive action a nearby Flak burst caused the rudder to overbalance with the result that aircraft turned over on its back..." It appears that the mid gunner baled out during this manœuvre but I wonder if he fell out, having got ready to bale out. In any case, he is reprimanded for having left the A/C without permission. Caught again in searchlights, bombs were dropped somewhere between Cologne and Bochum and they made for home by the shortest route. While over Holland two JU88s attacked and Sgt. Compton, the rear gunner, fought them off but they returned and attacked from 30 yards on one side and 300 yards on the other. Sgt. Compton fought them off again and the captain took evasive action. After two more attacks, the aircraft returned to Melbourne with none of the crew injured, though minus the mid gunner.[55] "Damage sustained was the port tail plane, elevator, rudder and port outer tank hole and one gun rendered unserviceable."

Jack would never fly ZA-X DT732 again because the ORB reports that early on 14th May, south of Ijsselmeer, it crashed or was shot down, it "failed to return" home from Bochum.[56] To fill the gap left by DT732, Melbourne later took receipt of a 102 Squadron Halifax, serial number BB324, which became the new ZA-X and flew for the Shiny Ten for the first time on 23rd May to Dortmund.

London Hospital Students Hostel,
Philpot Street.

Monday 7.45 a.m.!

Hello, darling.

Isn't this an uncivilised time to write a letter, but I find I'm not on orderly until 10.0 a.m. When I've finished this short epistle I'm going off to sleep for an hour – I can't be bothered unpacking yet, though I've swept the room.

I hope you managed to get up in time to catch your bus. I thought of you as I stood on the platform at Kings X waiting for the tube. It was not until I had bathed & changed that I found that I was not on orderly until 10.0 – what a sell.

So here I am – 199 miles away from you but I don't feel you're so far away really.

What a marvellous leave I have had, & how lucky to be able to see so much of you – though don't get the idea from this that I've forgiven your camp-quitting escapade. I suppose I shall eventually shelve it with 10.30 Euston Square!

I managed to get a seat quite easily on the train and slept most of the time. We got to Kings Cross about 5.45 a.m. Incidentally, after all that fuss I left my handbag at home – Fortunately I had two sixpences on me! What a stupid thing for me to do – I'm afraid I must plead guilty to negligence & put forward the defence that when one is in love one can't be expected to think of everything.

This is only an interim report, darling. I'll probably write again this evening when I know I'm going to miss you terribly; and so until then darling, all my love.

Freda.

London Hospital Students Hostel,
Philpot Street.
Monday evening [17th May]

My darling,

I can see that if I don't watch my step this will develop into what is, I believe, termed a love-letter, because these past few days with you have been so happy and I miss you so much that it's difficult to keep one's mind on day to day affairs. I blame you, for instance, for the fact that I spent about 15 minutes this morning trying to get through to Ronald Joynes at Museum 5986 before I realised that I was in fact dialling Bishopsgate 8425, which is the telephone number here!

I've just been doing a spot of wangling and have swopped my sloping & uncomfortable hospital bedstead for a divan which promises to be much more comfortable (I'm lying on it to write this). It makes the room look much better too.

I hope you had a good night's rest on my brother's none too comfy mattress. I can hardly get used to it myself. I do hope you won't fight shy of dropping in at home should you ever feel like it, Jack. Mother & Dad will be very glad to see you I know, though mother's standards & mine being rather different I can't guarantee you always finding the house in apple-pie order – also she is rather short sighted, which doesn't help. However, I don't suppose you will get into York much but you know where to go if you are stranded or anything.

It's been terrifically hot to-day. This morning I scrubbed the bathroom floors and stoked the boilers & helped in the kitchen until 2.0, and then I changed into a summer dress and went for a walk down Whitechapel High Street before going to the Play Centre. What a Play Centre too, it was pretty hectic I must say. Bring on your five children by your first few wives my sweet; they would be heaven after the mob we had to-night!

That sums up my activities to beginning this at about 8.0'clock. I'm going to bed early this evening, mainly because there is little else to do, though I do feel a bit drowsy. This room just catches the rays of the evening sun, which makes it rather pleasant.

I do hope mother sends on my hand-bag tomorrow; at the moment I've got tuppence, as Marjorie owes me 6d! How very stupid to forget it anyway.

I'm wondering what sort of day you have been having; I suppose you've been to an odd lecture or two, and done some flying. I suppose the picture of the Halifax I've got is out of date now that C for Charlie has got a dorsal gun-turret – 'ark at 'er going all technical! Anyway it's not the plane I want a picture of, but you – I'm going to remind you about this every time I write until you become a bundle of nerves and you scream and your fingers tremble every time you open a letter from me so H.Y.H.Y.P.T.?!

I phoned Ronald for a chat this morning – he had evidently wondered if I would come back married – I only wish we could have obliged him! I've just never known what happiness is until now Jack, when I've spent so many happy hours with you, though heaven knows the time went far too quickly. Loving you has been well worth waiting for. I've always known that I would know real happiness when it came my way, though I must say that until I met you I had never dreamed that it would come to me via the R.A.F.!

Are you getting any more sleep now – or are Norman's words of wisdom nearer the mark! I felt very guilty about robbing you of so much.

Have you heard any more about your commission. Please take it if you have the opportunity, darling, and the way seems clear to you. I don't see that it should make so much difference to us financially, because I shall not be drawing on any of your money while I am in the Unit, and if it means a check on saving, I shan't mind. However, I always want you to please yourself in whatever you do, but let me know what happens, won't you?

Oh dear, after seeing you so often last week it's difficult to realise that I shan't see you again for some weeks to come but I must accustom myself to your absence like so many other people. We have been engaged almost a month now, have we not? I hope when your allotted two months are up you will specially point out the date to the crew!

I'm sorry if this epistle is rather jerky in style. I never know quite what to write for my first letter after leaving you because there are so many thoughts I would like to express & things I would like to say if I but knew how, but I know you will understand well enough, darling, just what you mean to me, and will be able to read behind this seemingly aimless prattle.

>Good night, Jack, and good-luck wherever you are or are going.
>All my love, always.
>Freda.

This week the pressure is high. The mornings are misty with rising dew, the days hot, the nights clear and the heat is on: Melbourne is on ops again. At dawn birdsong echoes round the base and the fields blaze red and yellow – poppies, buttercups and dandelions in the slanting morning sun. Early summer in God's Own Country, Yorkshire, when all nature blossoms, grows big and healthy and generous. Hedgerows soften with great waves of Queen Anne's lace and elderflowers perfume the air, their faintly remembered smell of banana and lime seeps through the oily petrol haze which hangs over the base. It was dark shortly before midnight in May, double summertime, and it was "broad daylight at four in the morning." (Brennan, 1953, p. 6) and without cloud cover, heavy bombers were easy targets for night fighters.

The weather of course remains changeable and on 20th and 21st there were "No operations. No flying due to bad weather at Base. Low cloud and rain" (ORB, 20th May, 1943). "Weather at Base was fair to cloudy, wind was light and variable" (ORB, 21 May, 1943).

>Melbourne.
>Tuesday [18th May]

>My Darling Freda,
>Many thanks for your letter which arrived here this morning. So sweet of you to make such a sacrifice by writing to me so soon – I bet you were tired by the time you started your orderly duty. I guess I was much more fortunate in this respect since I must have been having a marvellous deep sleep whilst you were travelling. I awoke in time to hear 6 a.m. strike but I did not get up until your papa came to

wake me at 6.10 giving just nice time to catch my bus at 7 a.m. – and that's how a perfect 10 days ended, at least those days I spent with you were perfect, except that they were all too short.

Naturally the "reaction" I mentioned to you has set in but the remedy is already in full operation. By this I mean that the high-ups have pounced on me now that they know I am again in regular circulation & they are flying the hides off us. & they don't fail to remind me that I have a couple of nights flying to make up either.

Maxie had the misfortune to break his ankle a short while ago & so until just recently there has been bags of panic in the hut with the full crew all trying to display their knowledge of first-aid – I being of a modest nature (ahem!) fulfilled my duties by going for the ambulance. So it looks as though I shall have to look for a new engineer to tide me over the next few weeks.

What a silly girl you were to forget your handbag after all your "panic". How long did you have to wait on the platform before the train came? I bet it was over a quarter of an hour. I take a very poor view of York station for not issuing platform tickets.

I hope you are getting into the way of things at Gordon Square by the time this reaches you but don't work quite as hard as you threatened will you, Darling?

Now that we are back to letter writing I become very stuck for words. I guess we shall have a further natter shortly if I can get down to see you on a 48 hour pass – if I am very lucky this will be sometime in the next 14 days unless I receive a promise of leave at a fairly early date in which case I won't waste our precious cash. I guess it would be rather extravagant to have a 48 in 2 weeks time, for example, much as I am already bursting to see you again. However economy is my key word now & I have already cut down on what few things I can cut down on. And well I might with a marriage &, of lesser importance, a commission, both coming to hand at such a quick rate of fire.

> I am only thankful that we did get ourselves straightened out a little bit whilst you were on leave as this will give us both a foundation on which to base our plan of attack. When I can think clearly once again, if ever, I hope to do quite a bit of thinking & then perhaps the next time you ask me what suggestions I have, I shall be able to offer a sensible answer for a change.
> However I trust you will not expect too long a letter this time, as the only things I have been thinking are how beautiful you are & how wonderful to be with & like things – but I promise to get down to the thinking business shortly & then I shall surely give you the gen.
> At present I am missing you much too much, darling, and will do until I hear from you again.
> Until then,
> All my Love,
> Jack.

"Naturally the "reaction" I mentioned to you has set in but the remedy is already in full operation." Initially I thought "reaction" meant melancholia, Freda being so far away again. A more careful reading suggests that Jack refers to leaving base without permission – a serious offence for which he seems to have got off lightly, probably because his skills were valued highly by his C.O. Comments Freda made on returning to London, suggest Jack went AWOL at the end week, probably on Sunday, when he stayed away from base for the night. How did he get away with it? How often did this happen? The only reference in related record books that I have found was to the Court Martial of an airman who went AWOL from R.A.F. Leeming. 614507 LAC Randall was absent for twenty nine days "and was awarded 56 days detention", a punishment which appears to me lenient. However, being absent without leave would threaten his chances of promotion, or so Freda remonstrated in her letter of 17th May:

> I'm sorry if at times I seemed "panicky" as you put it. It isn't really that, but you know I should just hate to feel that I ever came between you and your upward progress. ... I'm afraid it annoyed you more

than somewhat; if it did I'm truly sorry, but it was very stupid of you dear, wasn't it.

Every month the ORB concludes with an appendix of lists: lists of operations, of commissions, of postings in and postings out, of sickness, etc. Maxie's broken ankle is recorded under 'Postings of aircrew out during May 1943'. "Sgt. Steele, R (F.E.) to R.A.F. Base, Pocklington N/E Sick w.e.f. 19th May 1943."

There was no operational flying on Monday and Tuesday that week but although no bombing raids took place, Tuesday 18th May was a busy day because there had been intruder raids throughout the country the night before and many lone bombers of the Luftwaffe strafed the streets in Northern and Eastern towns after dropping bombs, so crews were detailed to keep their air defence skills up to date (bullseye practice).

> No operations. W/C.D.W. Edmonds proceeded on leave and S/Ldr A.I.S. Debenham, O.C. 'C' Flight, took over command of No. 10 Squadron. F/Lt Badcoe assumed command of 'C' Flight. Five C Flight crews carried out fighter affiliation, two B Flight crews did bombing practice. Nine crews set off on BULLSEYE practice but were recalled. Weather at Base was fine with light cloud at 6000 ft. South Easterly wind. (AIR 27)

Of the half dozen letters written to people other than Jack, which Freda kept in the make-up bag in her trunk, one was written to Margaret on 20th May. Margaret had recently been posted to Bengal to help with famine relief and she was busy nursing.

> As you know by now via Ronald's airgraph, I've been a target for the R.A.F. and am now engaged to Flt. Sgt. Denton of that service. Last week I introduced him to my some-what sceptical parents (Mother keeps muttering that I'll change my mind, and in the next breath offers me a table cloth or pillow cases or something!).
> We are hoping to drop in on York Registry Office in October if all goes well. If your puce chiffon is going begging, Margaret, "Honi soit qui mal

y pense" which of course, being translated means "My need is greater than yours!"

Jack is very ordinary, and can't do anything except fly, so what we shall do after the war I don't know. I shall probably finish up in an L.C.C. flat in Wapping sending a batch of kids to the Play Centre every night and a Care Committee Visitor coming every week!

He's a darling really Margaret – I'm sorry you can't meet him.

I wish you were here to help me plan our getting wedded on my £12.0.0d. clothing allowance – what fun we could have. Roy (Mortuary Joe) Jarvis, has given me 6 coupons, which is very sweet of him – I want some blue material for a nightie – I'm afraid chiffon will be financially out, which is rather sad! I've also had given me some peach satin for a set of pyjamas (not by Mortuary Joe of course). It would be nice to start off with a splash, even if I do finish up with American Bundles for Britain! Ah well, if I will be a conshie! I still am, by the way, and have no intention of going over in spite of my R.A.F. interests – as you can imagine though, it's a more than somewhat worrying business but I shall have to get used to it and trust to luck and the poor aim of German flak.

It's terrifically hot here – Ronald and I were working on the roof all morning and I'm already getting quite sunburnt. I'm thrilled to find that I'm minus a lot of surplus flesh since I started biking to the Square, and can get on one or two summer dresses from the year before last.

Ronald is busy swotting for some Accountancy exam or other. If he's not careful he will crack up. He goes on leave next week and will spend all the time swotting. End of page, so I will close. Hope all the above don't bore you – I forget that others are not so interested in us as Jack and myself!

Freda.

London Hospital Students Hostel,
Philpot Street.

Thursday. May 20th

Darling Jack,

How nice to get your letter this morning. I hope you are cooler reading this than I am writing it. It's terribly hot and close. It's about 10.0 p.m. and I finished a shift of evening orderly about an hour ago. There's no point in going to bed because the siren is sure to go around midnight to-night & tomorrow (and yesterday & Tuesday when I was on the fire team).

We're getting two or three nuisance alerts every night and I'm getting rather fed-up with crawling out of bed and getting half-way to Wapping & then turning right about on the All-Clear. It isn't as though we are much use when we get to the shelter as we've no equipment & are forbidden to give first aid as our main function is medical aid – it's just a waste of time and we're all getting pretty sore about it. It's not likely that anything will develop & if it did the L.C.C. would reinstate their paid staff and I think we're just being mugs. However, we're hoping to withdraw from the commitment fairly soon – and about time too. Until then we continue the force, so I'm sitting around waiting for the siren

The big shelters are filling up again. I went for a short walk after orderly and everyone was trailing down with their bedding. Phew – it must be terribly hot in the shelters tonight – and the frightful smell of human bodies ----- I would sooner stay in bed any time, but I suppose everyone is fearing a reprisal for the Mohne Dam business. What a ghastly thing that is, though of course I recognise its value from a strategic point of view. Nevertheless I'm glad you were not in on it.

Ronald goes on leave next Wednesday for about 10 days, which reminds me, darling, that much as I should obviously adore seeing you on a 48 hr. pass, in view of the fact that I should be unable to get any time off during the day while Ronald is away I think it would be rather extravagant for you to come down just now. Incidentally, however can you be getting leave so soon – its only a month since you had your last leave?

By the way, I did not have to wait on the platform at York at all, because the train that had just come in was a London one and I got straight on it. I expect you think me silly darling, but honestly I hate hanging around on stations saying goodbye. I'm glad to hear that you managed to get some sleep before going back to camp.

It's terribly sweet of you to think so much of economy, dear. I feel very guilty about it. Please don't cut down too much on too many things will you, or I shall feel even worse and, lipstick or no, be getting a job as barmaid or something to do my bit.

I had quite a pleasant spot of floor scrubbing this evening, Jack Smith (the other orderly) and I, making a heck of a din singing in and out of harmony as we scrubbed the kitchen floor. I donned my slacks and a red aertex blouse for the scrubbing, which was pretty tough going in this heat.

You would laugh darling if you could see me now. My hair is very wild and falling onto my shoulders. My blouse is very red, my slacks are very brown corduroy, and I'm wearing sandals and sitting on my bed to write this – what a type you will say! I certainly wish you could see me as on the whole maybe I look rather nice!! What a modest violet I am!

I love hot weather though. What a pity we can't get married in the summer and have a lazy sunny holiday. Never mind, we'll have one next year instead.

I'm so sorry to hear about Maxie – which girl was he running away from when he broke his ankle! He'll have both his girlfriends sending him comforts etc. Give him my kind regards and good wishes for a speedy recovery, won't you. Are you catching up on your sleep, or does George still say you've got dark patches under your eyes. I always knew he was a sensible fellow.

I feel very sleepy but there's no point in going to bed only to get up about 10 minutes later, as I did last night. I think I will lie on the bed and doze, however,

& day dream and think of all the nice things you said to me last week and the happy time ahead of us.

Goodnight darling, or should I say Goodmorning – well, goodnight AND goodmorning, & write when you can and don't ever forget to go on loving me as you do now.

All my love,
Freda.

P.S. The siren is just sounding – darn it.

P.P.S. (20 mts later) Back again – I'll doze on the bed until the next siren which is due in about 2 hrs!

Freda mentions the "ghastly" Möhne Dam business, an attack called Operation Chastise to destroy the Möhne, Eder and Sorpe dams during the night of 16/17 May and now called the Dambusters raid. She knew Jack was not on the raid because it took place the night he stayed at her parents' house in York and maybe she also knew it was carried out by a specially formed squadron. After this raid, attacks on the industrial heart of Germany were called The Battle of the Ruhr, a description coined by Churchill, according to Bruce Sanders in *Bombs Away* (Bowman, p. 92). The description gave Happy Valley raids a form and a distinct objective for attacking squadrons. A battle could be won, a battle had a beginning and an end, it was less amorphous than what were endless single missions to this well-protected group of towns, each of which seemed to pick itself up and start again after even the worst attacks.

Sergeants Mess
RAF. Melbourne
[21st May]

Darling,
There is still a decided lack of activity around here & for this reason I am answering your letter whilst the going is good. For a start I have good news for you (I hope).

Having actually been offered a 48 hours pass I decided to accept same greedily & with small loss of time. The aforesaid 48 hours pass comes into force as from after-duty Monday & covers Tuesday & Wednesday. Will you be able to get a spot of time off during these 2 days if I come down, without Ronald swearing everlasting vengeance on me? Anyhow I have got the 48 whether I want it or not now, since the rest of my crew, keen as ever, have already submitted their passes so you might just let me know just how serious is the pressure of work!

Naturally I am still missing you a great deal & just dying to see what you look like once again – of course I could appease my mind in this respect by looking at your photo but this is hardly satisfying, beautiful as your photo is.

I am sorry to hear that you have been afflicted with absent-mindedness since you left me – perhaps this is an exaggeration but you have quoted 2 instances in 2 consecutive letters – maybe you had better produce a certificate from a psycho-analyst before we proceed with this marriage. If he certifies that you are madly in love then that is fair enough. By the way I.H.N.H.M.P.T.Y. owing to the fact that the great metropolis of Melbourne does not boast a photographer. Well I hope that excuses me as far as this first letter is concerned.

With regard to your enquiries re my commission I am destined to see the Air Commodore tomorrow morning & Derrick also shares my fate. I guess there will be bags of spit & polish going on in the hut after this letter is written.

Maxie is in hospital in York still. His broken ankle turned out to be a fractured ankle so I guess he won't ride with us any more during this tour. I wrote to him this afternoon & I expect I shall go into York to see him as soon as I can legitimately get the time off. Whilst I am around that part of the universe I will also call in & see your mama & papa. I did not thank them very well before I left for putting me up for the night because I only saw your papa for a few moments at a rather early hour & words don't come to me very easily at that time of day.

I'm afraid I started writing this letter pretty late in the evening & there have been many disturbances since, so I think my best plan is to prepare to meet this big cheese tomorrow.

But when I see you again next I'll try & tell you how much I love you (without having to be reminded either). I do love you more than anything else as you most likely know & all my thoughts are of you.

Until I see you again I'll just keep right on thinking of you & us!

Goodbye, Freda Darling.
All my Love,
Jack.

This charming letter shows Jack to be thoughtful, sensitive and with a gentle sense of humour, much more than the "dull and agreeable" fellow, he describes himself to be. Throughout Jack's letters his youth and friendliness shine through. He is more interested in Maxie's well-being than in the problems his hospitalization will cause and when Maxie first fell, Jack was the one to keep his head and run for an ambulance. Maxie was not on Jack's recent raid to Bochum and he would not fly with Jack again. Sgt. Maurice Harrison took his place from now on.

Figure 29 Maurice, who took over from Maxie

The crew's 48 hr pass was probably given because they had not had a break for some time and Command wanted their boys to be fresh for work. A 48 hour pass began when the crew returned from the previous night's bombing, "after duty on Monday" Jack says, so if the crew are to fly on Sunday 23rd May then their leave will begin after debriefing in the early hours of Monday 24th. If not slated to fly on Sunday, Jack planned to get the earliest train he could on Monday but if they were flying that night he could not leave until after debriefing on Monday morning. All Jack wants is for them to be together again, however short the time.

On Friday 21st there were

> No operations. Seven crews of A and B Flights carried out formation practice. Three C Flight crews carried out air to sea firing practice and two crews carried out night cross-countries for training purposes. Weather at Base was fair to cloudy, wind was light and variable. (AIR 27)

Air to sea firing practice for 10 Squadron took place up and down the Yorkshire coast, from Flamborough to Spurn Head. Rescue boats normally moored at Bridlington kept constant patrol before and during exercises to make sure nobody was hurt. According to Mac, a mid-upper-gunner at Melbourne, this was the only time the boats were used.

Jack's next letter was collected from the letterbox at Melbourne in the early evening of 23rd May and was franked in York post office at 8.15 p.m., at the same time Jack was getting tooled up in Flights.

> RAF. Melbourne
> Saturday May 22nd
>
> My Darling Freda,
> I am in rather a perplexed state of mind whilst writing this letter since I have received a letter and a telegram from you today & they are of a somewhat contradictory nature. In your letter you state to the effect that I am to do nothing so silly as to arrange a 48 in LONDON and then by the looks of your

telegram it seems you have done a spot of wangling to make it possible for me to come.

You see I had noticed that Ronald is due for leave on Wednesday so by rights I calculate you should be working on that day. However since everything now seems clear for me to come I guess I shall be seeing you on Monday night. I guess I shall catch the 3.10 train which usually arrives in the region of 7.30 p.m. I guess I shall ring you up in one place or another when I arrive – however this will depend on the circumstances prevailing when I do arrive.

And, Darling, please don't think I don't appreciate that this short stay is going to be a somewhat extravagant gesture, but since I had the 48 thrust upon me & the rest of the boys lost no time in making out passes I should have been left with 2 whole days on my hands & I could hardly get full benefit from these in York. I'll make a promise that we shall get down to hard & fast facts when I do see you so as to get the maximum results & benefit from the time I shall be spending with you. If I fulfil this promise will it compensate for the extravagance involved in this trip?

I seem to have a guilty feeling that I have not been quite fair with you in not discussing anything very much & the blame is partially yours since you are not strict enough with me. During Tuesday & Wednesday you must make a point of keeping me to the point and then perhaps we shall achieve something. I, in turn, will try very hard to pass a few helpful suggestions for a change, instead of being just dull and agreeable, as I usually am. However I must not make my promise too rash or I shall be finding myself in an awkward spot.

I am so sorry to hear of the hardships you have been enduring on account of the nuisance raids, and I hope you will have made up your beauty sleep by the time I see you next. And of course you are beautiful, aren't you? By the way I have caught up with my sleep marvellously well. The two nights flying I was supposed to catch up on seem to have gone by the board as all my flying has been done by the light of the sun recently – its rather a pleasant change but I should hate to stick to day flying permanently. I am rather too fond of the comforting protection of darkness – this sounds a bit yellow for a "gallant & dauntless member of R.A.F. air-crew", doesn't it?

That reminds me to tell you that Maxie is in pretty bad shape, most unfortunately & does not now expect to be out of hospital for a further 8 weeks. Norman went to visit him yesterday & he appeared to be in great pain although he did not complain. He also told Norman that he will probably have a permanent limp when he is released from hospital & naturally we all feel pretty upset about this as he was such a popular member of the crew (& the squadron for that matter). However we have done very well in replacing him since we now have his boss flying with us, namely the engineer leader.

Whilst on the subject of the crew I have some exclusive news regarding Norman who tells me he intends to get engaged to Betty, in spite of the fact that his mother wishes him to marry his old girl friend at Belfast. As I have stated this was given to me as confidential information but I feel I had to pass it on to you as it strikes me as being a somewhat amazing coincidence that 2 members of the same crew should have fiancées from the same school.

I think this must be the end of this topsy-turvey epistle. I guess when I arrive in London I will either ring you up at the hostel or Gordon Square depending on what gen is contained in your letter to me, and what time I arrive.

So, Goodbye for now, Darling,
All my Love,
Jack.

While Jack was writing to Freda, she was writing to him. Their letters crossed in the post.

F. A. U.
London Hospital Students Hostel,
Saturday 6.30 p.m.

Darling,

I'm not sure which of us is the more weak-willed, but as you should already know from my telegram I can get some time off on Tuesday & Wednesday by working on Sunday & Monday, so your luck is in as usual! I'm on orderly Sunday night but instead of sleeping much on Monday I'll go round to the Square and knock off some work, so that I shall probably have Tuesday & Wednesday free from about 11.0 a.m.

If you arrive on Monday night phone Bishopsgate 8425 and let me know – if I've gone to bed early leave a message to say that you've arrived or something; if I don't hear anything I'll take it that you will be phoning me at Gordon Square on Tuesday morning or when you arrive if you don't arrive until the afternoon.

I hope you will come prepared to treat me gently, my sweet, on account of I seem to have pulled a muscle in my back – I don't know how, probably carrying my bike down to the cellar – & at the moment it's rather painful but it will probably be O.K. when you are here – but if it isn't no boxing ring stuff!

I hope things went off O.K. with the Air Commodore. I'm longing to hear the result.

I've got lots to do tonight, wash my hair, iron some clothes, clean the room etc.

I was up again between 3 & 4 this morning with a wretched alert – had to shelter from a shower of shrapnel on the way down to Wapping.

Sorry to be to brief darling, but I want to make sure this reaches you Monday morning by catching the 7.0 p.m. post.

Isn't it marvellous to be seeing you again so soon. I'll get as much work cleared off at Gordon Square tomorrow as possible.

Gracious, its nearly 7.0.

Au revoir, darling, until I hear from you by post or by telephone & until I see you again.

All my love,
Freda.

Jack presumably saw Air Commodore Roddy Carr. Carr, a New Zealander eventually became the longest serving AC in the war.[57] Carr had joined Shackleton's Antarctic Expedition, had served in the nascent RAF in WW1 and flew in support of the White Russians – Jack must have been impressed. Jack's commission came through on the 10th May, as recorded in the Gazette and in his service record. I don't know why he did not tell Freda at the time. It is a puzzle, as is the engagement ring Jack bought, which I found in the trunk, still in its box from J. Parton, 20 The Walk, Norwich which he also presumably did not tell Freda about. The photograph of Jack was also a puzzle but I wonder if he had forgotten all about it and told Freda that IHNHMPTY (I have not had my photograph taken yet). Maybe his commission needed to be confirmed or he needed to accept it from the AC in person. More likely, I think, is that Jack was planning to tell Freda about the commission, to have a formal photograph taken, give it to her and place the ring on her finger when he came down to London in the next few days.

There were no operations that night at Melbourne, Saturday 22nd May. It was, as Jack says, all daylight flying.

> No Operations. Seven A Flight crews and four C Flight crews did formation practice. One B Flight crew and three C Flight crews carried out bombing practice. Weather at base was fair after mist in the early morning, with a light variable wind. (AIR 27)

"I keep wondering where the catch is" Freda had written, thinking how she and Jack made such a perfect couple. She does not sleep on Sunday night, 23rd May because she is on night orderly. There are no nuisance raids, so she scrubs the stairs and the passages and spends the rest of the night stoking the boilers, doing blackout rounds, dozing from time to time in the rocking chair in the kitchen. At 3 a.m. on Monday morning she poaches an egg the cooks left out for her and finally, at 6 a.m. she wakes the cooks and orderlies and staggers up to bed. She sleeps until about 10 a.m. and then cycles over to Gordon Square. She works until the early evening, then she cycles over to King's Cross to meet the York train. No Jack; no Derrick. It's too early to expect them anyway so she buys a paper and she pedals back East to Whitechapel, has a quiet evening and goes to bed early, fully expecting to be woken through the night by intruder raids.

While Freda scrubbed floors and stairs at the Hostel, Jack and his crew took off for Dortmund. A Scotsman, Sgt. Ian Inglis, 2nd Pilot, sat on the dickie seat. Sgt. Harrison, the engineer leader, was still flying in Maxie's position but as he had now been part of the crew for a couple of weeks, everyone was familiar with his way of doing things and he with theirs. The weather was so bad that they all expected a scrub.

In London and York, Monday's war news headlines screamed "GERMANY'S HEAVIEST ATTACK YET. CONCENTRATED RAID COSTS US 38 BOMBERS. ... Dortmund, 30 miles from Dusseldorf, has now had 41 raids." An accompanying map shows Dortmund to the East of Essen, about as far East as Duisburg is West. German reports of the raid stress, as usual, civilian casualties:

> Enemy bombers last night dropped numerous light explosive and incendiary bombs on Dortmund. There were casualties among the population and considerable damage. According to reports so far to hand, 33 of the raiding aircraft, mostly four-engined bombers, were shot down. Fast German bombers yesterday made a surprise daylight raid on Bournemouth and Hastings. Last night Luftwaffe again attacked the shipbuilding town of Sunderland with strong forces. (Yorkshire Evening Press)

In York, below the report about Dortmund, and in slightly smaller typeface, the Press reports that Hull and other "North East Coast Towns" were badly damaged that night and, "people were trapped in demolished houses". Sunderland was attacked and 84 people died, 221 were injured and much of the town was damaged. Rescue work was still going on after the daylight attack on towns on the South East coast. In Bournemouth 128 people were killed and 3,000 buildings damaged: "soldiers dug all night by the light of flares" and "bodies were discovered during the night". "Digging is still going on in the ruins of a public house where it is feared that other bodies are buried."[58]

Reports such as this were repeated more or less verbatim in all major papers because they were drafted by the Ministry, but local news was not so controlled and Maxie, as he lay in bed, probably also read, at the bottom of the war news page in the Yorkshire Evening Post, that Lieutenant Commander David Cecil Lycett Green R.N. has finally managed to divorce Angela, his wife, because she mentioned Lord Grimthorpe's name in her sleep, a full ten years after having an affair with him.

Meanwhile, Freda was reading that a damaged Halifax destroyed a Ju88 and may have wondered, as I do, whether it was Jack's. She cut out the article and kept it.

> **COMBATS WITH FIGHTERS**
>
> Many night fighters were sent up in an effort to stem the tide of the attack, and several bombers reached home after having indecisive combats. One Ju88 was probably destroyed by a damaged Halifax.
>
> The ease with which the crews could identify their targets permitted a highly concentrated attack. The procession of bombers over Dortmund proceeded so swiftly and smoothly that in a short time whole areas were carpeted with incendiaries, causing many fires to break out simultaneously. The work of the civil defences was still further impeded by the rain of heavy high-explosives which followed almost without a break.
>
> All the preliminary reports point to such tremendous havoc having been caused that, to

Figure 30 Cutting found among letters

Sunday .. Main target: Dortmund, a very heavy raid but the paper says the percentage of losses is low. She searches for a list of lost aeroplanes. Among the 826 aircraft on the raid, 199 were Halifaxes, 18 of these did not return.

On Tuesday morning Freda catches the tube to work (when Jack arrives she doesn't want to be encumbered by her bicycle) and buys a paper. She turns on the radio when she arrives at Gordon Square. It's Ronald's last day before he goes on leave so they are very busy but time goes by slowly in the morning, when she expects Jack to phone her and, though it is only Tuesday, she feels she's been spending all week sitting around waiting for him. By 2.45 p.m. Jack has still not arrived in London and although the next train is due in half an hour, she writes him a letter:

Darling,

This doesn't seem to be our lucky day does it?! I'm getting heart attacks every time there's a tinkle on the telephone, and as the day wears on and there is yet no word from you I'm regretfully coming to the conclusion that your leave has been postponed or cancelled.

What happened at your interview? I hope you remembered to take the chewing gum out of your mouth?!

I do hope your leave isn't postponed for long, darling – I've been so looking forward to it, but I suppose these disappointments are part of the business of plighting my troth to a member of H.M. Forces, and I shall have to grin and bear it –what a life! I won't make this a long epistle, just in case you do arrive and meanwhile I will hang on to the telephone – not literally of course – and put my trust in God and keep my powder dry, so to speak.

Write as soon as you can, darling, or, better still by far, arrive in person – but legitimately of course!

All my love,
Yours ever,
Freda.

Another sheaf of airgrams arrives on her desk waiting to be transcribed.

On Tuesday evening, Freda buys a platform ticket at King's Cross so that she can see everyone clearly as they get off the train; this is extravagant. The York train is forty-two minutes late and the platform is crowded and Freda is not tall. She's buffeted by all around her, seemingly the single stationary person. With a column behind her back she stands on tiptoe and looks right and left, from the back of the train to the ticket barrier and still no sign of Jack and his crew. Every day Freda listens to the radio and scours the papers for news of raids to see how hard Jack might be working. It is a busy week for Bomber Command. Monday, Berlin is the main target. Wednesday's paper reports another very heavy raid, this time on Düsseldorf. Because she cannot be with Jack, she writes instead:

>Judging from the radio and newspapers it sounds as if you are working hard once again, which I take it is why your 48 hrs has gone overboard. Never mind, darling, it will be all the more enjoyable when it does eventually come round, and another way of looking at it is that instead of your leave being nearly over, as it would have been, it is all still to come.
>
>This disappointment has made me realise that chances of seeing you are much more important than anything that might be saved by your not coming, darling, which I suppose is not very strong-willed of me, but so what!

When a new report lands on her desk to be transcribed, she complains, and apologises without looking up, because she cannot bring herself to smile. She finishes her letter to Jack angrily, as never before, but she cannot find it in herself to rewrite it. There isn't the paper even if she wanted to. This scrap of airmail is the last of a few remaining sheets of pre-war writing paper they have in the office and she doesn't want to write to Jack on the horrible thin yellow paper she has to use for work:

>It's the Play Centre this evening, I might as well go, "seeing as how".
>If I get into a bad temper I'll take it out on the little brats, so I hope they behave! I won't lose my temper though darling, because there's no point in it, and I know you'll be coming along soon.
>Au revoir, darling and all my love,
>Yours always,
>Freda.

On Friday Freda took a long detour to work and cycled via Fleet Street and the Embankment to Westminster. She cycled up Horseferry, down Broadway, turned towards the Park and bumped her bike down Cockpit Steps to St. James' Park. She had not the heart to cycle so she walked her bike. The tulips in St James' Park, which she had shown to Jack, were gone but the fig had sprouted large fresh summer leaves. Cygnets and goslings swam in the shade it gave. The pelicans were probably nesting. She stood still on the bridge and gazed at the French Château which is Whitehall; behind her, Buckingham Palace. Walking, following the route they took in

March, she scuffed through fallen plane blossom, soft as lambswool. Daffodil remnants, aged in the sun, sun-scorched bluebells, soft green leaves next to the shining metallic Ritz Jack had so admired. The ancient plane trunks, knobbled and aged, and the old buildings which line St James', gentlemen's clubs and such like, were solid against ethereal barrage balloons.

That week end, Freda wrote to Percy in the Near East and not to Jack but in the letter she relived her time with Jack in York.

> It was very strange – and very nice – to be able to walk through fields instead of on the pavement, and as milkmaids to let one's eye dwell on stretches of yellow buttercups and pale, hedges frosted with hawthorn, and ditches deep in black-man's oatmeal, speedwell, dandelions and even nettles and to listen to the lark as it soared high in the sky and to hear the cuckoo singing in some far off field. I spent a very lazy week doing absolutely nothing at all. Jack managed to get into York three or four times from where he is stationed, which was very fortunate.
> This week I had a lazy week-end, spending Saturday afternoon sitting in the sunshine in the Square and on Sunday I sat in the sunshine on the roof at the hostel. In the evening I went to a Service at St Martin- in-the-Fields which was conducted by Colin Sowerbutts. Very impressive to see young folk in uniform from all corners of the earth there. I find Church services very puzzling though, always jumping up and down; it made me appreciate Meeting more.
> Afterwards some of us went for a walk as far as Tower Bridge. While standing thereon, and watching a ship come up river, a man rang a bell and we all had to move off – what a sight to see the ship slip into the Pool of London.
> I was on night orderly in the Hostel last Sunday. It's a bit grim. Going down to the cellar every hour to keep the boilers going and scrubbing floors which are thick with those dreadful steam-beetles, and everything is so quiet, or worse, the stillness is broken by the steady drip-drip-drip of a tap, or the whirring of

the refrigerator. I must say I was glad when a cock crew loudly to announce dawn.

When I got down to the Play Centre I found that it had been broken into by the older boys, who had scattered the contents of the toy cupboard all over the floor: bricks, paint, crayons, jig-saw puzzles, books and as a piece de resistance, some red powder paint all over the floor. What a shambles. From this you'll gather that the East End flourishes as normal (it smells just as strongly too!).

On Monday 29th May, a week after Jack was due to arrive in London, Freda writes to her friend Alan McBain, in China. She is replying to his letter of April 5th, which has only just arrived. She describes Gordon Square in the summer heat.

> The trees in Gordon Square are thick with foliage, and looking out from the window it is sometimes difficult to imagine that this is a city at all. I can see nothing but trees, no houses, they are all hidden, but the steady hum of traffic soon brings one back to earth, the screech of tyres as the taxis swing round the corner on their way West from Kings Cross and Euston, and the clink of harness and the creaking of cart wheels as a horse and cart pass by.
>
> Gordon Square itself is at its best just now, the leaves are still fresh and are not as yet limp from the dust and heat. It is quite one of the most charming of Bloomsbury Squares, and more secluded than those nearer to Southampton Row.
>
> At lunch time there is a sprinkling of office workers from the nearby various Philanthropic Organisations – you know how Bloomsbury abounds in these – and in the morning and afternoon a few retired old gentlemen – liberal intellectuals – you will know how the W.C. district abounds in these too. On the whole, a very restful atmosphere.
>
> There are practically no Full Blood F.A.U. members at the hostel now –except me, I think. Those that are there are for the most part seconded to Friends War Relief Service. There are about 40 people living there altogether – a very staid and serious crowd.

If you have by now received my last two airgraphs, wherein I told you all about my getting engaged to Flight Sergeant Jack B. Denton of the R.A.F., you will appreciate that I am a much more subdued character than I used to be. I do hope you have received the airgraphs, Alan – you were the first of the Overseas Gang that I ever mentioned the matter to. I've written to them all since I got engaged, so they will know all about it by now though. I expect really they were very surprised.

I was home on leave two weeks ago, and had to face the ordeal of bringing Jack round to meet my mama and papa – phew! Actually, he is stationed about 14 miles from York, so I did not know how often I would see him when I was on leave, but fate was kind and he managed to get in five times altogether, which was very good going indeed. He got on with my family like a house on fire though, which was a relief – not that I thought it would be otherwise.

He is a darling, Alan. You must meet him some day when you come back. I've got a suspicion that he knows how to manage me, though, so I must watch my step – I suppose throwing a four-engined bomber around the skies has given him some practice for piloting a wayward wench like myself! We are hoping to get married before the end of this year – we are hoping somewhere round about October or November.

Actually, Jack should have come down this week on a 48 hours pass, but did not arrive, nor have I heard anything, and to say that I worry is to put it very mildly indeed. However, the R.A.F. have been very busy this week, and on these occasions they don't get such a lot of free time, so I suppose his pass has been cancelled and he's not had time to write.

Do you remember the airgraph I wrote some time in March, Alan, saying how far out of touch we were at the hostel with the war and how it affects people's lives? I never thought when I wrote it that before long I would be so much in the swim of it. I suppose I shall eventually get used to it – I shall have to, but it's making a nervous wreck of me, Alan.

Dashing downstairs for the 8'o'clock news in the morning, to hear if our bombers have been out, scanning the evening papers to see where they have been, and how many are missing; and then times like this, when I don't get any news for a few days, cycling to the Square from the Hostel every morning, hurrying at first, anxious to see if there is any post, and then, nearer to the Square, going more slowly, afraid that when I arrive there will be nothing, or worse. I promised Jack not to worry, and I do try, but it's so difficult.

When he does come down, life seems so good that I just can't imagine anything happening to break it, but it happens to other people, and all the time at the back of my mind is the knowledge that it might happen to me, and anyway, who am I that I should be more exempt than other women. Sorry to break out like this, Alan, this week has been rather more nerve-wracking than usual, and I can't keep myself bottled up forever – still, it seems hard to pull out the cork on you – I hope you'll understand.

Sorry, Alan, I'll have to give this up and try some other time – I can't put my mind to it. I do apologise, and will try again when I am in a more cheerful mood.

On June 4th *The Aeroplane* reported the Dortmund raid of 23/24th May:

> A new record in the bombing of Germany was achieved last week. More than 2,000 tons of bombs were dropped on Dortmund by less than 1,000 aircraft on May 23, and the week's total of bombs was only 1,200 tons less than the whole weight dropped on London during the "blitz" of the winter of 1940-1941. The raid lasted from 01.00 hrs. to 02.00 hrs, and was made in almost perfect weather. At first, the anti-aircraft gunfire was fierce, and the searchlights concentrated, but before the attack ended the gunfire had become desultory, and the few searchlights still working waved feebly and aimlessly about the sky. Night fighters were active and one Lancaster had an

encounter with a Ju88 which it probably destroyed. During the Dortmund raid Bomber Command completed the delivery of the first 100,000 bombs on Germany. (*The Aeroplane*: "The 195th week of THE WAR IN THE AIR", June 4, 1943, p.638-640)

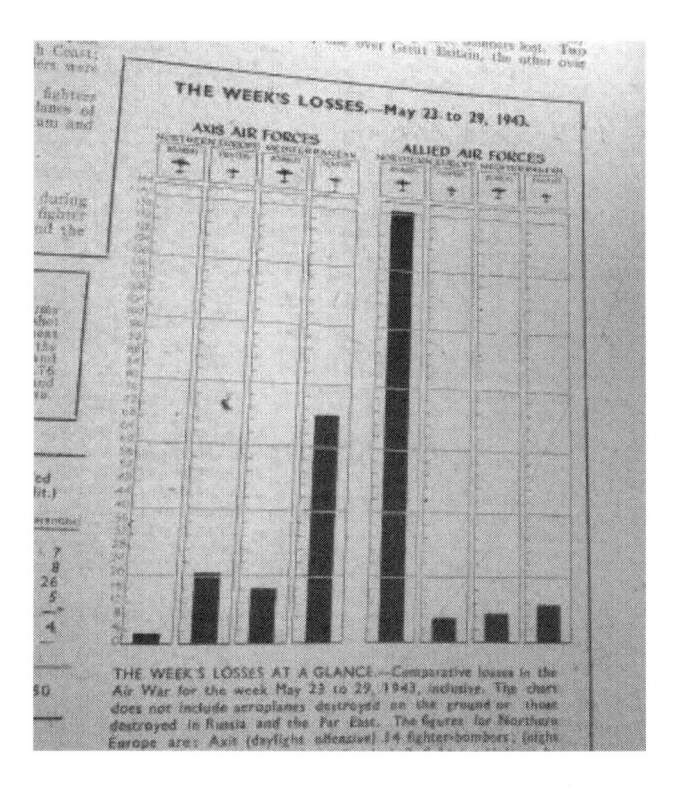

Figure 31 The week's losses at a glance. – May 23 to 29, 1943 ©The Aeroplane, June 4th

The four columns to the left are Axis fighters and bombers lost. The columns to the right show Allied losses. The very tall column shows how many Allied bombers were lost: 141. The graph does not include aircraft lost on take-off or landing, or those lost outside central Europe.

Freda read on to the section called 'Diary of the Week' for Sunday, May 23.

The heading, in bold, describes the previous week's "Offensive Operations of the Fighter, Coastal and Bomber Commands of the R.A.F. and of the U.S. Army Eighth Air Force."

> DAY .. Whirlwind bombers of Fighter Command, escorted by Spitfires attacked enemy shipping in the English Channel. Spitfire-escorted Venturas of Bomber Command bombed the coke ovens at Zeebrugge. Five FW 190 fighter-bombers destroyed over Great Britain, four by A.A. and one by fighters.
> NIGHT .. Main target: Dortmund (in the heaviest R.A.F. raid of the War). Thirty-eight bombers lost. E boats attacked by Albacores of the Fleet Air Arm operating with Fighter Command. Three sunk. One enemy raider destroyed over Great Britain. (*The Aeroplane*, June 4)

This was the 41st time Bomber Command had attacked the city of Dortmund. Melbourne Operations Record Book notes that 23/24th May brought one of the biggest raids yet on Happy Valley.

> 23/5/43 Bombing attack on <u>DORTMUND</u> (Twenty One Aircraft)
>
> Route: – Base – Cottesmore – 52.01 North by 01.30 East – 52.48 North by 04.40 East – 52.05 North by 07.25 East
>
> Target :-: 51.50 North by 07.10 East – Egmond – English Coast 52.47 North by 01.37 East – Cottesmore Light – Base
>
> Bomb Load: – 2.1000lb. (A/C H.D.A.F.E.G. and C – long delay, remainder G.P.TD.0.02) 7. S.B.C. (90 at 4lbs) 6 S.B.C. (8 at 30lb)[59]

Sgt. Beveridge again had trouble; this time a bomb would not release over the target so i/t had to be jettisoned live on the way back to base. Sgt. Watson had a close shave when two JU88s appeared and at the same time an ME109 closed in and another JU88 "came in from below". The rear gunner fired and saw it "dive into haze on fire".

The two other JU88s then came in from port quarter to dead astern, one above the other, our aircraft began to corkscrew and the ME109 then closed in from astern only to break away subsequently. ... JU88 made repeated attacks firing approximately five bursts in all, two of which hit ... Attack which lasted 45 minutes only ceased when our aircraft was near English coast. Aircraft sustained many holes in the fuselage, tailplane, rudders, starboard mainplane, starboard outer engine and port tyre. Hydraulics were also rendered unserviceable. None of the crew were injured. (AIR 27)

According to Rapier, "Twenty-one aircraft were available, a record for 10 squadron, for a raid on Dortmund during $23^{rd}/24^{th}$ May. One aircraft returned early with intercom problems and two others were attacked by night fighters.[60] Another Halifax claimed as probably destroyed, a Junkers JU88 after a running fight of three quarters of an hour, beginning over Amsterdam." (Rapier, p.46). A Junkers 88 certainly crashed that night over Holland, along with nineteen other RAF bombers, including ZA-Z W1217 which crashed into the Ijsselmeer, one of the three Halifaxes which failed to return to Melbourne that night. The other two crashed in Germany.

Twenty one crews detailed to bomb DORTMUND, seventeen attacked the target reporting a successful raid and moderate opposition. Sgt. Watson had an encounter with enemy fighters, his aircraft sustained heavy damage. S/LDR Baird abandoned the mission owing to failure of the 'inter com'. Three crews of FSgt Denton. Sgt Rees and Sgt Hine failed to return from this mission. Weather at Base was cloudy with occasional showers. West South Westerly wind. (AIR 27)

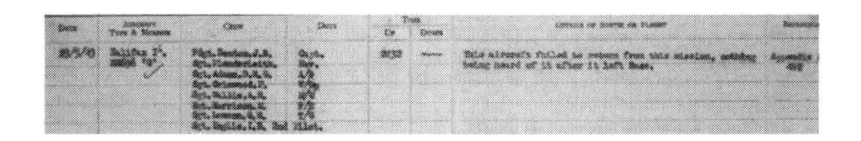

Figure 32 Crew list of HR696 ZA-G 23/5/43 © National Archives

Melbourne records note the three missing aircraft in the usual way, next to the crew list, under the heading DETAILS OF SORTIE OR FLIGHT:

> "This aircraft failed to return from this mission, nothing being heard of it after it left Base."

So many aircraft took part in the Dortmund raid that pilots jostled other pilots for position, some waiting a long time to drop their bomb load.

> On 23 May the biggest bomb load ever dropped anywhere in a single night – more than 2,000 tons – fell on luckless Dortmund. The entire Ruhr shuddered when its most easterly town was subjected to this fearful pounding. (Bowman, p. 92)

Sergeant Foster is quoted in the same book: " 'As I made my attack,' he said later, 'a Stirling came streaking out only 50 feet above us and we were bumped by its slipstream. By this time it was difficult to believe that it was a real town below; the place was so covered with fires and smoke'. " (Bowman, p. 93)

Tom Wingham describes this Dortmund raid as "something different. It was to be the heaviest raid of the war" (Bowman, p. 162). German defences tended to coordinate and home in on one aircraft so when the sky was full of aircraft, targeting a single aircraft was a problem. Wingham suggests that "it was the stragglers and those outside the stream, port or starboard, higher or lower, which could be guaranteed to get most attention." (Bowman, p. 162.) Presumably, this would include damaged aircraft, limping home after the raid.

On this night, Halifaxes of 4 Group were leading the attack with 102 Squadron in the van. I imagine that 10 Squadron was close on their heels as they flew south to manoeuvre into formation with the other 800 aircraft on this operation. The stream of aircraft approached Dortmund from the North this time and once the load was dropped, returned back home to the South of the Ruhr. "Everything was still dark, although it was a clear starry night with very good visibility" (Bowman, p. 162).

After dropping the big 1,000 lb bombs, other smaller incendiaries had to be dropped and the pilot kept a steady course for between 10 and 30 seconds to ensure that all bombs landed on the same target and to give time for the camera to photograph the damage. That 10 seconds, Wingham says, were very dangerous, especially for those heavies in the van. "We had been getting a bumpy ride as the flak intensified almost to the point of realization of the old line shoot, "The flak was so heavy you could get out and walk on it" "(*Flypast*, Dec 2009). As soon as the 10 second steady run was over, the pilot could jink to avoid anti-aircraft guns and turn for home.

Wingham now mentions that he had a terror of bailing out over the Ruhr or any of the towns they had bombed because the local people would probably tear the airmen, the terrorflieger, to bits: "This did happen in many instances, sometimes observed by their fellow crew-members." Tom Wingham's crew believed "It can't happen to us!" (Bowman, p. 165). When his aircraft looked likely to crash, the pilot was begged to save it and save it he does; Jack's crew probably also believed they were the lucky ones. When Jack's aircraft was hit, he also tried to get as far West as possible, if he had time to take any other than evasive action, that is. It is most likely that the aircraft dived too fast for any of the crew to bale out, but as their bodies, or parts of them, survived, it is unlikely the aircraft became a 'scarecrow'.

A12th Squadron Lancaster W4561, also crashed after bombing Dortmund that night. Sgt. Dew was taken P.O.W. and his story is recorded on Tom Forbes' memorial web.[61]

> We arrived over target on time, dropped our bombs and were immediately coned. By the time we got free we were down to about 8,000'. We set course for home and decided to gain height. In retrospect we may have been better staying at 8,000' and getting out quicker. We reached about 20,000' again over Holland and then we were shot down by August Geiger [a night fighter pilot of 3/NJG1].

Dan Brennan also flew that night. 10 Squadron record books record that his crew flew ZA-L, with Dan in his usual position of mid-upper gunner. The debriefing note reads:

> Visibility was spoiled by smoke and haze but the South of the town was seen to be well ablaze, fires being

visible for 60 miles on the return flight. Flak was fairly heavy at target. Searchlights were numerous but largely ineffectual. (AIR 27)

I believe Jack's aircraft was hit by flak over the target and that the crew tried desperately to evade the Ruhr. Norman calmly plotted a course to the South West towards Düsseldorf and they briefly discussed procedures with each other on the intercom, hoping at best to limp back home over the Channel or at worst to ditch over Holland – their normal route took them over Egmond, to the North of Amsterdam. Jack may have realised that he would not escape but probably trusted to his luck and experience to fly far enough to reach North Holland and level enough once there for his crew to escape. He probably warned the crew to be ready to bale out and may even have ordered them to, but possibly a night fighter finished them off because they were together when they died.

Then the fine weather broke. On 24th May: "No operations. Crews rested after operations. Weather at Base fair with intermittent rain and low cloud. Light variable wind," the Operations Record Book records. "Breathing Space for the Reich" *The Aeroplane* announced, followed by an article which began: "A break in the weather brought unexpected relief to Germany from Bomber Command's mighty blows." Melbourne reported to Bomber Command that rarely during the week were the heavy bombers able to set out. Ops began again on the 27th May, when eighteen crews from 10 Squadron bombed Essen.

Jack relied on reports of raids in the papers to indicate to Freda when he was too busy to write but by the same token, she knew when he was in danger and relied on his letters to confirm his safety. The papers were full of heroic adventures but "it was the lower-flying Halifaxes which suffered most." (Wilson, p. 54) Freda knew this. Along with reports of operations for the last week in May, she began to study the Roll of Honour.

All papers and many magazines carried long lists of missing airmen, killed or taken prisoner and this was called the Roll of Honour. Each list sent by squadrons to the Air Ministry was recorded alphabetically. There was no way to sort all the lists together, the way we do now using word processing, so each column, whether of MISSING, MISSING BELIEVED KILLED, KILLED OR TAKEN

PRISONER, consisted of many shorter lists, each in alphabetical order. The lists were not separated by squadron number, only by Group, so searching for Jack, therefore, meant working down through each section in turn, name by name. I did exactly this when researching Jack's career and found it inexplicably nerve-wracking because, even though I knew he was dead, I still could not bear to see his name. The multitude of names cannot have failed to dismay Freda but how she must have feared finding his name among them though she knew in her heart of hearts that sooner or later it would be there.

A week passed and his name was not among those listed in the *Aeroplane*. Still no letter from Jack so Freda, desperate for news, stamped and self-addressed an envelope and enclosed it in a letter to Jack's mother and shortly her envelope arrived back from Norwich. The letter inside was from Jack's sister Beryl. She wrote that "my dear brother Jack is missing." Her mother was too distraught to write but the family clung to a ray of hope that he could have been taken prisoner. Years later, Beryl told her daughters how it seemed that everyone in the street saw the telegraph boy cycle up to their house and how her mother went down to the gate in her apron to take the telegram and then collapsed on the garden path, her neighbours rushing over to help her inside.

Freda also wrote to Maxie at Melbourne and her letter was forwarded to him at Askham Grange, where he was in hospital.[62]

She did not keep copies of these letters but Maxie's replies were included in the bundle of letters stored in her trunk. It is easy to imagine how shocked and distraught Jack's right-hand man felt as he lay in hospital wondering whether he could have saved his pals. Their loss was "incredible" and he probably felt he had let them all down and worried whether their belongings had been disposed of correctly. His letter is literally stilted, written in short distinct paragraphs, as though written in between bouts of pain.

    7.6.43
    578363 SGT. STEEL,
    AUX. MILITARY HOSP.,
    WARD. 1.,
    ASKHAM GRANGE,
    ASKHAM RICHARD

Dear Freda,

Thanks for your letter received this morning. Excuse my writing please; only am sort of strapped in an awkward position.

Well I have bad news for you. I am terribly sorry, but Jack & the rest of the crew, have not returned from the big raid on Dortmund.

I know, though this will be a shock to you, you must have thought of it. It seems incredible to me. I cannot believe they haven't come back. They were so full of life & a <u>very</u> skilful crew.

He is so far officially posted as "MISSING". No wireless message was received from them, & so nothing more is known.

It will be approximately a month before any notification is given by Germany. That is, <u>if</u> they are prisoners.

I don't know what to say. Don't build up too high hopes, then again do hope. You know what I mean!

I will of course inform you of any further developments.

I don't know his parents, so I can't write to them, but I am very sorry for them. Also because he is such a fine pal of mine.

Personally I am okay, but very bored. I hate being in bed. Especially I would have looked after their personal kit.

I do hope I have helped & that I haven't caused you any distress.

Cheerio for Now,
Maxie.

Maxie gave Freda the address of Norman Plenderlieth's fiancée, Betty, who she then wrote to. Betty had found out that the crew was missing the previous Tuesday. Can she be correct that his squadron really did not send anyone to the hospital to tell Maxie his old crew had not returned? If so, were they protecting him in his illness?

Dear Freda,

Thank you ever so much for writing to me. When I went to see Maxie, he told me that you probably would not have heard the news but we were absolutely helpless as we did not know your address.

I received a telegram from Norman's sister on the Tuesday morning, telling me the sad news – although somehow it did not come as a shock to me. I remembered that Maxie was in hospital in York, so of course I wrote to him. My letter was the first he knew about it although he too had guessed something was wrong.

Cheer up Freda. I really feel that we shall have some good news soon, and if we don't there is always the possibility that they will have escaped. I shall not give up hope for a very long time yet.

The same day I received your letter, I also heard from Peter's mother. She seems very cheerful and had got in touch with Jack's mother in Norwich.

Norman thought that there wasn't a pilot like Jack, but I believe they used to argue when they were down on the ground.

It was funny how we happened to see you that day at the tennis courts. Norman just said that Jack was down there and of course I looked and then he said that must be Freda with him. I think Norman teased Jack that he knew all about you but actually that was all.

I used to hear a lot about you, for you must have made Jack a different person. Norman always used to be talking about the two of you. He once said he thought he was terribly lovesick but that Jack was far worse than him!

Still there was no news from Jack. Freda worked as hard as she could; she scrubbed her room clean each evening; she cycled to and from Gordon Square each day and after work helped Mary run the Sugar Loaf more often than usual. She did not lose her temper with the children but kept very quiet and in the evenings she did not go downstairs for coffee but embroidered in her room. She got soaked walking along the Embankment in unseasonable rain and had too many baths. Then, slowly, day by day, letters she had sent to Jack were returned to her unopened.

Figure 33 Unopened letter returned

Chapter 6: After Jack

Figure 34 Freda ready to leave for Cairo, Spring 1944

THANK YOU FOR YOUR AIRGRAPH of I forget when, which I received about 10 days ago. Last week I wrote you a longish air mail letter ...

On 17th June 1943 Freda wrote to her old friend Alan McBain in China.[63]

... but I'm afraid it is not very newsy, but more of a personal nature. In your airgraph you said that my December and (I think) January, airgraphs had not reached you, and consequently I am wondering whether this will reach you, also my airmail and my two previous airgraphs. I hope so; they make a nice little story of my activities over the last few months –

Chapt.I Meeting. Chapt.II – Engagement. Chapt.III Finale.

Yes, Alan, I'm afraid my steps towards matrimony have not been favoured by the Gods, and Jack (my fiancé) has been posted missing after a big R.A.F. raid on Dortmund on May 23/24th – just five weeks after we got engaged.

I won't give you any further details in this airgraph, as I have taken the liberty of pouring it all out in my airmail letter, which will probably arrive sometime after this. I'm sorry this news had to come so soon after my earlier joyful airgraph. I am of course hoping that he is P.O.W., in which case we should have news in a week or two, but I just daren't think about it – it would be too good to be true.

I am going home this week-end; it will be a nice change. Jack's engineer missed the raid because he had fractured his ankle, so I hope to see him when I am in York, as it will be interesting to talk to him, also to the fiancée of Jack's navigator – she was at the same school as me though I have not seen her since school days. Still, it's nice to be able to talk to someone in the same boat – people here are very kind, but I don't think can really understand just how nerve-wracking a business it has all been.

I was up at Millfield (new Transport/Worksquad Hostel) on Monday evening. After supper we went for a very pleasant walk across the Heath (Hampstead) to Ken Wood, and through the gardens. There was a fair on the Heath, and the sounds drifted up to us, but we yielded not to temptation and turned away, feeling rather like Christian in Pilgrim's Progress!

I hear you may want some typists in China, in which case I am thinking of being one of them if poss. London seems pretty grim at the moment, or maybe I'm prejudiced. However, I hope soon to be able to bring you better news – you may be sure I will lose no time in passing any further news on to you.

> I have not been much about London since I returned from leave four weeks ago, but the shops are amazingly well-stocked, when one considers how long the war has been going on.
>
> The hostel is very quiet now, and I don't think I will speak of it again, as it has quite ceased to exist as a Unit centre at all. I gather that there is some talk of a dance for midsummer's eve, but I'm not interested, and if I put in an appearance it will only be from a sense of duty (ahem!).
>
> Best wishes Alan, and apologies for the lack of news, but I know you will understand.

She uses one of Jack's phrases, "ahem!". Shortly after this she wrote to Margaret Smethurst in Bengal.

> As you will know by now, things have not quite gone according to plan. We have not heard any further news about Jack, but even if I do not hear that he is P.O.W. I feel fairly confident that the crew is alive somewhere, and shall not lose hope for some time but I'm afraid there is a very slight chance – there were 38 planes missing from the raid.
>
> I'm afraid it will be a great shock to his Mother as he never told her he was on ops so that she would not worry – I may go up to Norwich to see her next week.
>
> There's not much more I can say about it in a letter, and not much point. I shall have to readjust myself like everyone else.
>
> I was in York last week-end by the way. I saw the chance of a cheap and very welcome trip home because Gwendy had a microscope which she was sending out to Ethiopia, and as it would be rather risky to send it by post I went up to collect it. Actually, the week-end did not turn out so cheap, as, my mind being on other things, I left my little fawn hip-length jacket on the train and have not got it back – just my luck. I seem to lose everything that's irreplaceable, case, watch and now my coat – not to mention Jack of course.

> You will be amused to learn that in order to fill the long evenings I have taken to embroidery, and am busy embroidering an afternoon tea tablecloth. One certainly wants something to do in the evenings at the hostel – what a place! I don't see much of anyone because I sit in my room and sew after supper most days.
>
> We had a dance there last week, but I did not feel like it. However, Ronald came round and raked me out and we went to the Prospect for a drink – the parlour in the back was crowded with dancing couples, finishing up of course with 'Knees up Mother Brown' but we managed to get out before the crush.

Freda also tells Margaret how she has become friendly with Betty, Norman Plenderlieth's fiancée, and with Mary "19 year old wife of another fellow in the same squadron who went missing a couple of nights after Jack", married to Ted who went down in ZA-N after the raid to Essen on 28th May.[64]

> Between us we manage to keep very cheerful and we are all looking forward to the day when they land up on our doorsteps, having made their way back in some mysterious fashion, as I gather is often the case – so you see I have by no means given up hope.

Mary wrote to Freda that "it does not help us, nor anyone around us, if we show our feelings." Mary may simply be repeating propaganda, but she still yearned to visit Melbourne to see where her husband had spent his days and to talk to his friends.

> I have not been to Melbourne as planned. You see, a Pilot Officer, Ted's best pal, came to visit me and he explained how terrible it would be for the rest of the crews to speak to me. Also his Commanding Officer advised me not to go, much as I wanted to. I have now more or less given up the idea.
>
> He said they see nothing very much happen when up there. I can hardly believe that, but I guess he ought to know, having completed his first tour of "ops".

In the first week of June, Grace, Jack's mother, wrote to ask Freda to come and stay in Norwich.

> On that awful Monday – just two weeks ago – your name kept cropping up in my mind and how I wished I could have talked to you just then.
> I shall not trouble to write an epistle because my grief is something which I can't express.
> Please <u>do</u> come and stay. Just let me know the time of the arrival of your train and I will meet you – that is if you will tell me what sort of an identity disc you will wear and if (don't laugh) you will carry a few wild roses (just in case).

I imagine Freda looking for wild roses in the bombsites of Whitechapel. Two weeks later Grace wrote that Mrs Plenderleith, Norman's mother, had also written to her and said "it gives me great comfort to hear from anyone who knew my boy." Grace also spent time with Mary who could not resist going to Melbourne in the end, even though she had been warned very clearly against doing so.

> I went round last Tuesday to say "Goodbye" to Mary but she insisted on seeing me alone so she came round on Thursday morning. Sylvia made tea in her little cups and this tickled Mary to death, but she drank the tea.[65] She said she was going to Melbourne and would mention Jack. Poor Mary. She is such a young girl.

On July 14th, after Freda's visit to Norwich and a month after her first letter, Jack's mother wrote again to Freda. The family had finally had news of her son's formal status, Missing presumed dead. Grace used Jack's R.A.F. notepaper to write to Freda.

> Dear Freda,
> I have been going to write you so many times, and will now, dear. I feel somehow I can't write at all, in other words, I am at a loss to tell you the inevitable.

I have just received a telegram from the Air Ministry to say that my dear boy is believed to have lost his life as a result of Air Operations on May 24th.

You know, dear Freda, what it is costing me to write you these few lines, so I trust you will forgive me if I sound casual. I am to have a letter and then when I know details I will be perhaps able to write a little better.

Meanwhile, please bear up as he would have wished you to do.

Excuse me, I simply cannot write more.
Yours With Love.
G. D. Denton.

By the middle of August 1943 Jack and his crew had not landed safely and escaped back to England and none of them was listed as a prisoner of war. Then there he was, listed as MISSING, BELIEVED KILLED IN ACTION. Freda cut out the notice from the newspaper. Sgt Ayres is also listed as missing – Jack's 2nd Pilot on the Bochum raid of 13th May. Freda immediately wrote to tell an old friend that she felt very depressed at times but remained hopeful.

However, I will give myself until October and then try to get things straightened out. Mrs. Denton has just been informed by the War Office that Jack is now "Missing Believed Killed" – it seems rather early to be put into this category to me, and I am waiting until she receives further information from the Air Ministry because unless she learns something definite, I am not believing anything of the sort.

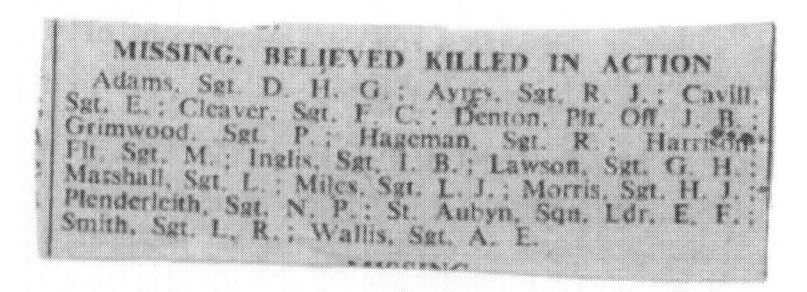

Figure 35 Missing, believed killed in action

Freda then wrote again to Alan in China. She's been thinking of a holiday with Marjorie, one which she had already planned as her honeymoon with Jack.

> It is very cold here today – typical July weather, with a faint mist over everything, reminding one that the summer is well under way and before long the September mists will be upon us.
> Marjorie and I are thinking of planning a holiday together next October, where there are moors and lots of trees, but I don't see how we are going to rake up the cash. It would be marvellous if we could manage it though. When I think of the moors in September and October, vast expanses of heather; misty mornings and the slight chill in the evening; walking all day and then returning to a good, plain meal in the evening and a roaring fire.
> 'Holidays at Home' are in full swing here. Shadwell and Wapping park producing shows of all kinds; Regent's Park giving 'As You Like It' and Victoria Park 'Lilac Time'. The Bombed Site around St. Paul's is to be utilized for a Fete next week, with Inter-Service Sports etc, Dog Shows and heavens knows what else.
> I am sorry to report that one of Philpot Street's landmarks, the bombed synagogue, will soon be no more. The demolition workers have attacked it and daily it loses its familiar silhouette as the stones are loosened and crash to earth.
> I need to think about going to China as a typist on 5/- a month but to go out for the duration seems an awful long time. My optimism and feeling that Jack may be alive somewhere, rather tie me. One has to face the fact that probably he is not alive, but I really can't get used to it, and keep expecting to see him back, and it would be dreadful to get under way for China and then have good news of him – you see my dilemma. I am drawn to China but if Jack has been killed, I would feel drawn to Europe to complete the work which he, in his way, was doing.
> I see so many girls running through the war as if nothing had happened, other than that they are earning

a lot more money than they did before. I didn't expect anything from the war and don't want anything but at least I did not expect just to go on having things taken away.

When the remains of the crew of HR696 G for George were retrieved, they were buried in temporary graves at the northern cemetery, Nordfriedhof, in Düsseldorf, barely 50 miles from Dortmund and only a few more from the Dutch border. The Ruhr valley was still reeling in shock from the Dams raid and had, in any case, been bombed most nights for the last three months so downed R.A.F. airmen, whether dead or alive, received little pity. Representatives of the Luftwaffe arrived at dawn to record details of ZA-G and other crashed aircraft and to examine identity tags. The crew of DT789 ZA-B, which also crashed in Germany that night, were buried the day after they were found. That same day, Luftwaffe personnel rescued the bodies of Jack and his crew, what remained of them, protected them from the general anger of residents, and took care that they were buried with respect. By writing this forcefully, I will it to have happened this way.

The International Red Cross were informed of all air crashes and they in turn reported back to the British Red Cross and then the Air Ministry confirmed who had been flying in which downed aircraft that night. Years later Freda met and wrote to John, her future husband.[66]

> That you believe I might need to be reminded of comparative values under the sun's brighter days, falls strangely on the ears of one who has spent weary months hoping for the return of a missing bomber pilot, whose ashes, had I but known, had long since been extracted from the wreckage of his plane & buried in the Ruhr. I long since, you will see therefore, ceased to expect any gold in my life.

The British Red Cross finally confirmed Jack's death. Freda wrote to two Unit friends, Jack Butterworth and Percy Brown, in August after Bank Holiday leave in York.

> Travelling on Bank Holiday Friday was fairly hectic, everyone ignoring the 'Is Your Journey Really

Necessary' notices. The train was terribly hot and stuffy, the country being in the throes of a heatwave – for the first time I understood the meaning of "to stew in your own juice"! It did not help matters to get a tantalising whiff every time the soldier next to me removed the stopper from his water bottle, filled with lemon squash, utility of course.

As the train travelled out of London, the harvest was a refreshing sight to pavement-sore eyes, acres of wheat of all shades of yellow, from a pale biscuit to the burnt gold associated with those 'TEAS WITH HOVIS' signs one used to see outside at least one cottage door in every country village

The recent raids on Milan have been preceded by the heavy drone of bombers flying over London on their way out, a rare sight for Londoners. I don't know why they have suddenly started to fly over us, probably partly propaganda.

The International Red Cross have had what must, I'm afraid, be taken as fairly accurate information from German sources that "the eight occupants of the plane in which Pilot Officer Denton was flying were killed on May 24th ". He was commissioned the day before the raid. So, in R.A.F. slang "I've had it". I suppose casualties must happen even with the best air-crew and, as I've probably said before, it's not for me to make a fuss when it happens to so many other people.

I guess it sounds rather funny for a conshie to be proud of a bomber pilot as I am of Jack – I suppose that's life. I've written to the Red Cross to see if they can find out where the crew were buried – it would be rather nice to know. You will appreciate that recent events have made me very unsettled.

To turn to brighter things – had you heard that Marjorie Whittles had got engaged to Ken Llewellyn – one of the Ethiopian doctors?

Freda then wrote to Margaret in Bengal and reminded her of the peach satin pajama material she had been given in May.

The best thing to do is to be glad that I had been able to make Jack so happy – my regret is of course that if this had to happen I should have liked it to have been after we were married when he would obviously have been even more happy, but thinking on these lines could go on forever without getting anywhere.

I was home on leave two weeks ago – it was a change I suppose, but I was rather glad to get back – there were too many aircrew in York for my liking, and it seemed such a contrast with my last leave when Jack managed to get in so often.

You remember I told you I had had some peach satin given by a friend of mine? The donor has herself just got engaged so it just tickles my sense of humour nicely to give it back to her – I hope she will accept it, because it's no use to me stuck away in a drawer. What a world.

When Freda received a copy of the RAF condolence letter, which Jack's father kindly copied out for her, it came as no surprise, though I find it very stark. The letter was copied in pencil on green lined notebook paper, and I found it enclosed in the envelope containing Jack's letter of 8th April.

Sir,

I am commanded by the Air Council to inform you that they have with great regret to confirm the telegram in which you were notified that, in view of information now received from the Inter.l R. Cross, that your son – Pilot Officer Jack Banfield Denton, Royal Air Force, is believed to have lost his life as the result of the Air operations on the night of 23/24th May 1943.

The Committee's telegram, quoting official German information, states that the eight occupants of the Aircraft in which your son was flying on that night were killed on the 24th May. It contains no information regarding the place of their burial of any other details.

Although there is unhappily little reason to doubt the accuracy of this report, the casualty will be recorded as "missing believed killed" until confirmed by further evidence, or until, in the absence of such evidence it becomes necessary, owing to lapse of time, to presume for official purposes that death has occurred.

In the absence of confirmatory evidence, death would not be presumed for at least 6 months from the date when your son was reported missing.

The Air Council desire me to express their deep sympathy with you in your grave anxiety.

I am, Sir etc etc

After this, her anger showed, most notably in a letter to one of the doctors in Ethiopia.

You will pardon me if I laugh when you say that your young lady is already writing saying you have been out of the country over a year and that it is time you were thinking of returning. You might tell her from me that she should thank her stars that you will be able to return eventually. These, dare I say it, selfish madams seem to be at the root of half the unsettlement of chaps overseas, and I just wish I could write round to them all and give them a piece of my mind!

By the way, whoever's was the idea to put the news of my engagement in your Ethiopia News Letter, it afforded me great amusement - I only wish Jack could have seen it. Also all the nice letters from chaps overseas when they heard that I had got engaged, but they all arrived after he was killed.

Once Freda accepted his death, once she stopped waking in the sunny morning feeling it was good to be alive, her heart flying for a moment weightless, then crashing down, she embarked on a course of action not open to many women in her situation. She applied to be sent abroad.

She persistently made a case to be sent overseas and at the same time, Freda volunteered for every exciting job that came her way, which was how she came to test medical treatments and the bravest of these was testing malaria medicines. Gordon Square staff typed up reports from the F.A.U. medical teams in Syria, Ethiopia, China and Bengal, all of which described the urgency for efficient treatment for bilherzie, kala azar and malaria (still the three most common killers in Africa).[67] Years later, Freda told me excitedly that Oxford University had discovered a cure which might lead to the eradication of malaria. To my shame, I did not ask her why she was so interested, thinking she was simply making lively conversation. She left her body to medical science but it was only when I read *Pacifists in Action* that I understood her serious concern. Angela Sinclair-Loutit describes the malaria experiments in a Reading hospital. Next to Angela's description, "Some of us volunteered as human guinea pigs", Freda wrote in the margin of her copy: "F. S. Angela Sue".

> ... we had to go twice a week to laboratories in Reading where we were bitten by malaria-carrying mosquitoes. We were given a glass jar covered with a piece of gauze with about twenty mosquitoes flying around inside. We were told to take off our stockings and hold the jar to an area where its mouth covered the flesh of the thigh. These mosquitoes, by then starved and very hungry, bit through the gauze. You could see them swell up with blood. This was done for about fifteen or twenty minutes until enough of them had a bite. Then some of us were given the proper treatment tablets and some given controls. Some of the guinea pigs got malaria but I never did. I didn't care, I was prepared to get malaria. I was only too delighted to do what a lot of other people didn't dare do. (Smith, p. 75-76)

After reading this I found a flimsy letter Freda had written to Jim, one of the China Convoy, in Kutsing. She writes from her Friends War Relief Service course in Hampstead that

> Angela, Susie and I and the Unit have been crashing the "news" of late in the Evening Standard and the News Chronicle and Sunday Dispatch (of all papers!). 25 members of the Unit have been acting as sort of guinea pigs for the Sorby Research Institute in connection with a malaria experiment. We have been bitten by malaria-infected mosquitoes in order to try out some sort of pill which is supposed to cure malaria (and prevent it). It's the last stage of the experiment which is more or less proved already so there is no risk attached to the business, but the newspapers got hold of the story, first one and then another – I gave

> an interview to a Sunday Dispatch reporter and Susie and Angela had their photos in the News Chronicle or somewhere – a lot of silly fuss but I suppose it all helps publicity! One result of taking the pills is that we are apt to go somewhat yellow in the face at times. Some days I turn a very Chinese hue.

Elsewhere in the letter she says that they all had to go to Epsom to have their blood examined for signs of the inoculation working. Freda did not contract malaria, though, she writes to Percy in Syria, "I forgot to take my pill last night. I don't suppose it will make much difference. We have to take the pill every night except Sunday at 9.0 p.m!" (letter dated 3rd Sept. 1943)

On the same day, 3rd September, Freda wrote to Jack Green in Ethiopia about post-war plans almost as though she is counting on the war not ending.

> Although the public are naturally optimistic, I think it would be true to say that most people anticipate at least another two years yet, before the war finishes in the West. 1945 is the latest calculation by some prominent American or other. After which, of course, there will be the war in the East to finish off, and there will probably still be some form of national registration of manpower until that is finished.

That summer and autumn Freda continued to write amusing letters to her colleagues abroad and in one she describes London road works.

> It's the 'Road Up' Season in London, and in almost every other street one sees the familiar British Workman with his pick-axe and can of tea, and the hole in the road, and the red flags diverting traffic and, of course, a collection of spectators.
> In an effort to induce people to buy wooden-soled shoes, leather soled ones have got up to 9 coupons a pair for men and 7 for women – a rise of two coupons a pair! We are now allowed ¾ lb of sweets a month but chocolate will be scarce soon.

The Govt. have warned us of this because vitaminised chocolate is recognised as the best method of feeding the starving and under-nourished people of occupied territories when the Second Front opens.

I dashed into Oxford Street this lunch time to buy some pyjamas, and bang went 8 of my clothing coupons, leaving me with 10 to last until March, and I shall want a winter coat which costs 18! We only get 32 coupons a year now, and they really don't go very far. I'm feeling a bit mad at the moment because I lent a girl two prs. Stockings (two coupons a pair) and she has left the hostel without returning them – what trials we have!

Almost six months after Jack's death, and after three months training, Freda was accepted for overseas duties in the Middle East on November 12th 1943. Her report from Course 11 at the Emergency Relief Training Centre describes her as not leadership material but with plenty of practical sense. Under the heading 'Reliability and Thoroughness' it is recorded that she is "Very dependable : always the first woman up in the morning" and socially she was "A very sensible, self-respecting influence : takes the trouble to dress well. Good fun withal." However under the heading 'Adaptability', it is said that "She tends to resist change" which couldn't be further from the truth.

Before November was out, Freda received a letter from Maxie's mother in March, Cambridgeshire. The last member of Jack's original crew had died. Even as late as March 1944, the Luftwaffe showed no signs of weakening. In fact they introduced new jets. RAF casualties did not decline as the war progressed and, for example, more aircrew were killed in the bombing of Nuremberg on 30th March 1944 than in the whole Battle of Britain (Nichol and Rennell, p. 53). Jack's engineer was flying with 10 Squadron again and on 19th November the Squadron attacked Leverkusen, a decoy raid for the main target which was another strike at Berlin. On returning, the aircraft crashed at Tangmere on the South coast. Maxie's mother wrote to Freda almost immediately. Her son, who she called Jimmie, was the youngest of the crew, aged 19 when he died.

My dear Freda,

    I can't be formal with you, as you were a friend of my darling Boy's and I had heard so much about you from him. He admired you so for your efficiency.

    Thank you so much for the letter to you sent in answer to mine. I appreciate your sympathy so much. We know words seem to mean little but if you feel they are meant, they mean a lot.

    I am so glad my dear boy was a help to you in your time of sorrow. I know he really felt it deeply when Jack and the boys were lost. My boy used to tell me so much about his life, I felt I lived it with him.

    Jimmie was taking a course at the time and off ops but they wanted an engineer for another bomber and he volunteered. They did not get back to Melbourne but crashed at a fighter station, Tangmere, just over the coast. We thought as you did, that Jimmie was perhaps going to be lucky as he was safe at the time of the other dear boys' loss, but I feel they will all be lost, only those that go in the R.A.F. just at the end will live.

    The thoughts in your letter are similar to mine: the war being over does not seem to matter to me now. I know it is frightfully selfish. I do <u>have</u> to think that others are suffering as well as me, to try to make things bearable but the loss is awful.

    I do so hope you spent a nice week-end with Jack's people and that they were feeling a little better.

    I would like to wish you the best of luck in your future abroad.

    We shall never forget our dear boys.

    M. M. Steel.

Working overseas meant wearing uniform. The Quaker Friends War Relief Service, which Freda worked for when she first arrived in London, refused to allow members to wear a uniform and certainly not khaki, not even the Red Cross uniform. The Friends Ambulance Unit was not so strict and most Unit members understood the necessity to wear uniform. All the same, the Unit tried to remain separate from the armed forces. They refused to carry arms in their trucks, for instance, even when rescuing wounded soldiers. Freda expresses the difference between the two organisations in a letter to

Percy Brown in Palestine at a time when there was discussion at 3 Gordon Square about how close to the FWRS the FAU should be.

> I'm all for maintaining cordial relations with F.W.R.S, but I think we might as well recognise the fact that in the main the Unit is suited to emergency work and the F.W.R.S. to long-term, and plan things accordingly. It seems to me that if anything does crop up F.W.R.S. will want to dash in just because it's something overseas, but they are so frightened to death to contaminate themselves by touching a bit of khaki and want, so to speak, all jam and no bread. I'm not so much speaking of individual members as Friends' House. Many individual members are quite prepared to wear B.R.C.S. uniform and work with us, but they've got a pretty good proportion of what I, perhaps somewhat intolerantly, call cranks, who think that because the F.A.U. wears uniform and cooperates with Govt. and military authorities, we're the devil's own offspring.

Although Unit members wore uniform when necessary, the informality of the F.A.U. was refreshing for members who had already proved that they were unafraid to be different. Even during wartime, men on official business rarely left the office bare-headed and there are amusing descriptions of 'the Unit hat' held at Gordon Square: formal meetings for the use of. The hat was called The Conqueror and "rendered ... notable service to the Unit in Whitehall and Princes Gate".[68]

When working with the British Red Cross at home or abroad, Unit members wore the British Red Cross khaki uniform with F.A.U. embroidered in black below an embroidered red cross. Based in Cairo, Freda was attached to the Middle East Forces and affiliated to the International Red Cross whose uniform she wore.

Freda was lucky to work for interesting "cheeses": at Rowntree's, she began work in Arnold Rowntree's office; at Gordon Square, intrepid accountant Ronald Joynes was her boss. Now in Cairo she worked for the archeologist John Rose.

Figure 36 I have Freda's British Red Cross F.A.U. epaulette here, in front of me, on my desk

It was generally accepted that work overseas might not be terribly safe and getting there was even more dangerous but, as Freda explained to her parents, in a letter written on 12th February 1944, she was determined to do it. Her parents, specifically her mother, were angry their daughter was leaving England.

> Ronald is coming up to see us off. Angela & Susie will I think be in the same convoy, but not in the same boat as Margaret Briggs, Rita & I and the 3 men.
> …
> I do hope that as time goes by you will not feel so upset about the step I am taking; I do realize how upsetting & worrying it is for you, and I am very sorry to cause you such distress, but I am sure that you will come to see that I have made a wise move, and everything will turn out right in the end.

A popular F.A.U. motto was GADA, go anywhere, do anything. One week-end Freda was fire-watching in the East End – "I was glad to be able to shelter in the little pill-box when the shrapnel started to fall. Two or three fires were started in the surrounding Bethnal Green district – big blazes two of them, but the other seemed to be soon put out" – and the next week-end she was crossing the Bay of Biscay on the way to Africa and braving U-boats. There is no doubt that this was an adventure and she knew how lucky she was to be able to take part. It was now a year since she had met Jack at a dance in York.

Landing at Port Said, she went immediately to her job in the local office in Cairo. In Bab-el-Louk, the Cairo office, she was a short-hand typist, as she had been in London. Later she helped to run Naples HQ and then helped to set up Rome HQ, from where she ordered and dispatched equipment. She also accompanied Unit officers on their tours of inspection, during which her main occupation was to transcribe and dispatch their reports. Freda relished her job and enjoyed addressing letters to the great and the good in her secretarial job in Gordon Square, and later in Cairo and Italy. Her work was demonstrably not as unimportant and uninteresting as she suggested to the interviewer from the Imperial War Museum; her role was pivotal, for without funding, with no equipment or transport, the F.A.U. welfare and surgical teams could not function.

The Friends Ambulance Unit raised funds effectively because of frequent reports dispatched from Gordon Square. After reading reports many American Friends provided the Unit with funds and hardware, such as ambulances, and the Foreign Office was persuaded to contribute £50,000 towards the British Fund for Relief of Distress in China. The *Report on Relief Work in Ipriros (West Greece) March – July, 1945*, found among Freda's papers, is a good example. Forty pages long, it contains details of food costs and names village officials, and even lists the number of horses, donkeys and mules in the village. Chapters include Welfare, Recrimination and Corruption. The local knowledge and evidently disinterested concern for a community are persuasive.

While waiting in Cairo for the green light to go into Greece or Italy, Freda enjoyed an active social life and told me about Shepheards and other famous Cairo watering holes, though she was not allowed into Shepheards often.[69] She enjoyed picnics, parties and excursions to the Nile, the pyramids and souks. Molly Izzard's biography of Freya Stark describes Cairo when Freda was there as a round of "glittering social occasions where enormous quantities of Mediterranean food, supplied by French and Italian and Greek grocers, were devoured in settings of gilded Levantine splendor" (Stark, p. 165).

It was now just over a year since Freda had agreed to marry Jack. All the time, wherever she was, she continued to write to colleagues. She preserved carbon copies of most of her letters but not one which, she tells Stephen Peet, she wrote to Sylvia, Jack's little sister, for her 6th birthday on April 21st. She wrote a number of letters to Stephen, who had been in the Cairo office for some time but was captured on Cos and was now in Germany, a POW in Stalag XVIIA.[70] On 15th May, 1944 she describes her life in Cairo. Stephen had sent her a letter from Cairo a couple of years before, with some sand in the envelope but she cannot return the favour.

Her most memorable experience was when she accompanied her boss on a tour of the Syrian medical stations, most of which were part of the Anglo-French Hadfield Spears Mobile Hospital teams.

Syria and Lebanon were French protectorates, as Palestine and Egypt were British. This is how Ralph Davis describes the F.A.U. Hadfield Spears men who were the first Englishmen in Paris at its liberation in 1944.[71] It provides a flavour of the camaraderie Freda was to find working in Syria. The Unit followed the Free French to North Africa and England and then to France, when they were invited, to De Gaule's annoyance, to join the Paris victory parade:

> Of course you will never understand the story that I am going to tell if you think the "Spears" was just another hospital.
> It was an Anglo-French mobile hospital and it had nurses and Quakers ("my girls and boys"). But it was more than that; it was a club, membership of which carried virtual exemption from military formalities; it was a hotel for visiting generals and an FAU hostel; it was the only remaining French source of English cigarettes, gin and whisky, and the sort of place where you really did find a bull walking into the pharmacy the day before it was slaughtered in the laundry. It was an *institution unique* and the First Free French Division treasured it as its mascot. They were delighted to see our trucks chugging up hills or breaking down with *éclat*, an explosion and a cloud of smoke issuing from the exhaust. So they said of course we must be in their *défilé* in Paris, all of us. (FAU Chronicle 74)

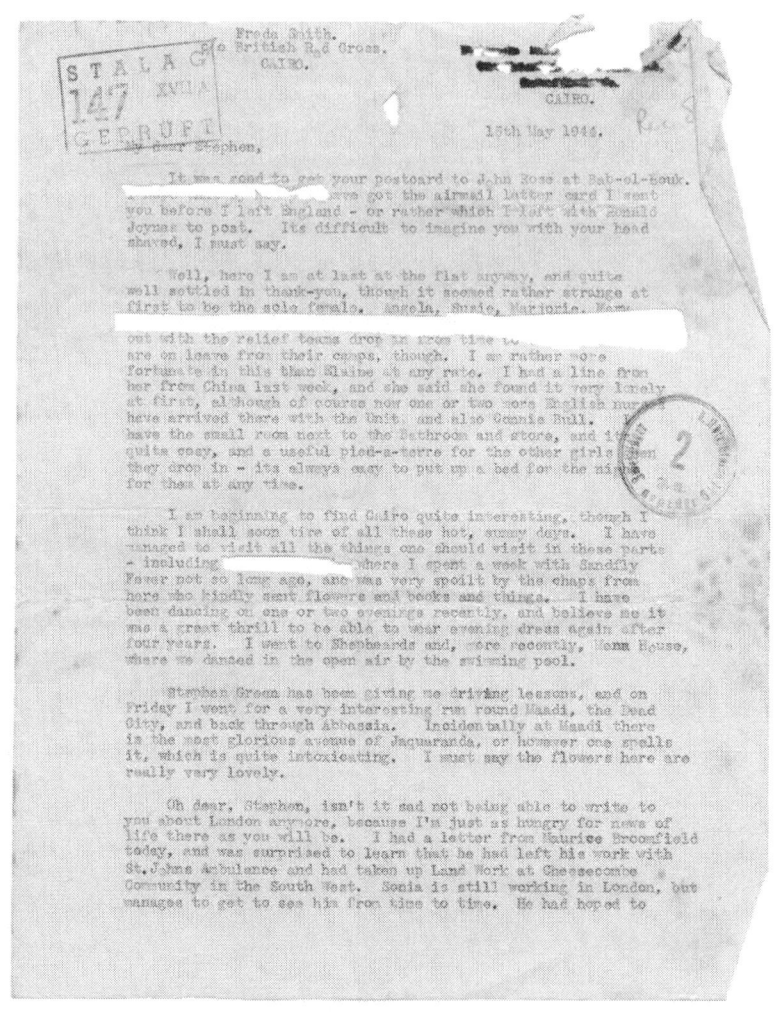

Figure 37 Freda to Stephen Peet, POW in Germany

The F.A.U. Syria tour of inspection began at 7 a.m. on 30th May, 1944, Freda records in her Public Service note book.[72] Agricultural scenery along the Nile, long since lost under urban sprawl reminds her of a Wordsworth poem about London.

> After a somewhat noisy start (Jack Frazer and other members of the HQ Section having tied sundry

> tin cans to the back of the Staff Car, which we discovered as we moved off along Sharia-el-Kassied and hastily removed before a quickly gathering crowd of amused Egyptians), we left Cairo.
>
> The workers were already in the fields as we slipped out of our Cairene Cocoon and emerged onto the open road and countryside. On either side of the road was the green patchwork of Nile cultivation – greens and yellow, with here and there a clump of tall palms silhouetted against the blue sky, and the squat mud-roofed houses of the villages "all bright and glittering in the smokeless air".[73] The road is the one to Port Said, along which I came when I first arrived in Egypt. It runs for a long way parallel with the Sweet Water Canal – an unfortunate name for a canal teeming with Bilherzie, and source of many of the country's diseases.

The team of four in two vehicles drove north from Cairo, to cross the Canal at Ismailia.

> At Ismailia, some 90 miles from Cairo, and a residential town built up largely round the officials of the Canal Company, we stopped for 15 mts. at the Y.M.C.A. where we had an ice, and then, having presented our Movement Orders and papers to the Military Police at their check post, and assured them that my typewriter case did in fact contain a typewriter, we left Egypt and the last bit of greenery for some 200 miles, and crossed the canal by ferry to begin the long 170 mile journey across the Sinai Desert.

Roald Dahl crossed the Nile by car three years before Freda, which he describes in *Going Solo*.

> It was simply a wooden float that was pulled from one bank to the other by wires, and I drove the car onto it and was taken to the Sinai bank. But before I was allowed to start the long and lonely journey across the Sinai Desert, I had to show the officials that I had with me five gallons of

spare petrol and a five-gallon can of drinking water.
(Dahl, p. 187)

The small convoy drove through Sinai towards Gaza along a narrow road through almost empty desert and "later, towards Palestine, a few camels grazing if that's what they do". The journey took only a few hours.

> By 3.0 p.m. we were feeling pretty hungry, and not sorry to arrive at the NAAFI at Aslug – aptly called The Travellers Rest, where we had a meal of Steak and Kidney Pudding and green peas, and then set off on our last lap to Nuseirat, near Gaza, leaving the desert behind us, through BirSheba and Gaza, and eventually to the Refugee Camp.

Nuseirat camp of 9,000 was mainly for Dodecanese Greek islanders. Nuseirat is still a refugee camp, but when the British left, it became a camp for displaced Palestinians, and it is now part of the besieged Gaza strip. Marjorie, who was at the De Grey Rooms when Jack glanced up the staircase and saw Freda for the first time, was now working on the isolation ward in the hospital along with Mary Shaw, who had helped run the Sugar Loaf in Wapping. After tea "Marjorie and I went for a stroll along the beach which, like the sea, was bathed in brilliant moonlight."

The camp was just recovering from a measles epidemic and Freda comments that the shortage of nurses was "rather neatly solved by the mothers of the children, who spend the whole day at their bedsides." This system was unheard of in England at the time, when parents were banned from hospitals except during short visiting hours, and it was not adopted by British hospitals for many years. Colleagues on the China convoy would have seen hospitals in Free China run with this holistic approach to medicine, and may have encouraged parental involvement in the care of sick children to F.A.U. colleagues elsewhere.[74]

Major problems in refugee camps were boredom and poverty, and so the F.A.U. made sure transferable skills were taught to the refugees, to occupy time profitably until repatriation and in some cases to provide an income in the camp and on returning home.

From the hospital we walked across to the Workshops, where Norman Kay and Hubert Busby have a group of men making things for the camp out of what small salvage they can get – knitting needles of straightened out bed springs, bin lids beaten out of salvaged corrugated iron. From Workshops we looked in at the Information Centre, and the Shoe-making Centre, the Welfare Centre, etc.

Freda and Mary Shaw bathed in the Mediterranean before tea and then the group from Cairo drove to Jerusalem for supper. She wrote Bill Spray that "Jerusalem by night has a neat continental flavour, and by day it is really rather wonderful." It was strange to be in a city with no black-out. "I derived great pleasure from being able to drink a glass of hot milk – a liquid I had not tasted since leaving England". They lodge opposite the King David Hotel in what is now West Jerusalem. Her diary records sightseeing on June 1st.

An energetic day. We went to the top of the high tower at the Y.M.C.A. and looked out across the city and to the Dead Sea beyond, and then made our way down to the old city - a delightful maze of narrow cobbled streets and white walls and buildings. We visited the Church of the Holy Sepulchre which, originally a Crusader church, is now an unholy conglomeration of Catholic, Greek Orthodox, Coptic, Russian and Byzantine "art" and Edwardian decoration at its worst. The guide duly recited for our highly skeptical ears all the various events which are conveniently supposed to have happened on the ground over which the church was built. We then made our way to the Church of St. Anne, a rather delightful Crusader church and the pool of Bethesda and back along the Via Dolorosa to the Wailing Wall and into the new city for lunch. … John Rose and I took a bus up to the Mount of Olives, where we climbed the tower of the Church in the Russian Convent and surveyed Jerusalem and, turning, the Dead Sea and mountains of the Transjordan beyond.

Cecil Beaton describes the same scene in *Near East*.

> The view from the tower of the Russian Church is like a model in relief of a pastoral country. Below us they are threshing corn ; in the far distance are the old city walls. There is the Dome of the Rock – there the Church of the Holy Sepulchre ; those are the ruins of the 1927 earthquake. Perched high among the cypress trees in the Garden of Gethsemene, the air scented with wild thyme and roses, the nuns hurry on their chores, hiding their heads from the view of the soldiers from Norfolk and Cheshire and from the airmen rather self-consciously sight-seeing. (Beaton, p. 110-1)

Cecil Beaton's interest in history, his description of the WW2 Desert Campaign and the vivid account of his visit to the Arab legion, which was previously lead by T.E. Lawrence and now led by Philip Brocklehurst, an Arctic explorer who, like Jack's C.O., had travelled with Shackleton, along with descriptions of Cairo and Tobruk and of the "extraordinarily fragrant" hills behind Beirut, all made Freda value his book. It is a remarkable memoir, with striking photographs but marred by a certain lack of humanity and by racism common at the time, such as: "After the gloomy ugliness of modern Cairenes, the Irani people, of Aryan stock, ... are a delight to the eye" (Beaton, p. 98).[75] Freda's descriptions, written in the field as were Cecil Beaton's, show none of his impatience, though written in the same summer heat which Beaton calls "frightful", "calamitous", "phenomenal – a sort of plague of heat" (Beaton, p. 92-3). It was only when I read *Near East* that I realised how fresh and humane Freda's reports must have sounded at the time.

Freda persuaded me to keep a diary of my trip to Palestine in 2004 and I wrote about the owner of a shoe shop on Sultan Suleiman road near the Damascus Gate, who talked about 1943.

> The shop owner begins to talk to as soon as he finds out we are British. He is 68 years old and has lived in Jerusalem all his life. He remembers being shot at by Israelis while on his way to school from when he was 7, in 1943, in what is now West Jerusalem. He blames the British for the present situation.

In 2004 the view from the highest point of the Old City is different from the view Freda saw in one big respect:

There's not much of the Crusaders left in the Citadel but it is still a spectacular castle. We can see a large empty area that looks like a rubbish dump but it is called the pool of Hezechaiah / Birket hammam el Batraq and must have been one of the cisterns fed by Solomon's Pools. How marvellous it must have been when full of water and reflecting the bright blue sky, with birds swooping down to drink.

At the foot of the castle we can see Police stables, possibly where stables have always been. We see the whole of Jerusalem from the battlements: the windmill, the King David Hotel, French Hill, Mount of Olives and, Oh no, the Wall at Abu Dis. Walls are all around, but most especially the Wall at Abu Dis to the right of the Mount of Olives, curling round the hill top like a venomous snake.

That night in 1943 the F.A.U. travellers set off for Beirut and stayed on the way at the Quaker Boys' School in Ramallah. I also sat there, in the same peaceful rose garden which Freda had described sixty years before; the heat was intense and the earth hard and red. Their route took Freda's group past the Sea of Galilee and up to the "Check Post" at Rosh Pinar. The Unit jeep broke down only once during the journey but imagine it: bouncing all over the road, zig-zagging to avoid potholes and skidding to a halt for stray goats and then bumping over stones and round boulders as they roared up inclines and, to save fuel, freewheeled down the other side, the occupants thrown from one side to the other and holding on for dear life.

> By a neat piece of timing we arrived in Beirut,
> after dropping 5,000 ft. by way of the winding road
> over the Lebanon, just in time to catch the sight of the
> sun going down, red and fiery, behind the sea.

It was under the influence of John Rose, leader of the expedition, that Freda began her love affair with medieval castles. From this point on, Freda's Syrian letters and diary are littered with descriptions of ancient monuments and ruins. She and I shared this interest in Crusader castles with romantic names: Krak des Chevaliers, Kerak, Acre, Tripoli. On the way to Lattakia on the Syrian coast, their base to visit the hospitals in northern Syria, they stopped at the castle at Jbail, ancient Byblos.

> We stopped for a while there and ran the car down through the narrow streets of the old town to the ruins of a Crusader Castle which stands on the cliff edge commanding the sea. We attempted to climb to the top of the keep – all that really remains standing of the castle, but found our way up the stone stairs blocked with sheep so we retired defeated!

It is a surprise to see the Norman church in Tartouss sail like a ship among low flat-roofed houses, and Freda is sad that they do not have time to visit the castle of Marquab.

> A few miles before Tartouss an island rises out of the sea – the Island of Ruad. This is a great ship-building centre, and it is here nearly all the white-sailed caiques are made which sail up and down the coast. I should love to visit this island some day – I am told it is just crowded with houses, and there are so many of them jumbled along the narrow streets that nothing is grown anywhere on the island at all, and all supplies have to come from the mainland, from Tartouss.

It's Tuesday 6th June in Lattakia. The Second Front in Europe has opened and Freda, overcome by memories of Jack for the first time in many weeks, cannot stay to join in the excitement.

> To be told of this historic and momentous occasion, for which the world had been waiting, in the cool, white-walled, red-tiled parlour of an American Missionary in a small Syrian sea town, was the last place I ever thought to hear the news.
> For the nine-o'clock news we went to the house of some Arab friends across the street, they having the all-important radio, and there, the coffee having been handed round and our cups returned, we listened to the announcer's clear voice giving the news. ......of the 11,000 planes backing the operations, of the 4,000 vessels. A grim and busy time.

> I had always thought that I would feel very far away from it all when it did begin, but somehow I felt strangely involved in it, together with Betty & Jack & Norman & Wally & George & Derrick & Peter, as though we were all alive and being part of the whole universe.
> After the news we drank some delicious coffee then I made my excuses and returned to bed early, to spend my first night under a mosquito net.

In a television interview, Freydis Sharland, who flew fighter aircraft from factory to RAF station, spoke of celebrations which she too felt unable to share. While Freda recorded in her memoir in 1996 that she left the Invasion Day [D Day] party in Syria to be alone, Freydis shook her head in 2009 as she remembered her melancholy on VE Day:[76] "I felt then terribly sad, with everybody dancing and jumping about I suddenly realized all the people we'd lost and that wouldn't be celebrating this. I just felt terribly sad."

The next day the small group travelled with the Clinic inland to the Turkoman village Seraya. The ambulance stopped at a village on the way. The village was " a cluster of miserable houses by the road".

> The ambulance was standing under a few trees outside the small and rather naked-looking mosque. Against its walls sat the village worthies, young and old, while around the back of the ambulance gathered a crowd of patients, men, women, mothers and children, clutching in their hands bottles and tins of all shapes and sizes in which their medicines and ointments could be put. The women wear trousers almost to the ankles, and a full-skirted dress almost as long, with kerchiefs over their heads, all originally gaily coloured but now somewhat faded and shabby. We were given chairs under the tree and coffee brought to us, while the doctor chaffs and teases his patients in a very jolly manner.
> Within the mosque waited the more well-to-do village maidens – Moslems, who waited for the doctor to attend to them after he had dealt with the other villagers. As a girl I was allowed to go in with him when he went to see them. The girls, seen without

> their veils, were very attractive; two of them were really lovely. One, a shy raven-haired black-eyed girl of 12, with a modern orange velvet dress which glowed brightly against her olive skin made a very colourful picture against the bright walls of the mosque. Munira, aged 16, was an exceedingly merry and lovely creature, who I thought must find very trying the lack of freedom which is her lot. She was dressed in a neat mauve dress, and puce jacket, and wore her veil with quite an 'air'. I was sorry not to be able to speak with them, but we all smiled at one another from time to time in friendly fashion.

Freda also met a three-year old child suffering from kala-azar, whose father brought her to the clinic from another village three miles away. Like bilherzie, kala azar attacks the body's organs and often leads to death if not treated early. Unlike malaria, both are water-borne diseases, caught from either snails or worms. None of the three diseases have yet been eradicated.

> The doctor brought across to us a little girl of about 3 yrs. She seemed quite bloodless, her eyes, nails and skin showed no traces of any blood. Her face was swollen and yellow with the 'earthy' look typical of the disease.
> The child cannot be helped as her father will not take her to the hospital in Lattakia because it has a bad reputation, and the villagers do not trust it, so the last we saw of the child was as her father untethered the donkey, which he had left in a field across the road, and seating the little girl on it with great tenderness, he led the animal and its burden up the ravine and away to their village.

One day should have been spent helping at a clinic a few miles inland from Lattakia, but Freda writes in her diary that car trouble prevented them being any help at all.

> I have written Wednesday's report as I am sitting by the roadside in yet more lovely country, this time rather resembling Wales, the car having broken down

> again on the hill. This has no connection whatsoever with the fact that I have been driving it for the last 20 miles but a return of our old trouble with the petrol pipe. The blockage was removed but the car still won't start.
>
> Now we are joined by one or two curious villagers and an anxious-to-help member of the Transjordan Frontier Force, who seems to have done the trick. We eventually got away to meet the Clinic, which was being held by the roadside a few kilos further up.
>
> By the time we arrived the pressure was slackening and I talked as best I could with some young boys who sat by a stream looking after sheep and goats which were gathered in the shade. The boys wear very neatly crocheted caps, and some wear woollen ones of a Fair-Isle type of design.

In Lattakia and over supper with friends they suddenly hear gunfire and an air raid siren. People scatter to their respective homes and Freda notes a certain nostalgia at "the old familiar wail of the siren". It was only "a practice gunfire". A couple of days later, Freda visits two Moslem girls, the Haroun sisters, who want to practice their English.

> We drank once again a cup of sticky delicious Turkish coffee, and they were very amused when I said 'Daimen-in-shallah' as I returned my cup to the tray. I thoroughly enjoyed my visit there – the girls were very pleasant and attractive.
>
> They told me that when English soldiers pass by they (the girls) listen at the lattice to hear the soldiers speaking, but find their English difficult to understand!
>
> At the moment they are just sitting around awaiting marriage – the world must seem a weird place from behind a black veil.

When Freda left Lattakia the girls gave her "four delightful hand-made lace mats", which I found after Freda's death, carefully preserved in tissue paper. One now hangs by my bedroom mirror.

The Unit returned to Beirut, and Freda found letters from home, Ronald, Grace, Maxie's mother and Mary Curtis. As women were not allowed to go with the men to Aleppo, she explored Beirut on her own.

> I spent the Tuesday wandering around Beirut,
> into the Suqs, looking at the shops, where everything
> was far too expensive, and then strolled along the
> corniche below the University.

The group travelled from Beirut to Damascus, where Freda was taken to a Deanna Durbin film by the daughters of her Syrian hostess, "Damascus was the last place I expected to see Deanna, I must say!". After seeing the great mosque in Damascus, they visited Sednaya clinic.

Figure 38 Hadfield Spears / FAU mobile clinic in Maloula, near Sednaya

> Sednaya is a most attractive village, pushed right
> back against the rocky cliffs. Towering over the
> village and commanding a superb view of the valley
> at its feet, is the Convent of Sednaya, where I was to
> sleep during my stay there.

> The walls of the clinic are lined with British propaganda posters, which are found everywhere in Syria: Britain at War, Nursery Schools, Evening Schools, with the appropriate captions and information underneath in Arabic.

The clinic at Sednaya was run by a Syrian doctor and Marie, a nurse, with the help of an F.A.U. member. Here Freda "tried to watch an operation but felt sick & had to come out." She and Marie corresponded for some years. From Sednaya, they visit the clinic in Chtaura. Freda is not allowed to camp down with the men and has to stay at Massabky's Hotel. Burnell, one of the Unit has created "a swamp drainage scheme" near the village to try to eradicate mosquitoes. In the hills, at Maloula, they "walked up a track through a narrow, rocky gorge, to visit the Monastery perched high above the village", but the "most memorable" event for her is hearing Aramaic spoken.

After a month on the road, they returned to Cairo. Throughout the tour, Freda typed reports which were sent to Bab-el-Louk and from there to Gordon Square by airgraph to the secretary of the Middle East section. Though she had told Jack she was not the type to be homesick, she wrote home to one of her London colleagues at the end of June, to say she missed Wapping and Whitechapel.

> Have you been to the Prospect again? I can just picture it on a calm June evening, and the steady chug of a boat going up the Thames, and the swish of the water on the gravel below the balcony.
> Life in Cairo flows along very quietly. Sometimes on Sundays we go out to the Gezira Club for a swim and tea there – all very English and at 2/- entrance fee, rather expensive.
> One of the nicest features of life here is the open air cinema, and a ride back in a garry, which is really delightful.
> We find things much easier in uniform of course, which is I suppose, immoral. Some things we draw the line at e.g. services clubs like the one which has just been opened for the ATS, or getting tickets for Irving Berlin's "This is the army". However, Goppi's

ices and cakes are the same price for civilians and the armed forces so we have no qualms there! [77]

A letter from the Red Cross now arrived for Freda. An official German report has identified Derrick's grave. Jack's has still not been found.

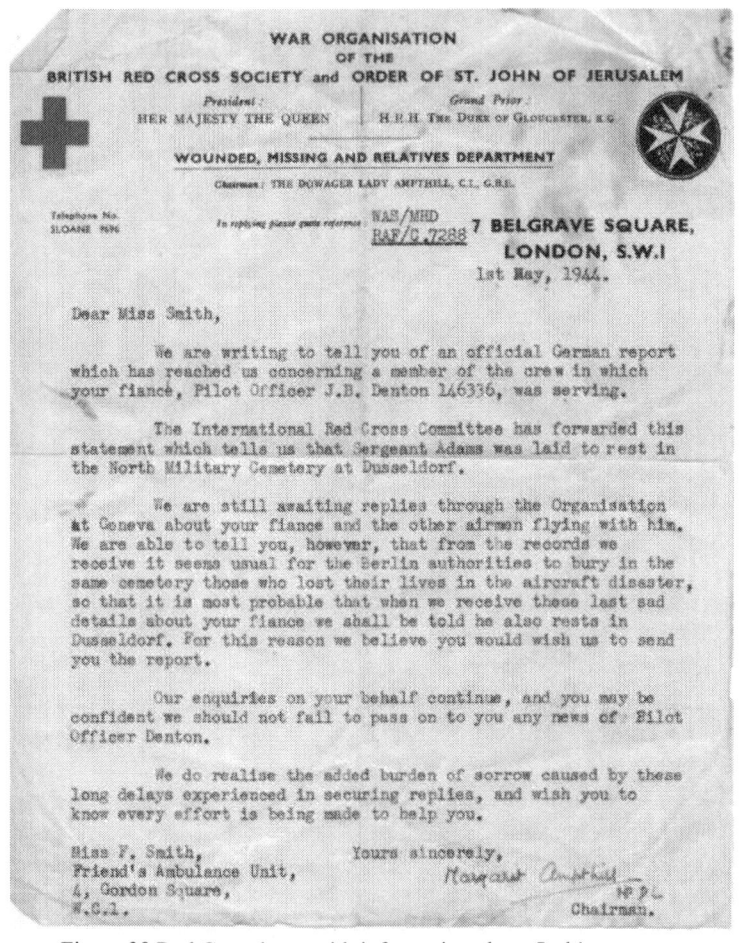

Figure 39 Red Cross letter with information about Jack's grave

Extensive negotiations with established relief agencies which were recognized by the military, as the F.A.U. was not, determined that it was safe enough for F.A.U. relief workers to set up offices in the newly liberated territories. Freda was offered Greece or Italy and chose to be sent to Italy. It was now safe to fly and the journey from

Cairo to Naples was via Tripoli, to an old German landing ground known as Marble Arch. The flight took her out over the sea from Egypt to Libya, a route described by the poet Keith Douglas: "over the minute wrinkles of the Mediterranean Sea, the deep blue gave way, not to brown or yellow desert country, but to an almost European pattern of towns and cultivation" (Douglas, p. 155-6). This was her first flight: "in a Dakota (bucket seats) via Marble Arch (Tripoli) and Malta and I was horribly sick over Italy." She does not record whether the experience of flying moved more than her stomach but one of the first things she did in Italy was go dancing in Naples with the Dakota pilot and this was the first time she heard the song about Lili Marlene.

Freda's impression of the city is more than confirmed in another book she kept by her always, Norman Lewis' *Naples '44*. Freda has marked this section. The Allied powers continued to advance North through southern Europe and by September 1944.

> People camp out like Bedouins in deserts of brick. There is little food, little water, no salt, no soap. A lot of Neapolitans have lost their possessions, including most of their clothing, in the bombings. (Lewis, p. 46)

In Naples for a month, Freda helped run the office, wrote reports and visited refugee camps. She wrote to her parents:

> I saw a ragged, barefooted little boy going along the street yesterday, with legs like sticks. The Black Market here is a huge organization – petrol, all sorts of things, and Olive Oil here is a fantastic price, though I can't quite yet understand why, in a country where there is so much of it.
> It is astonishing to witness the struggles of this city so shattered, so starved, so deprived of all those things that justify a city's existence, to adapt itself to collapse into conditions which most resemble the Dark Ages.

Once Rome fell and the Unit had found quarters there, Freda travelled up to organise HQ and was in Rome for V.E. Day. The Army requisitioned an apartment in 13 via Pietro Borsieri for the F.A.U., commandeered from an Italian General, "and his nephew,

Stelvio, visited us for a meal once or twice." The Unit lived and worked there and Freda worked in the kitchens as well as the office. One of her tasks was arranging food for the Unit and its visitors. Her Public Service note book lists menus for April and May 1945. Daily menus are recorded sometimes in Italian and in another hand but mostly by Freda and in English. She also cut out menus from English language newspapers listing "dried egg reconstituted", "household milk" and such like. On 25th March they had Zuppa di pollo for lunch and Carne agradolce con piccolo with Gelato de crema for dinner. The next day they had Lancashire hotpot. 30th May saw them eating Salad with mashed potatoes and Spam for lunch and for supper they had Boiled mutton and fig pie. Hidden in the pages of the note book I found a photograph of York Minster on Easter Sunday, cut out from the Union Jack, an armed forces newspaper.

The battle of Monte Cassino had taken place in March 1944 and in October Freda wrote home about her journey from Naples to Rome and her first impressions of Italy:

> I wish you could see some of the towns and villages we passed through on our way – house after house, street after street, a pile of rubble or just the shells of houses – in some districts not a house but it is damaged in some way. How people are living in them I don't know, and how they will keep warm this winter, I can't think. We've been told that it is worse near Cassino. Here and there is still the odd burnt-out tank or lorry by the roadside. Such is the road to Rome in 1944.
>
> All the people evacuated themselves, of course, when the fighting was on, but are now drifting back to what is left of their homes, and queuing for water at the few available water-points.
>
> All last week I was in the south of Italy. On Monday we set off by car and crossed the mountains down into the plain at Foggia and on to Bari to see one of our sections there. At Maglie we visited the Yugoslav Refugee Hospital. This is housed in the local school and is mainly filled with children with infectious diseases and of course they all have skin diseases through malnutrition. They are mainly from

the poorer peasants of Yugoslavia, and Partisans, and look tough enough – the adults, that is.

We visited another hospital at Poggiardo for the older chronics and the next day the hospital at Leuca, which is right on the tip of the heel of Italy. In peace time this is a small seaside resort for rich Italians, but their houses are now filled with Yugoslav refugees. The hospital is right on the edge of a cliff, overlooking the sea.

The roads in Italy, the main ones, just run in a straight line from one town to another. Our road ran through olive groves and vineyards. The grapes were all being picked and we passed cart after cart with barrels full of grapes. There are no hedges by the roadside, so on our way back we stopped and picked some to eat – the wine grapes are very small and deliciously sweet.

As soon as the road gets to a town or village, it gets into a shocking state – rough and with huge potholes, which are filled with water in wet weather, and bumpy, you have to go very slowly over them. At some towns, the army has installed one-way traffic, so that all south-bound traffic goes one way and northbound traffic the other.

The people are very poor in the south.

The F.A.U. began to do the type of work Freda had always envisioned doing: post-war reconstruction. Freda visited Ruvo section with John Rose and Peter Gibson, her new boss, where they stayed in an old hunting lodge and "it was bitterly cold, with snow on the ground, and in the evenings we all huddled round an enormous stove". The medical centre at Leuca, which she visited in the summer of 1944, was paired with one at Maglie. These two small centres were dealing with measles, otitis media, enteritis, broncho-pneumonia, diphtheria and scarlet fever. They were understaffed so the arrival of seven F.A.U. "made all the difference between the collapse of the work and its continuance" (Davies, p. 374). Undernourishment aged some of the children who, "with the drawn and haggard faces of old people and bodies that looked not more than skin and bone, were textbook cases of child starvation, and they quickly succumbed to epidemics." (Davies, p. 374)

> Practically all the work, whether it meant welfare activities in camps or working out statistics in an office or visiting billeted refugees in the provinces in the south, was concerned with some aspect of the life of the refugee from the time when the war shattered his home and spoiled his crops, through the weary progress from camp to camp, through the period of forced billeting, generally as an unwanted guest in some commune hundreds of miles from home, down to the final stage of returning to a ruined village to be re-established and begin life anew. With each of these stages members of the Unit had something to do. (Davies, p. 376)

Tegla Davies describes the Yugoslav refugee camps in the South with unattributed quotations and descriptions, some of which may be from Freda's reports. In the F.A.U. report dated 2nd June 1945, which Freda typed up, the northern section called Team 2, based at Forli, turned up to find 5000 refugees installed in inadequate lodgings and in a fortnight the team had processed between 12,000 and 20,0000. The Unit helped at Riccione, Palombina and Rimini and wherever they were needed; ministering to the lost and ill and getting them on their route as best they could.

> At the moment, tens of thousands of refugees, ex-internees, ex-prisoners and Todt workers of all nationalities are making their way south, some through official "camp channels", and others under their own arrangements. ... The large numbers of non-Italians, Yugoslavs, Poles, Russians in particular, will be housed temporarily but no long term solution to their plight is yet in sight.[78]

Freda was involved in negotiations to requisition run-down buildings which could be cleaned up and equipped as medical centres by the F.A.U., including a German poison gas factory at Cesano! The centres were then taken over and run by local councils or the UN's nascent refugee relief agency, U.N.R.R.A. The section Freda was attached to distributed clothes to about 30,000 refugees scattered in 400 communes as well as completing a survey of conditions in six provinces (Davies, p. 383). For some time there were pockets of German resistance, but after the war ended the unit's task was mainly repatriating displaced persons who had travelled many miles to escape the fighting. Freda has marked a section in Davies about four U.N.R.R.A. camps in Frosinone, in the devastated area around Cassino and the road to Rome. Frosinone fell to the Canadians on 31st May 1944 and Rome fell on 4th June. The Frosinone camps were run by the Unit for around 5,000 repatriated people who had come home but found no home to return to. It was at around this time, in early June, when the Germans were fighting for Rome, that the Allies bombed Tivoli. The damage Freda saw in Italy was still very fresh.

> Frosinone had been devastated by the heavy fighting around Cassino and on the road to Rome, and was in no state to receive back its homeless people from the communes of the south. But home they came. (Davies, p.385)

After a description of the Sangro Valley villages, which the Germans had systematically mined "so that the valley is dead in every sense of the word", Freda does not mark any more passages in Davies' book and I think this coincides with her return to England:

> My responsibility has been – besides dabbling about with odd things like registration – issuing of blankets, chlorination of water, the important question of rehabilitation. Nearly all these people come from around the provinces of Littoria and Frosinone and they are to be returned commune by commune. This has necessitated dashing about the countryside in a jeep, contacting *sindaci* and Civil Affairs officers, and several approaches to the venerable Jesuit hierarchy in the Vatican, who have a concern for *assistenza*. The Jesuit-Quaker association, under the invigilation of the Major, has succeeded in producing Vatican transport for rehabilitation of refugees. (Davies, p. 378-9)

Freda probably typed up this report, it was the type of report she was making, the type of work she was doing. For instance, I found a letter sent to her in Rome dated August 1945 by Susie Carter in Rhodes, H.Q. of the Middle East Forces in the Dodecanese where the F.A.U. had its base. Susie asks if Freda can rustle up some towels from somewhere. In late October Freda sent a brief description of Rome H.Q. to the Chronicle for the 'Near and Far' section.[79]

Rome Headquarters

Freda Smith writes: Our office is in what was the library, which is furnished in Tudor style. Where we sit in the evenings is decorated in Moorish style, somewhat reminiscent of the Brasserie at Oxford-Street Corner House, and has leopard-skins and spears and things on the walls, and a little chintz settee. There are four bathrooms, but no means of getting hot water. (F.A.U. Chronicle no 65)

In Naples Freda visited the theatre and ballet and she continued with gusto her cultural education in Rome. In both cities she was rather lonely and she made her own amusements from travelling as a tourist to spending a few days in the summer at Rome Y.W.C.A., as a holiday from the Unit H.Q. On 12th October 1944, she saw 'An exhibition of Masterpieces of European Painting' in the Palazzo Venezia (arranged by Region IV Allied Military Government). Usually she was one of a group of people. On V.E. Day she saw Verdi's opera *La Forza del Destino* and her companions signed her programme, mostly illegibly. Tucked into the programme for *La Forza* I found a letter written to her parents. She describes a visit to Hadrian's villa and to Tivoli, where a steep and powerful waterfall provided Rome's electricity. The RAF bombed the Power Plant in June and as it had still not been repaired, the fountains remained dry. A visit to St. Peter's to see the Pope's first Mass after liberation turned out to be rather a scrum. When I read through her letters to her parents describing how much fun she has as a tourist in Italy in an effort to allay her mother's fears, I realised that, however cheerfully her letters began, she always wrote about the sad situations she found. She writes of honeysuckle and about the fate of the Dodecanese Greeks:

A recent report gave harrowing descriptions of caique (boat) loads of starving and some dying refugees putting in at the islands after being at sea for 7 days with no water and little food, and packed like sardines, so that when they got ashore some could only crawl – they were returning from Turkey to their homes on the islands.

While in Rome, all F.A.U. members were given a privileged status by the Rome Area Allied Command:

Figure 40 Freda in Rome

"Freda SMITH BRCS No. 21647, being a British subject specifically assigned to this theatre of operations ... and being a person considered suitable for privilege of the undermentioned facilities normally available to a Commissioned Officer of H.M. Forces ..."

She is allowed to drive in staff cars and enter hotels and restaurants off limits to other ranks. Many Quakers in the F.A.U.

would feel uncomfortable taking such privileges because they only allowed themselves to be officially linked to armies of occupation in order to minister to the needy, but Freda left those qualms behind in London. Ever practical and not one to stand on ceremony except for royalty, she had enjoyed herself when she could. As Bill Spray recalls, she was one of the sybarites.[80]

In later life she turned to the philosophy of Seneca and Marcus Aurelius but young and in wartime, she had fun whenever she could. Freda played hard because her world was spiritually draining. Rome in Spring 1945 is more pleasant than Naples, Freda tells Alan McBain in April. The fountains are turned on again to cool the hot dusty air and water shot into the sky, sparkling. She mentions an opera singer to her friend Alan, called Beniamino Gigli. Raleigh Trevelyan in his book *Rome '44* describes a gala performance of *Un Ballo in Maschera* at the end of May 1944, which Kesselring ordered Rome's senior staff to attend to show the Romans that Germany was not abandoning them. Gigli sang in *La Forza* on V.E. Day and went on singing. He was a collaborator, as Freda suggests, if singing for the German High Command in Rome is collaborating. The taking of Rome cost 82,000 lives and this does not include civilians (Trevelyan, p. 310, p. 320). Freda was there only three months after the Germans left and reprisals for collaboration with one or other side were taken for many months longer. She mentions women having their hair shorn for being with Allied soldiers. Trevelyan records the brutal killing, the lynching in the Tiber, of the Italian governor of one of Rome's prisons, who the crowd wrongly believed had collaborated with the nazifascisti. "His body, followed by at least ten thousand people, was hauled by the legs to Regina Coeli [the prison] and hung by the head from the bars of a window" (Trevelyan, p. 323). This took place in September 1944. Freda had every reason to be on her guard.

> It is glorious weather here. We have a balcony at the back of the flat where I take out my typing most days. In the afternoon I went for a long walk towards the Vatican and then into the town and round by the Forum, all strangely deserted, most of Rome's 1945 citizens having gone to St. Peter's, it being Passion Sunday, to hear the Pope speak. I passed long processions, mainly of women and children, from

every church in Rome, making their way to the Vatican, some of them must have walked miles.

Rome is a tiring place to walk in, and after my long stroll in the warm sun I just about staggered into the Y.W.C.A. for tea. Rome YW.C.A. is rather a pet place of mine – I seem to have passed through its portals on so many occasions, taking people there to tea or for a meal or letting them take me there – chaps in the Unit on leave, friends meeting me to go elsewhere. I met there a very nice Capt. in the King's Own down from the line, who was on leave recently and who needed a partner for a dance that night. What a collection of memories it holds for me – grave and gay, funny ha-ha and funny peculiar! It was a large hotel before the war. All the big hotels here are Officers' Messes of some sort, British or American, with the Americans usually in the best ones – no malice about that, just fact.

About 10 of us went to the Opera on Tuesday to hear Beniamio Giglio in *Tosca*. He is appearing in public again after lots of controversy as to whether or not he collaborated with the Germans or sang for them and whether he should be allowed to sing in public. You have no idea of the hysteria which threatens Europe on this point of collaborating, war criminals, etc. It's all rather terrifying. Italian youths of late have got into a habit of lopping off the hair of Italian girls seen out with Allied soldiers – it's making me wary of going out with the Unit or forces in civvies.

Sundry Unit people are attached to Displaced Persons camps in a Welfare Officer capacity but I'm afraid UNRRA is proving a big disappointment to everyone, in its slowness off the mark and general top-heaviness as regards administration. The big hold-up as regards relief work is the fact that the Germans obstinately refuse to vacate Bologna and the Po valley, and this half of Italy seems to be full of Allied personnel waiting to go to their appointed jobs. I don't suppose the line will move before the end of the war now, and beyond patrols and things reported in the papers each day, nothing much happens. My

Y.W.C.A. Army Captain friend is in the infantry up north.

Two years after Jack's death Freda came to the conclusion that going overseas was cowardice on her part and that the brave ones are people who stay at home in hum-drum lives and make the best of a bad job. "It's just two years this month" she writes to Percy Brown, "since I got engaged, and it seems a long, long time ago in many ways, though very clear."

> I had not known Jack long, I knew him for three months in all but I do certainly feel very much the richer for the experience. Jack was a very ordinary person by Unit standards, with no money and little post-war prospects, but he wasn't afraid of life and living – so many Unit members seem to be? Maybe I'm wrong.
> Jack's young sister has a birthday this month and I want to send her something – she will be seven! It's funny to think of my meeting her two years ago when she was only five. She must have grown a lot by now.
> It was my birthday two weeks ago and Mother sent me a huge birthday cake, complete with white and pink and almond icing, which travelled very well and arrived safe and sound. It was very kind of her to go to so much trouble and I feel guilty, when I think of all the worry I've caused her.
> I was just writing to Ronald Joynes, that it's just about two years since he gave me the day off because Jack was in town, and if he had not given me the day off, I probably wouldn't have got engaged, and if I'd not got engaged I probably wouldn't have landed up in Cairo by sea, or Naples by air, and thus on to Rome by road!

On 5th September, 1945, after a year in Italy, my aunt came back to England. She flew back in a Dakota but I have not found a description of her flight or whether she flew over the Alps. She became Warden at Gordon Square until January 1946 and then helped to wind-up the Unit, which had officially ended in June 1946, until January 1947. I leave her then, living in Baker Street, looking for a job back up North, still young, still melancholy from time to time but with a 'good war' behind her and a satisfying future ahead. She never lost her brilliant smile. As for me, her biographer, I leave subdued but wiser for having told this story of love and courage in the Second World War.

🕊✈   🕊✈   🕊✈

Well, I would like to be able to end Freda's story this way. Whichever way it ends, it is a story which tells of the bravery of women in war. The men are brave, or not, but for the most part they take an active part in world events but it is the bravery of the women which strikes me as I read through Freda's letters. Freda herself says that without the women at home keeping the home fires burning, literally, the men would not be able to do the work they do: the lovers and mothers and sisters of all those lost boys, women who did not allow their grief to overwhelm them, and the erks, typists and nurses waiting by silent runways and busy in refugee camps or in the front line.

Why is Freda not acknowledged in Lyn Smith's book on the F.A.U.? I know that some of the information in the book came from her, or was at least confirmed by her. I know that because I have listened to the tapes of her interview.[81] Why did she ask not to be quoted? The best years of her life were her war years but maybe she felt she had not given enough back to the Unit which had given her so much. Her letters express guilt that she let down Ronald when he really needed her, when he was embarking on an accountancy course and was overworked but she wanted to be sent overseas. She let down Rome H.Q. when she asked to come home early and they had nobody to take over her secretarial tasks. Am I harsh to think she had every reason to feel at fault? Cecil Beaton recalls conversations with soldiers in the Near East:

> Whenever I was asked when I would be going back home and I replied, "Soon perhaps", the eyes that had regarded me in a friendly way suddenly looked at me with loathing. The men are resigned to remain out here in one solid block; but to see a man who is going back to England is as disquietening as if they were to see someone from another world. (Beaton, p. 122)

All Unit members requesting to go overseas were asked to sign an agreement. Tegla Davies, as Chair of the Executive Committee, wrote to Freda on 24th November 1943 asking her to agree to certain "terms of service".

> You are asked to serve with the Unit overseas until you are free under the National Service Acts to return to other work, or for three years, which ever is the shorter period.

Freda had been overseas for 1 year and 7 months when she asked to be repatriated so she had not completed her agreed tour of duty. Tegla's letter continues.

> In sending members overseas, the Unit takes upon itself considerable responsibility in applying for Exit Permits for them. There has recently been some trouble over members of the Unit resigning overseas to undertake other work, and we ask you to give an undertaking that you will not do this, since in war time you could not leave this country at all except under the Unit's auspices, and it is unfair to accept that privilege, and then let the Unit down.

However, though she asked to be posted home, she did not ask to be relieved of duty to the Unit and once back in London she worked hard for the F.A.U. until it disbanded.

Freda's letter to Lyn Smith, where she dismisses the importance of her own work, cold give a clue to why she felt she had let down Rome H.Q and rereading it, I noticed a comment about her being engaged briefly while in Rome, which, she writes, was a mistake. I must have ignored this while writing the book because I was writing about a world-without-end love affair, but now it bothered me: it would be dishonest to ignore Freda's second engagement.

Phillip Gleave, the man she was engaged to, was a Captain in the 10th Indian Division (Tanks), Freda noted on the fly leaf of Cecil Beaton's *Near East*. He had fought in the desert war and was in Rome at the same time as Freda. He was waiting to be posted North and was staying at the YMCA when he asked her to dance. Tourist guides to Florence and Venice which I found among Freda's letters now made sense: she must have visited him there. The 'Congratulations' section in *Chronicle* no. 74 announces:

Freda Smith and Lt. Philip Gleave, on their engagement

Freda was given permission to leave Rome by the Unit Executive Committee because her fiancé was returning to England – not a valid reason by her own standards, hence her guilt.

Brenda Bailey, who Freda first met before she was posted to Cairo, remembered that her husband Sydney mentioned Freda in his letters and she allowed me to read Sydney's letters, written in 1944-5. She told me that "Freda was always secretary to the top person, whoever that was." Freda and Sydney Bailey worked closely together in Gordon Square and he rather took her under his wing.

Sydney's letters to Brenda, which are the only surviving record of Freda's life in the F.A.U. post-war, were written when he was running the Unit in London and Brenda was a very young relief worker in, coincidentally, Dortmund. Brenda's main task there was the de-Nazification of the Red Cross which was run, at that time, by upper-class ladies of position in society; maybe the very Deutsches Rotes Kreuz contacts who had informed the International Red Cross when Jack's aircraft went down. She was also tasked with setting up playgroups and finding occupations for mothers in the extensive camps around the city. When there was nowhere to house people, they were put in one of the enormous air raid bunkers. As we chatted about Dortmund, Brenda mentioned a complete Polish village, nearby, which had been removed from Poland and recreated in the Ruhr in order to train horses for German officers.

The F.A.U. sent many volunteers to the Ruhr:

Teams of 11 or 12 each are stationed at Essen, Duisburg, Dortmund, Gelsenkirchen, Bochum and Oberhausen in the Ruhr, and in Aachen, Hannover and Berlin. (F.A.U. Chronicle 80)[82]

The first time Freda is mentioned in the letters is on 17th November 1945 when Sydney describes the new warden, i.e. Freda. She is "a nice unaffected girl and adds a very pleasant air of sweetness to the place". They go out for coffee or cider occasionally. She even manages to give Sydney an egg and bacon for lunch one day. It sounds as though a number of staff at FAU HQ stayed in London over Christmas 1945, Freda among them, and Sydney confirms that Freda is still fun. He admits to Brenda "I am often very irresponsible, but Freda incites me." At the same time, she is accused of being "casual" with Sydney's feelings. For instance, when she is ill, he finds her some Horlicks, which was hard to obtain, and he expects her to treasure it and have some left for him when she is better, but she gives it away. On another occasion, she fails to clean his room after Philip Gleave has used it. She is slow to anger but on one occasion, early in 1946, she is furious with the current warden who refuses to scrape together some food for Peter Leyland, back in London after four long, gruelling years in China.

Sydney rather despairs of Freda's relationship with her Pip. He writes that "officially their engagement is off but actually they intend getting married as soon as possible". Philip seems to have been posted to Germany at this stage and Freda toyed with the idea of following him there but she would have been missed as "she's a good warden."

Sydney's letter of 28th December tells the whole sorry story of Freda's second engagement.

> Freda has been telling me all about her affair and I really feel sorry for her. Apparently she and Philip got engaged in Italy and very nearly got married, but eventually decided to wait until they got home.
> They arranged to come home at the same time, but actually Philip arrived a fortnight earlier. His mother is apparently selfish, who resents the idea that anyone would take away her darling boy, and so she kept all the letters Freda was writing to him after he'd left Italy.
> He, getting no letters from Freda, assumed she'd given him up and stopped writing to her. So, Freda arrived in London and found no letters waiting for her. After hanging around for a few days, she decided to go to his home in B-d. She arrived one noon and found he wasn't in but was expected around midnight.

> His mother never asked her in for a meal or a wash or a rest, and she had to hang around for hours for him.
> When he arrived he was apparently in such a daze, not knowing whether he loved her, or what his mother wanted, or anything, that Freda decided to break it off. They both seem to think it will turn out all right and will be on again after Pip's leave in February. But what a mess for them, isn't it?

Sydney realises that "she wants somebody to be devoted to her rather than just fond of her, and it'll have to be someone else." By 13th February 1946, Brenda hears that "Freda is rather low these days" and she regrets leaving Italy and that is the impression Freda always gave me: she should have stayed in Europe and helped with post-war reconstruction over there instead of coming home to England early. Poor Freda, and poor Sydney too. This, then, is why she felt that she had let down her friends in the Rome office. She never mentioned Philip to me when talking about that time and I never asked her why she came back early.

A revealing description of Freda's demeanor comes on 18th February. Had Sydney known about Jack, I believe he would have understood her fear of flying but he has no conception that what she has been through made her too frightened, or too brittle, to fall in love again.

> After tea Freda and I went for a long walk before supper. She talked all the time about her love life. She is depressed again and I think she's going to have it all out with Pip. But the worst thing she told me was that she'd determined that she wouldn't fall in love until the day she gets married. ... No man would marry a woman if he thought she had that attitude. I think people must let themselves go without restraint, and I told her so, but I don't think she's convinced ...

This is as much as I have been able to find out about Freda and Philip, even though their engagement dragged on for five years. Brenda told me that she had no idea about Jack, and probably neither did Sydney, but it was Jack's letters and photograph Freda kept, not Philip's.

Jack was always on her mind, a fact proven by her continued correspondence with his family, which ended only, according to Jack's family, when she married my uncle John. Freda's address books yield no information about Jack's family or the families of his crew so I believe all ties to them were severed in 1953-4 but I have not given up hope of finding a note from Jack's mother hidden in a book. Of course I now wish I had gone through each and every one of Freda's books with more care and attention before allowing them to be boxed and discarded.

According to her school friend Sybil, Freda visited Bridlington soon after the war. Sybil thought it strange but did not think to question her; she only now wonders if it was because Bridlington was one of the places were Jack had been. Freda never saw Peter Naylor's memorial at Lissett near Bridlington to 158 Squadron, also part of 4 Group. She died the year before it was created. Steel silhouettes of seven aircrew walk over a field near the road, on the site of the Squadron base, with their backs to the sunset and ready for night ops, or backs to the dawn as they trudge to debriefing. The memorial was created 64 years after the end of the war and is, at the time of writing, the only memorial to Bomber Command and is dedicated to the 851 people based at Lissett who died during the war as well as to those who survived.[83]

On Peter Grimwood's birth date in 1946 Freda asked one of her Unit friends in Germany to put flowers on his grave for his mother. It is hard to remember that photographs were not so cheap or easy to copy and that there were no internet mapping tools, smart phones or indeed personal computers. How simple it is now to load an online map and narrow a search and see Jack's grave. Peter is remembered in the war memorial in his home town Wroxham and Jack's name is engraved on his school's memorial tablet but none of the mothers of the boys in Jack's crew was able to visit their son's grave for many years.

This letter, written by Norman Plenderleith's mother on 10th February 1946, betrays the helplessness and loss many thousands of mothers felt and went on feeling.

My dear Freda,

It was very kind of you to write and I got your letter on my dear boy's birth-day. It cheered me a lot to know if possible there were flowers on his grave.

It seems even now almost impossible to believe he and his friends won't come back. I often lie at night and feel he must come in. You will thank your friend for us won't you, dear, and ask him to tell us what we owe him.

My husband does not say much but I know how pleased he was with your letter. So are my other boys – they think it will be so nice to have a photo. I wrote to Mrs. Plenderlieth and told her about the graves as she has said how she tried to picture them. She wrote by return to thank me for letting her know and says when I get the photo, will I send it for her to see and she will return it to me. Also she asked me if I would ask you if you could, would you have some flowers put on Norman's grave for May 10th. She does not mind what it costs. I hope we are not troubling you too much dear. I feel your friend is my friend too to do this for us and I hope he will let us repay him.

Have you seen Betty lately? I don't wish to write to her as I don't want to keep reopening the wound. She is young and I hope she will meet someone who she can be happy with. Give my love when you see or write to her.

When you come to Norwich again do please let me know. I would like to see you. I hope to see Mrs. Denton again soon and when the days get longer I hope she will come out to see me with the little girl- she is a sweet little thing.

Again thanking you my dear for your kind thoughts and for all you have done for us. I often picture those graves now. My Norman was 25 last Wednesday.

When the flowers were laid in 1946 the boys were still buried where the Luftwaffe had laid them in 1943.[84] Therefore the photograph Freda had taken was of their graves in the North cemetery in Düsseldorf. On 4th October 1946 they were moved to their final burial ground in Reichswald War Cemetery.

Maxie is the only crew member to have a grave in England. It can be found by the entrance to St. Mary's Church, March. "On sun-tipped wings he loved to fly proud son of England's heritage" says his gravestone.

The last mention I found of R.A.F. Melbourne was in a letter Freda wrote to York Meeting in 1948. She was now working for the Manpower and Welfare department of the Coal Board. She had just attended a course in Oxford on "The problem of the absorption of European Volunteer Workers into the mining industry." She writes to ask if any of the York Quakers can help:

> One of the speakers was the Warden of an Education Centre which the Coal Board is running at Melbourne, ex-R.A.F. Camp, near York, and one of the points he made was the difficulty of these Displaced Persons in accustoming themselves to English life.

How strange that Melbourne should reappear in her life in this unexpected manner.

The last mention of Jack, is in a letter from the War Graves Commission, written in reply to a request for information Freda made when she became engaged to my uncle John. I do not know whether she visited Reichswald on the 10th anniversary of his death but I think she did and that she did so alone because I read through all her correspondence with John and found no reference to Reichswald.

> Imperial War Graves Commission
> WOOBURN HOUSE, WOOBURN GREEN,
> HIGH WYCOMBE, BUCKS.
> 3rd February 1953
>
> Dear Madam,
> In reply to your letter of the 28th January regarding your proposed visit to the grave of the late Pilot Officer J. B. Denton who is buried in Plot V, Row D, Grave No. 7 in Reichswald Forest War Cemetery, Cleve, Germany.
> Reichswald Forest borders on the German-Dutch frontier, about twenty five miles North of the Ruhr

and three miles from Cleve, the nearest town. The cemetery is sited in the centre of the forest on the left of the road from Cleve to Gennep, Holland.

Arrangements for visits are not made by the Commission but a relative made a successful visit to Reichswald Forest War Cemetery, and I am enclosing the information which he gave which may be of assistance to you.

It is suggested that you place yourself in the hands of a reliable travel agency who would be able to give you full information regarding the cost of your journey, etc.

Flying into the Rhur on the 69th anniversary of Jack's death, the cloud cover was 10/10. Düsseldorf is an enormous city build by the Rhine and as we turned downstream to land, the northern cemetery, Nordfriedhof, was clearly visible. We were flying low, far lower than Jack would have flown to make a bombing run.

Düsseldorf's north cemetery itself lacks historical information. There might have been histories and photographs in the church. I could not get inside because funerals were being conducted, one after another. I found no plaques, however small, to remind visitors that multitudes of British airmen were once carefully buried there by the Luftwaffe in temporary graves. It was terrifically hot so I may have missed information. A young attendant, raking sand by a large pond, told me where the WW2 area was and I could see her wondering why I wanted to visit that part of the graveyard. I walked in the shade whenever possible. Was it hot like this on 23rd May 1943? An old couple walked by with a wheelbarrow, a fork sticking out and a watering can, and I wondered (as I always do on the Continent but never in England) what they remembered about the war.

I think the airmen were placed in an area near to where victims of the bombing now lie. I walked along lines and lines of them, flat stones set in the grass, like a strange flattened township baking in the sun, some unknown, some complete families, most of them either women or very young or very old or whose names suggested they were not from Germany. Large ochre-coloured crosses made of what seemed to be lava stood at irregular intervals. It was unforgettable. I was alone. Elsewhere old folk, almost all were old folk, tended graves. I looked longingly at the bridge which crosses Danziger

Strasse and wanted to walk through to Nordpark to sit and watch the magnificent Rhine flow by but I had to run for the train to Kleve. Later, the train took me past Krefeld on the opposite bank of the Rhine and past a cement works and numerous other industrial sites: the Ruhr.

In Kleve, after a heavy storm, I took a taxi along Grunewaldstrasse to the cemetery in the forest and wondered if Freda had done the same. Kleve is now rebuilt and modern but if Freda came in 1953, it would still have been littered with building sites and ruins.

The forest, on the Siegfried Line and once the scene of battle, was calm. It is mainly beech trees and at the end of Spring, fresh leaves were still light green and new. The trees dripped dew, and the grass though short, was soaking wet. Click open the brass gates and step down into the cemetery and the vast number of graves is almost overwhelming. Early morning birdsong echoes from tree to tree, the mist rises in the hot morning sun, a buzzard shrieks and I walk to the left, to row 5.

It was peaceful but it was so unlike the fens Jack loved. This made me unutterably sad. The airmen's greatest fear was to touch the land they bombed. If only the British cemetery had been close to fenland, or if Jack had come down in Holland rather than the Ruhr then maybe he would have been in a Dutch cemetery, below the migration route of birds who had fed and rested in Norfolk, under wide open space, his sky wheeling swallows and streams of conversational geese.

It is said on message boards that Jack's tail gunner is separated from the rest of the crew.[85] Crews are, in the main, buried together and in this section, which seems to represent the Battle of the Ruhr, each crew is buried according to the date they came down. George Lawson, though not in the same row as Jack and the others, is at the end of the row before and you come to George's grave first. As tail gunner he was always out on a limb, separated from the others and the first to warn of danger.

Figure 41 British and Commonwealth Cemetery, Kleve, Row 5, Jack and his crew; taken very early on a misty morning

I have seen Jack's name listed four times: on a brass plaque in his old school in Norwich, and in the cathedral, in York Minster and at Reichswald. In the cathedrals, a church official unlocked a cabinet holding the book of remembrance and carefully turned the pages until we found Denton, J. B. The books were left open at that page until the next mourner asked to see a name. At Reichswald I sat alone with the book on my lap. To remember at a grave, to run your fingers over a name or read a name written with care in a book – these were denied the mothers of Jack's crew for many years.

My flight home followed the Rhine to Nijmegen, then the Meuse and crossed the Channel by Rotterdam, not far from the Ijsselmeer and Amsterdam, not far from Egmond and the North Sea, much as bomber streams would have flown 70 years ago. We flew over the Channel and skirted Norfolk, down the coast to Suffolk and the Thames. On finals, the plane jumped and bounced and yawed and I imagined Jack trying to hold the wheel, sweat pouring down his back with the effort, yelling down the intercom for Maxie or Derrick to come get the throttle and then the landing gear banged down and we landed with a thump.

My tour back to 1943 began as a transcription of letters which needed a small amount of context, but turned into a journey over territory I'd never charted before. Cairo connected Freda with Jack and with her future husband John, but also with Eleanor, my mother. Freda may not have known when she chose to be posted to Cairo, that Jack spent four years there after he was born in 1922 and that his sister Beryl was born there in 1926. Freya Stark, who wrote about Cairo when Freda was there and whose books Freda valued, had a secretary called Lulie Abdul'Huda who took English lessons from my mother in Oxford before the war. In 1940 my mother was invited by Lulie's family to live with them in Egypt but she was refused an Exit Permit. She hoped to be nearer to her fiancé David Hunt, who was in the Desert Campaign, where, two years later, in 1942, John Wood was taken POW at Tobruk, where Philip Gleave also fought. One of the camps FAU Rome HQ inspected was PG 21, the Italian camp at Chieti where John, her future husband, had so recently been incarcerated as a POW. My father's eyesight prevented him for fighting in the war but he did post-war reconstruction work with youth clubs in Germany. Back in England trainee pilots circle over the house I used to live in, sometimes so low they seem to lick the tops of the fir trees at the end of the garden. They come from Brize Norton and, long before I knew anything about Jack, I used to walk up the hill nearby and watch the airfield lights and aircraft landing and taking off.

One year, maybe more often, Freda had Jack's name added to the In Memoriam column with the words "Thy sweet love remember'd such wealth brings."[86]

IN MEMORIAM

"THEIR NAME LIVETH FOR EVERMORE"

BLOCKLEY.—In proud and loving memory of my son, BERNARD ALFRED BLOCKLEY, Paymr.-Midshipman, R.N., late H.M.S. Hood, lost at Crete May 23, 1941.

CARIELLO, ANTHONY P. J., B.A.O.C., died May 26, 1945, while serving in S.E.A.C. Ever dearly remembered.

COCOLLIS.—In proud and cherished memory of Lt. GEORGE BERTRAM COCOLLIS, R.A. (formerly H.A.C.), killed in action in Crete, May 24, 1941, aged 36.

COOTE.—In proud and undying memory of dearest MICHAEL, F.O., R.A.F. Mentioned in Despatches, killed on active service May 24, 1942; also remembering those who died with him.—Mother, Daddy and Mary.

DENTON, Plt.-Offr. JACK B. DENTON, R.A.F., Bomber Command.—Lost with his crew in operations, Dortmund, May 23-24, 1943, "Thy sweet love remember'd such wealth brings."—P.

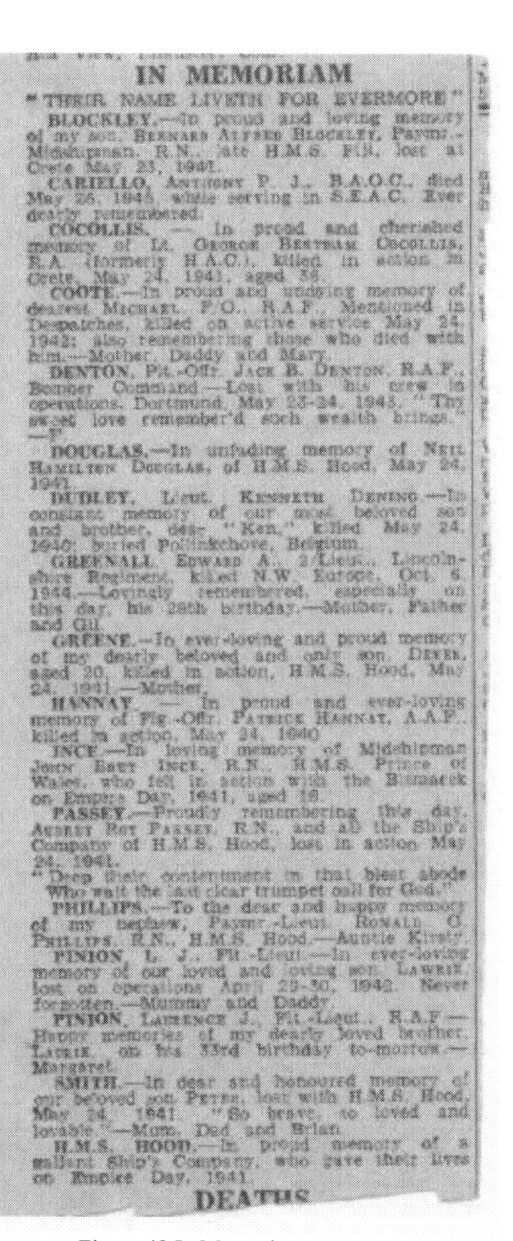

DOUGLAS.—In unfading memory of NEIL HAMILTON DOUGLAS, of H.M.S. Hood, May 24, 1941.

DUDLEY, Lieut. KENNETH DENING.—In constant memory of our most beloved son and brother, dear "Ken," killed May 24, 1940, buried Pollinkchove, Belgium.

GREENALL, EDWARD A., 2/Lieut., Lincolnshire Regiment, killed N.W. Europe, Oct. 6, 1944.—Lovingly remembered, especially on this day, his 28th birthday.—Mother, Father and Gil.

GREENE.—In ever-loving and proud memory of my dearly beloved and only son, DEVER, aged 20, killed in action, H.M.S. Hood, May 24, 1941.—Mother.

HANNAY.—In proud and ever-loving memory of Plg.-Offr. PATRICK HANNAY, A.A.F., killed in action, May 24, 1940.

INCE.—In loving memory of Midshipman JENY EAST INCE, R.N., H.M.S. Prince of Wales, who fell in action with the Bismarck on Empire Day 1941, aged 18.

PASSEY.—Proudly remembering this day, AUBREY ROY PASSEY, R.N., and all the Ship's Company of H.M.S. Hood, lost in action May 24, 1941.
"Deep their contentment in that blest abode Who wait the last clear trumpet call for God."

PHILLIPS.—To the dear and happy memory of my nephew, Paymr.-Lieut. RONALD C. PHILLIPS, R.N., H.M.S. Hood.—Auntie Kirsty.

PINION, L. J., Flt.-Lieut.—In ever-loving memory of our loved and loving son LAWRIE, lost on operations April 29-30, 1942. Never forgotten.—Mummy and Daddy.

PINION, LAURENCE J., Flt.-Lieut., R.A.F.—Happy memories of my dearly loved brother, LAURIE, on his 33rd birthday to-morrow.—Margaret.

SMITH.—In dear and honoured memory of our beloved son PETER, lost with H.M.S. Hood, May 24, 1941. "So brave, so loved and lovable."—Mum, Dad and Brian.

H.M.S. HOOD.—In proud memory of a gallant Ship's Company, who gave their lives on Empire Day, 1941.

DEATHS

Figure 42 In Memoriam

Epilogue

"WHAT'S SHE SAYING?"

The nurse called me over. I looked down at my aunt Freda. She was mumbling so I leant down beside her bed to listen and rested my shoulder on the cushion put there to stop her head rolling uncomfortably. She had not opened her eyes more than a couple of times all day and had stopped reacting to people but still felt pain and cried out in a reedy scream when being washed. The rhythmic swish of the syringe driver and my aunt's gentle breathing filled the silence in the room.

"John." Her husband's name.

Today was February 23rd 2009 and John had died almost twenty years earlier. He and Freda married in 1953 after meeting on a package holiday to Majorca; they'd been very happy together. They met late in life, so Freda was a relative newcomer to the family and was never fully accepted by my mother. With her Coal Board background and Yorkshire accent, she did not fit in readily with my mother's family. Nobody, of course, could have been good enough for John, my father's brother. He was gentle and intelligent and had not had a good war, so to speak. "So to speak" was one of Freda's favourite phrases.

"Yes, Freda. John's waiting for you."

She repeated the name twice more and it was not John this time. Maybe it had not been John at all. I turned away to look out of the small window at the reflection of clouds rushing across the pond. Then

"Jack. Jack." I looked towards the nurse.

"OK. I know who she means. Thank you for fetching me." My aunt began to talk very fast and incomprehensibly in a breathy whisper. I held her hand and stroked her hair but I could not hear a word she said.

"Freda, Jack's waiting for you too."

Acknowledgments

Quotations from Churchill are reproduced with permission of Curtis Brown, London on behalf of the Estate of Sir Winston Churchill. Copyright © Winston S. Churchill.

Friends Ambulance Unit *Chronicle* and other publications used by permission from the Library of the Society of Friends.

Quotations from the Yorkshire Evening Press (1943) are reproduced courtesy of The Press, York.

Bombs Away! by Martin Bowman is quoted by kind permission of Pen & Sword Books Limited.

Stephen Peet's photographs used by kind permission of Olive Peet. Jack's photo with bomber jacket is used by kind permission of Sylvia Martin. Photos of other crew members are used with kind permission of Dawn Hatton, Maureen Stoneman and Harri Harrison.

Thank you to RAF Hendon librarians who inspired me to discover what Jack did in the war as I sat in their small library and listened to Mr. Eliot describe crewing up. Thank you also to the librarians of Friends House, York Railway Museum and York Public library, to the Imperial War Museum, London, to the archivists at RAF Elvington, and to the librarians at the National Archives. The National Archives librarians must be congratulated for putting online the ORBs (only not in time for my research!). Thank you also to the librarians at All Souls College, Oxford and of the Bodleian Libraries electronic resources section who offered helpful advice.

A memorable day in Yorkshire included lunch with 10 Squadron society followed by a tour of RAF Melbourne with Mike Wood who has reconstructed Melbourne control tower. Thank you also to Mac who flew with 10 Squadron as Mid-Upper Gunner and told stories which made me laugh and cry and to Iris his wife from the Royal Observer Corps who was based in the war on the Knavesmire racecourse.

Sybil, who knew Freda all her life, described wartime York to me. Bill Spray and Brenda Bailey and Angela Sinclair-Loutit knew Freda in the F.A.U. added context to Freda's letters.

Thanks also go to Kevin Sharpe, Warren Chernaik and Nick Neale. Thank you to Imogen Rigden for painting the cover image, and for being a travelling companion to Berlin one cold November and to Norfolk one hot March and to Rome. To Janet also, who came to Norfolk on a different occasion, and to Jenny, Ruth, Michelle, Kay, Althea and many others have given support and encouragement.

Neil Haverson of *Let's Talk*, East Anglia, published a letter from me when I had almost abandoned the search for Jack's family, and it is thanks to him that I met Jack's sister-in-law Margaret, his nieces Sue and Caroline, his nephew Steve and his sister Sylvia.

List of figures

Figure 1 The leather frame with photographs of Jack, Freda and John 5
Figure 2 Freda Smith 7
Figure 3 Freda's first letter to Jack 8
Figure 4 Jack's first letter to Freda 9
Figure 5 Batholomew's pre-war map 20
Figure 6 Hermitage Wharf park in 2010 22
Figure 7 Freda's Conscientious Objector identification card 23
Figure 8 Letter written by BPR, once Freda's manager at Rowntree's 26
Figure 9 The Middle East Section Office, Gordon Square 30
Figure 10 Jack Denton at home in Norwich 37
Figure 11 Sprogs training in Canada, Derrick top left 46
Figure 12 Briefing room, R.A.F. Melbourne, 2010 54
Figure 13 The runways at R.A.F. Melbourne, still visible. Jack's dispersal to the east of Seaton Ross © Google Maps . 55
Figure 14 Member of Jack's crew. George? Wally? 58
Figure 15 Peter, radio operator 59
Figure 16 Norman, navigator 60
Figure 17 Derrick, bomb aimer 61
Figure 18 Member of Jack's crew. Maxie? 62
Figure 19 De Grey Assembly Rooms, York 64

Figure 20 The postcard of the "4 engined" which Jack sent to Freda. She attached his R.A.F. sweetheart brooch. The picture is of a 76 Squadron Halifax heavy bomber. 65

Figure 21 Freda photographed by Stephen Peet in Autumn 1942 on her sloping bed in the London Hospital Students hostel 67

Figure 22 Roofless Essen. ©Bomber Command Diary 80

Figure 23 The letter which never arrived at Melbourne 105

Figure 24 An aircraft like Jack's 121

Figure 25 At debriefing, Norman with his back to the photographer 124

Figure 26 Jack's new handwriting 130

Figure 27 Freda to Stephen Peet about her engagement 137

Figure 28 Jack, mid 1943 142

Figure 29 Maurice, who took over from Maxie 193

Figure 30 Cutting found among letters 200

Figure 31 The week's losses at a glance. – May 23 to 29, 1943 ©The Aeroplane, June 4th 207

Figure 32 Crew list of HR696 ZA-G 23/5/43 © National Archives 209

Figure 33 Unopened letter returned 216

Figure 34 Freda ready to leave for Cairo, Spring 1944 217

Figure 35 Missing, believed killed in action 222

Figure 36 I have Freda's British Red Cross F.A.U. epaulette here, in front of me, on my desk 233

Figure 37 Freda to Stephen Peet, POW in Germany 236

Figure 38 Hadfield Spears / FAU mobile clinic in Maloula, near Sednaya 246

Figure 39 Red Cross letter with information about Jack's grave 248

Figure 40 Freda in Rome 255

Figure 41 British and Commonwealth Cemetery, Kleve, Row 5, Jack and his crew; taken very early on a misty morning . 269

Figure 42 In Memoriam 271

Figure 43 An airgraph, actual size, 4 ½ x 5 inches 281

Figure 44 Sterling, 1943-2010 282

Figure 45 Jack's medals 291

Further information

The introductory quotation

Adapted from *Never So Young Again* by Dan Brennan (p. 153) who writes of a bomber pilot lost on a raid "… his memory will not die. It will only die when the fighting stops, and what he did will be forgotten by many but not by me. For here in this thinking he will live a little longer."

Freda wrote a reference in the front her family bible, Phillipians IV 8:

Finally, bretheren, whatsoever things are true, whatsoever things are honest, whatsoever things are just, whatsoever things are pure, whatsoever things are lovely, whatsoever things are of good report ; if there be any virtue, and if there be any praise, think on these things.

John Wood

When John enlisted, he was a geologist employed by the company which became Shell. In the 30s he spent many months in Iraq prospecting for oil. By the time he returned to England at the end of the war he had been very ill and his sight never recovered; he never saw green again, which seemed to me, even as a child, one of the cruellest hardships. This did not stop him cultivating his garden. Yellow roses were his favourite flowers but he planted and tended any flower Freda chose for him to grow in their garden.

Captain J.E.R. Wood, number 94175, Royal Signals, MEF was taken prisoner at Tobruk in November 1942, and he became POW number 1424. He was sent first to various camps in Italy but the one which he spent most time in was PG 21, Chieti, to the East of Rome. There from January 1943, he said it was a desperately uncomfortable camp.

In early June 1943, shortly before the Italians surrendered, senior British officers of Italian POW camps were ordered by MI9 not to allow any prisoners to escape. When Italy surrendered, their POW camps were taken over by the surprised but pleased Germans. Tom Carver writes in *Where the Hell have You Been* that "Out of the 80,000 British POWs in Italy at the time of the Armistice, 50,000 – more than half – were immediately captured by the Germans and shipped north. Of those who did escape, only 11,500 made it all the way home ... Some 2,000 were never accounted for." (p. 112-3)

When the Italian guards abandoned PG21 ... SBO Colonel Marshall threatened to court-martial any POW who left the camp, there was a near mutiny among the prisoners. He appointed his own phalanx of guards and ordered them to man the watchtowers. ... The entire camp population - about 1300 soldiers - was shipped by train to the Nazi camps in Poland and Germany. (p. 112)

In July (?) 1943 John was moved to Stalag VII A, Barrack 6B while Oflag VII B was being built (letter to his mother of October 1943). In March 1944 he was moved to Oflag VIII F i.e. Oflag 79 near Brunswick (a letter has Oflag VIII F crossed out and Oflag 79, COY 7 added). Each move was probably a gruelling march, as described in *The Last Escape: the Untold Story of Allied Prisoners of War in Germany, 1944-45* by John Nichol and Tony Renwell. Until I read this book I believed John when he wrote to his mother that the camps in Germany were better than Italian camps partly because the Germans had taken them on some nice country walks! When Oflag 79 was about to be liberated many prisoners including my uncle decided to set up a charity to help poor boys back in London and they called it The Brunswick Boys. (www.thebrunswickclub.org.uk)

Freda's ashes were scattered at Blewburton Hill and on the Downs at Langdons, where she and John often walked.

Tour of Duty

A tour of duty for an RAF bomber pilot in 1943 was normally 30 operational missions. Jack had flown on operations before he officially joined 10 Squadron at the beginning of March, 1943. He clearly flew to North Italy, at least once. Information about Brize Norton OTU states that trainee crews were often used on operations and he would have flown nickelling and gardening raids. Not each sortie was deemed to be an operation so far as the tour of duty was concerned; sea patrols, for example, were worth a third of a bombing raid. Jack told Freda in April that he should be off ops "in another three months" and I estimate that Jack had completed around 4 ops one way or another by the time he moved to Yorkshire for conversion to heavies. By the time he died in May, he had probably completed around 21 operational raids and at least two mining sorties. He had 8 or 10 more raids to complete. He might then have volunteered to do another tour – some aircrew did.

Inscription in Never so Young Again (1946)

My copy of Dan Brennan's *Never So Young Again* (1946) was owned by Lt. Eugene R. Mathis of the USAAF, who served with 10th Squadron at R.A.F. Melbourne. On the title page he has inscribed a poem by A.E. Houseman:

> With rue my heart is laden
> For golden friends I had;
> For many a rose-lipped maiden,
> And many a light-foot lad.
>
> By brooks too broad for leaping
> The light-foot lads are laid;
> The rose-lipped girls are sleeping,
> In fields where roses fade.

Following the poem, Lt. Mathis has written:

I always remember Jean Mickleburg, a lovely 19 year old who worked in a factory making parts for Spitfires: she married a squadron-mate named Young: came to the U.S. with him. I know not what happened to her.

Double summer time

GMT+2 During the war double summer time was introduced

http://www.bpears.org.uk/NE-Diary/Inc/ISeq_32.html .

Airgraphs

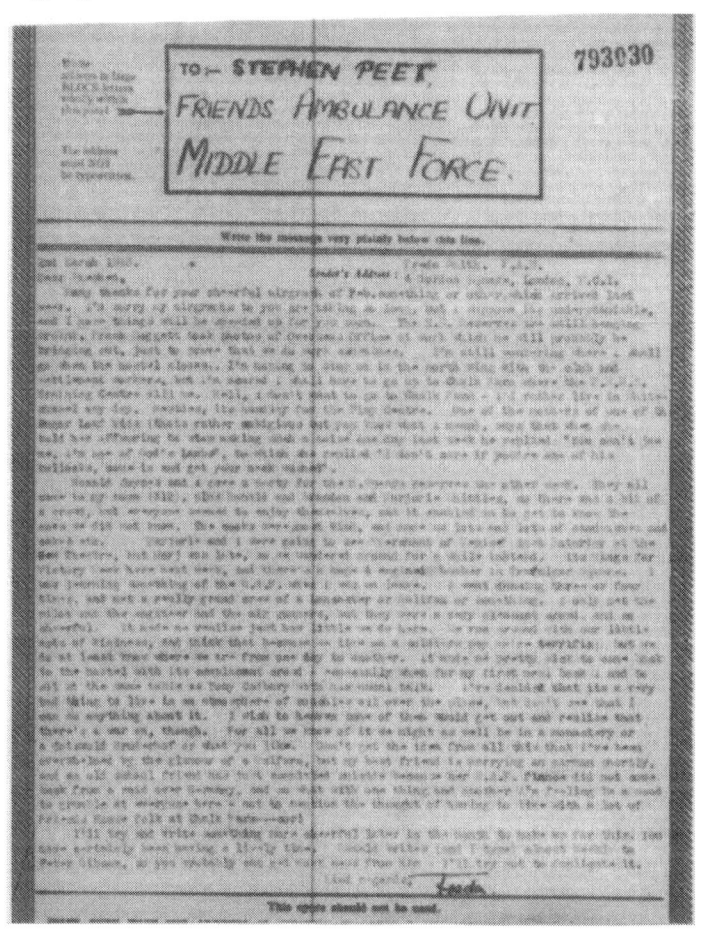

Figure 43 An airgraph, actual size, 4 ½ x 5 inches

The Airgraph Service provided a way of sending letters abroad using a minimum of space. Airgraph forms were available from Post Offices and were a single sheet of paper with space for the address and message. To quote the Airgraph Service: "A miniature photographic negative of the message and address will be made and sent by air mail. At the destination end a photographic print, measuring about 5 inches by 4 inches, will be made and delivered to the addressee. ... Very small writing is not suitable". Indeed! I have had to use a magnifying glass on some of Freda's airgraphs. This is Freda's letter of March 2nd 1943 to Stephen Peet, actual size, 4 ¼ in x 5 in.

Pilot training

It is unclear how many hours a pilot would have flown before becoming operational, the figure varied according to the year and Group but it was approximately 300 flying hours in 1942-3. Bowyer estimates that after initial training, pilots flew 120 hours at their SFTS (service flying training school). After the middle of 1941, this normally took place in the quiet skies above Canada or Africa. On returning, bomber pilots flew another 60 hours at a (P)AFU (pilot advanced flying unit) to accustom themselves to the weather and busy skies (fighter pilots flew 30 hours at AFUs). At the OTU (operations training unit), pilots flew at least 80 hours, some of these on operations, before joining an HCU (heavy conversion unit), when they flew another 30 hours (Bowyer, p. 31-2).

Money

1943 in pounds, shillings and pence.	Equivalent value in pounds and pence in 2009-2010
£150	£5,187
£100	£3,458
25/- (25 shillings)	£43.22p
6d (sixpence)	86p
1d (a penny)	14p
¼ (a farthing)	3 ½

Figure 44 Sterling, 1943-2010

I chose these amounts because they are amounts Freda and Jack mention.

Pay scales for recruits for aircrew Aircraftman 2nd class 2/- a day. If chosen as a pilot then an LAC (Leading Aircraftman) was paid 5/- a day + instructional pay of 2/- a day. Other aircrew seem to have been paid less for instruction. When the LAC became Sergeant he was paid 12/- 6d a day. Once operational, Jack must have earned quite a bit more but I am still trying to find out how much. 12/- 6d was worth about £22 in 2009. According to Nichol and Rennell an operational pilot earned around £24 a month.

List of letters and Jack's operations

Bar the last two, Maxie flew with Jack on most of these missions and listed them for Freda: "Jack has been to Hamburg: Cologne: Essen: Berlin: Berlin: Duisburg: Essen: Kiel: Frankfurt: Duisburg: mine-laying: Essen: Duisburg: Dortmund: Bochum: Dortmund."

Month, date	Letters	Jack's operations
Feb 3		Hamburg 2nd pilot
4		Turin 2nd pilot, scrubbed
14		Cologne 2nd pilot
15-28	F	"Heavy raids for 11 nights and 7 days"
21	J	Bremmen
23	F	
Mar 1		Berlin
3	F	Hamburg (Wedell)
4		Essen
5	J	
9	F	
12		Essen
14		Bremmen or Essen and a dingy search.
15	J	"a late raid"
20	F	Scrub
21		Scrub
22	J	Scrub

24	F		
26		J	Duisburg
27			Berlin
29			Berlin
30	2F		
Apr 3			Essen
4			Kiel
6	F		
7	F	J	
9	F	J	
12	F		
14		J	
10			Frankfurt
21	F	J	
23	F		
24		J	
26			Duisburg
27	F		Gardening
28			Gardening
30	F		Essen
May 1	F	J	
3			Essen
4		F	Dortmund
7		F	
10	F		Scrub
11	F	J	Air-sea rescue practice
12			Duisburg
13			Bochum
15			Formation flying training
17	2F		
18		J	Bullseye training
20	F	J	
22	F	J	
23			Dortmund
25	F		
26	F		

Though Maxie says Jack flew 16 missions in all, he also suggests that Jack flew to Cologne again after February 14th but I cannot find proof that he did. Maxie does not mention the Italian missions.

Radar

Operations Record books mention bombing by **Gee Fix**, or G-Fix, when a radar signal was fixed onto a target. It was used mainly when the cloud of smoke cover was too thick to see the target.

Oboe was good for short distances and used three points of reference: two on the ground in England and one on the aircraft. The curvature of the earth made it unusable for distant targets. Also it was easily intercepted.

H_2S radar was top secret and there are a number of explanations as to why it was called H_2S and I like to think it was named for the poison hydrogen sulphide.

Monica was also used but by all accounts pretty useless. Monica alerted a tail gunner of the approach of a fighter but by the time Monica picked up the signals it was normally too late to take action.

AI stood for Airborne Interception which, like Monica, worked only up to a point.

Freya radar was used by the Luftwaffe to locate bombers using massive Wurtzburg dishes and, in conjunction with the Himmelbett system of dividing the territory in to neat squares, each night fighter was given adequate warning of approaching bombers as they lay in wait in their pre-arranged quadrant. It was effective.

Window released from bomb bays blinded Würzburg radar and therefore incapacitated the accompanying flak. Eventually German radar was recalibrated to recognize the different velocity and directional movement of chaff and an aircraft.

Maps

For interesting detailed old maps, largely out of copyright see http://www.parishregister.com/moddoclarge.html and http://www.parishregister.com/areamaps.html .

Old Ordnance Survey Maps: Whitechapel, Spitalfields & The Bank 1913, which does not include the whole of Wapping.

I found a pre-war Bartholemew's map at a Fly to the Past airshow in Kidlington airport which includes most of London in details even showing the tramlines on Whitechapel Road.

Acronyms, jargon

Ack Ack	Anti aircraft guns
AI	Airborne Interception
ARP	Air Raid Precautions
ATS	Auxiliary Territorial Service
FIDO	Fog Investigation and Dispersal Operation (clearing fog from runways)
Flak	Fliegerabwehrkanone
F.A.U.	Friends Ambulance Unit
F.W.R.S.	Friends War Relief Service (earlier acronym Warvics)
Gardening	Mine laying
Gee fix / G fix	Radar
HCU	Heavy conversion unit
I.R.C.	International Red Cross
Kite, bird, a/c, flying coffin	Aeroplanes
l.s.d. / £.s.d.	pounds, shillings and pence (librae, sestertii/solidi et denarii)
NAAFI (stores)	Navy, Army and Air Force Institutes
Nickel	Leaflets
Oflag	Offizierenlaager, prison camp for officers.
ORB	Operations Record Books (held at National Archives)

OTU	Operations training unit
(P)AFU	(Pilots) Advanced flying unit
PFF	Pathfinders, with the Master Bomber, found the target area, marked it and often stayed in the target area during bombing
Scarecrow	exploding aircraft, airborne
Schräge Musik	Luftwaffe fighter aircraft cannon which pointed upwards
SFTS	Service flying training school
S.B.C.	Small Bomb Containers. For example, Jack carried 2 long delay 1000 lb bombs to Dortmund on 23rd May along with 7 S.B.C (90 at 4lbs) and 6 S.B.C. (8 at 30lbs).
u/s	unserviceable
U.N.R.R.A.	United Nations Relief and Rehabilitation Administration
U.N.W.R.R.A.	United Nations War Relief and Rehabilitation Administration
w.e.f	with effect from

Window, also called Chaff. Not used until the Hamburg raid of 24/25 July 1943, Window was a radar jamming device.

ZA-X

The aircraft with call sign ZA-X which Jack flew was serial number DT732. It was delivered by 26 Jan 1943. He often flew it but when it crashed over Ijsselmeer on 14 May 1943 after a raid on Bochum, it was being flown by an American volunteer pilot, Flt Sgt Mills, whose body was never found. The rest of the crew also died.

There has been some confusion about dates, in for example *Osprey Combat Aircraft no. 14, Halifax Squadrons of World War 2* where ZA-X BB324 is given incorrect dates: BB324 was the serial number of a replacement ZA-X, transferred from 76 Squadron at Linton-on-Ouse after 14th May and before June 23rd, when it too crashed, while bombing Mulheim.

Nose art for BB324 also shows Wings for Victory (though one web site reads it as "Haighs for Victory") written below a picture of "a terrier's head wearing a sailor's cap". Near the picture are four bombs denoting four completed raids. BB324 only flew for a month with 10 but it had flown earlier missions with other Squadrons so it is unclear which squadron the 4 bombs painted on its nose apply to.

The archivist at RAF Elvington thought the photograph used by Chris Davey for his painting of ZA-X in *Osprey Combat Aircraft no. 14, Halifax Squadrons of World War 2* (pages 50 and 103) was adapted from an official HPH photo. Looking carefully at the original, you can almost see the pilot. It was taken during the test flight at Melbourne, soon after delivery from 76 to 10 Squadron. This aircraft, ZA-X BB324, also featured in an article in *The Aeroplane* in 1943 on the differences between the various Halifaxes.

Wikipedia's photograph of ZA-X notes "Halifax B.II Series I (Special) *W1057, ZA-X*, No. 10 Squadron RAF, with a faired-over nose. During April–May 1942, this aircraft took part in a number of raids on the German battleship *Tirpitz* in Fættenfjord near Trondheim, Norway." It crashed on a raid to Mannheim on 19 May 1942 having successfully bombed the Tirpitz in March and April 1942. Another ZA-X crashed in January 1943 so presumably Jack's ZA-X was 10 Squadron's third of that name.

The aircraft Jack and crew were flying when they crashed

Information about the Jack's aircraft from the Lost Bombers web for 23/24 May 1943:

http://www.lostbombers.co.uk/bomber.php?id=6821

"Serial Range HR654 - HR699. 46 Halifax Mk.11.
Part of a batch of 250 HP59 Halifax Mk.11. HR654-HR699; HR711- HR758; HR773-HR819; HR832-HR880; HR905-HR952; HR977-HR988.
HR758 was used for engine experiments; HR845 and HR909 had experimental turrets. Delivered by handley Page (Cricklewood & Radlett) between 21Dec42 and 5Feb43. HR696 was one of three 10 Sqdn Halifaxes lost on this operation. See: W1217; DT789.

Airborne 2232 23May43 from Melbourne. Cause of loss and crash-site not established. All were buried in the Nordfriedhof at Düsseldorf. Their graves are now located in the Reichswald Forest War Cemetery. F/S J.B.Denton KIA Sgt I.B.Inglis KIA Sgt M.Harrison KIA Sgt N.P.Plenderleith KIA Sgt D.H.G.Adams KIA Sgt P.Grimwood KIA Sgt A.E.Wallis KIA Sgt G.H.Lawson KIA"

Jack and his crew on 23rd May 1943

Each plane carried 7 men and according to Maxie this is the crew of G for George. Many thanks to Chorley's Aircrew losses, v. 4 (1943) and the War Graves Commission site. I have also added information.

"The crew consisted of Jack, pilot: myself flight-engineer: Derrick Adams, bomb-aimer: George Lawson, rear-gunner: Albert Wallis ("Wally") mid-upper gunner: Peter Grimwood wireless operator air-gunner: Norman Plenderleith, navigator."

Halifax II ZA-G HR696 23 / 24 May 1943

Lawson, George Henry. Married, with a daughter.
658406 Sergeant (Air Gnr.)
Buried: Reichswald 5.C.18.

Harrison, Maurice. Age 21.
643364 Sergeant (Eng)
Buried: Reichswald 5.D.1

Inglis, Ian Bethune. Age 22.
1343173 Sergeant R.A.F.V.R. (2nd pilot)
Rutherglen, Lanarkshire.
Buried Reichswald 5.D.2

Grimwood, Peter. Age 22.
1331835 Sergeant (W. Op./Air Gnr.)
Wroxham, Norfolk.
Buried: Reichswald 5.D.3.

Adams, Derrick Henry George. Age 22. Engaged.
146446 Pilot Officer (Air Gnr.)
Buried: Reichswald 5.D.4.

Plenderleith, Norman Peter. Age 24. Engaged.
1504640 Sergeant (Nav.)
Balmoral, Belfast, Ireland
Buried: Reichswald 5.D.5.

Wallis, Albert Edwin. Married.
1578208 Sergeant (Air Gnr.)
Buried: Reichswald 5.D.6.

Denton, Jack Banfield. Age 20. Engaged.
146336 Pilot Officer (Pilot) R.A.F.V.R.
Volunteer Reserve.
Norwich, Norfolk.
Buried: Reichswald 5.D.7

All were buried initially at Nordfriedhof, near Dusseldorf and moved to Reichswald in October 1946 except for Maxie who is buried in March.

ZA-K HX1812 19 / 20 November 1943.
Steel, (Maxie) Raymond James Harry. Age 19
578363 Sergeant (Flt. Engr.)
March, Cambs.
Buried: St. Mary's, March, Cambs.

Jack's medals

The Aircrew, Europe, Star
The 1939-1945 Star
The War medal, 1939-1945

No Bomber Command medal was awarded, a bar was offered instead.

Figure 45 Jack's medals

A note on sources

Arfur Tegla Davies: *Friends Ambulance Unit: the story of the F.A.U. in the Second World War 1939-1946* is online: http://www.ourstory.info/library/4ww2/Friends/fauTC.html .

Sources of information about the early part of 1943 are varied. *The Aeroplane* reported bombing raids for the previous week. Each weekly report is numbered and the week Jack and Freda met was 180th week of the War in the Air. *Melbourne Ten* by Brian J. Rapier (1982) has been an incredible source of information, as have too many articles to mention of which 'It can't happen to us' by Tom Wingham (*Flypast*, Dec. 2009 also in Bowman / *Bombs Away* 2010) stands out. Of the books about Bomber Command, I will never forget Nicoll and Rennell's *Tail-End Charlies*. Of the television shows,

Revealed: Bomber Boys (Channel 5, Testimony Films 2011) is also unforgettable.

Newspaper cuttings are very hard to place. Freda always read the Manchester Guardian but could have cut information about raids from any newspaper. I cannot place the In Memoriam notice.

Many web pages added to my scanty knowledge, especially the discussion lists on the Professional Pilots Rumour Network (PPRuNe, www.pprune.org/), RAF Pocklington history and the many BBC history archives including "An archive of *World War Two* memories - written by the public, gathered by the *BBC*" www.bbc.co.uk/history/ww2peopleswar/

Pocklington History web describes the Halifax mid-air collision: http://www.pocklingtonhistory.com/ .

The pity of war is always present in paintings by Käthe Kollwitz, seen in her house in Berlin, and of Paul Nash among others, along with too much music to list here except maybe *The Lights of London*, quoted in Chapter 3, which I sang to myself when walking from Reichswald back to Kleve on a very hot afternoon in May.

Peter Naylor's memorial to Lissett's 158 Squadron and Philip Jackson's Bomber Command memorial in Green Park are powerful and moving.

Among Freda's books was an interesting novel by John Steinbeck called *The Moon is Down* (1942), a novel about the German invasion of an English town. Freda annotated or inscribed a number of her books. Freda's marginalia in her copy of A. Tegla Davies' *Friends Ambulance Unit* was enlightening. The inscription in a novel by Dan Brennan, which looked like a Boy's Own adventure story when I first saw it so it almost got sent to Oxfam, prodded me to research Bomber Command. First published in 1944 with the title *Never so Young Again* and reissued as *One of our Bombers is Missing* (1975) this book is written about the months Dan Brennan, a mid-upper gunner, was stationed with Jack at Melbourne. Freda wrote on the fly leaf of both these books "Flt. Sgt. J.B. Denton, No. 10 Squadron RAF, Killed Dortmund Raid, 23/24 May 1943. Freda Smith, F.A.U."

Bibliography

Newspapers:

The Aeroplane (1943) © Kelsey.
Flight (1943) © Air Age Media.
Yorkshire Evening Press (1943) © The Press, York.
10 Squadron Association Newsletter ©
http://www.10sqnass.co.uk/
Flypast (© Key publishing, Dec. 2009) Wingham, Tom 'It can't happen to us'

Lyrics:

Freed, Ralph *How About You* (1940) © EMI
Gilbert, Joseph George *You Made me Care* (1940) © Kassner Associated Publishers Ltd.
Pola, Edward and Tommy Connor *Till the Lights of London Shine Again* (1939) © 1939 EMI.

Online resources:

Bomber Command Diary, online
http://www.raf.mod.uk/bombercommand © Crown copyright (2010).
Swain, Harold WW2 People's War'
http://www.bbc.co.uk/ww2peopleswar/stories/88/a7212188.shtml . "WW2 People's War is an online archive of wartime memories contributed by members of the public and gathered by the BBC." Source - BBC bbc.co.uk/ww2peopleswar - © 2012 BBC.

Books:

Anon *A China Convoy Anthology* (FAU? [Chungking] 1945)
Arnhem Lift: Diary of a Glider Pilot (Pilot Press, 1945)
Conditions in Occupied Territories, no. 2: Rationing Under Axis Rule (HMSO, 1942)

Free Europe Pamphlet no. 3: the Soviet Occupation of Poland (Free Europe, 1940)

Ackroyd, Peter *London: the Biography* ISBN: 9780099422587 (Vintage (2000) 2001)

Ashton, Valerie *Bomber Jack: the Second World War and its Effect on One Man's Life* ISBN: 9781445273860 (Lulu, 2009, 2010)

Barber, C *FAU Postscript collated by Chris Barber* (Oxfam, 1984)

Barnard, Clifford *Binding the Wounds of War: a Young Relief Worker's Letters Home 1943-1947 from the Friends Ambulance Unit and the British Red Cross in North-West Europe* ISBN: 9780955618369 (Prounoun, 2010)

Two Weeks in May 1954: Sandbostel Concentration Camp and the Friends Ambulance Unit ISBN: 9780852453155 (Society of Friends, 1999)

Bailey, Brenda A *Quaker Couple in Nazi Germany* ISBN: 1850721319 (William Sessions, 1994)

Beaton, Cecil *Near East* (Batsford, 1943)

Bowman, Martin W., editor, *Bombs Away: Dramatic First Hand Accounts of British and Commonwealth Bomber Aircrew in WWII* ISBN: 9781848841871 (Pen & Sword Aviation imprints, 2010).

Bowyer, Michael J.F. *Action Stations 6: Military Airfields of the Cotswolds and Central Midlands* ISBN: 9781852603724 (PSL, 1983, 1990)

Action Stations: Military Airfields of Oxfordshire ISBN: 9780850598247 (Patrick Stephens Ltd, 1988)

Bridges, Robert *The Spirit of Man: an Anthology in English & French from the Philosophers & Poets made in 1915 by Robert Bridges O.M., Poet Laureate & dedicated by gracious permission to His Majesty King George V* (Longmans, 1915)

Brennan, Dan *Never so Young Again*, (Reinhard, 1946) (in the text Brennan, 1946). First published in Great Britain by Allen & Unwin in 1944 with the title *Never so Young Again* and reissued, with revisions and UK English spelling, as *One of our Bombers is Missing* (NEL, 1979), (in the text Brennan,1979).

Third Time Down (NEL, 1979), first published in UK with the title *Time Enough to Live* (Secker and

Warburg, 1953). Reissued in 1961 by Ace Books (in the text Brennan, 1953)

Carver, Tom *Where the Hell have you Been?: Monty, Italy and One Man's Incredible Escape* ISBN: 9781906021535 (Short Books, 2009)

Dacie, Anne *Yugoslav Refugees in Italy: the Story of a Transit Camp* (Gollancz, 1945)

Dahl, Roald *Going Solo* ISBN: 0224024078 (Cape, 1986)

Deneke, Helen and Norris Betty *The Women of Germany* (NCSS for the Women's Group on Public Welfare, 1947)

Douglas, Keith *Alamein to Zem Zem*, (c1946, Penguin, 1969)

Etherington, William *A Quiet Woman's War* ISBN-9781874739241 (Mousehold Press, 2002)

Farson, Negley *Bomber's Moon*: *London in the Blitzkrieg*. Pictures by Tom Purvis (Gollancz, 1941)

Fedden, Robin *Syria* (Robert Hale, 1946)

FAU *Reports* 1st 1939-1940, 2nd 1940-1941, 3rd 1941-1942, 4th 1939-1945 (FAU).

F.A.U. Report, December 1945 (FAU, 1945).

Shelters (FAU, 1941?)

Freeman, Denis and Cooper, Douglas *Panic* (Cresset, 1941)

Fuchs, K.H. (ed.) *Danzig: What is it all About?* ([?] 1945)

Gardner, Brian *The Terrible Rain: the War Poets 1939-1945, an anthology* ISBN: 0417020708 (Methuen, 1966; Magnum, 1977)

Gilbert, Adrian *The Imperial War Museum Book of the Desert War* ISBN: 9780283061745 (Sidgwick & Jackson Ltd, 1992, 1995)

Gollancz, Victor *"Let My People Go": Some Practical Proposals for Dealing with Hitler's Massacre of the Jews, an Appeal to the British Public* (Gollancz, 1943)

Harmon, Christopher C. *Are we Beasts? Churchill and the Moral Question of World War II "Area Bombing"* Newport Papers, v.1:1991 (U.S. Naval War College Press)

Hastings, Max *Bomber Command* ISBN: 9780330513616 (c.1979; Pan, 2010)

Hawkins, Chris *The Great British Railway Station: King's Cross* ISBN: 9781871608144 (Irwal, 1990)

Heckstall-Smith, Anthony *Tobruk: the Story of a Siege* (Blond, 1959)

Horner, Gordon, *For You the War is Over* ([London], 1948)

Izzard, Molly *Freya Stark: a Biography* ISBN: 0340589078 (Hodder, 1993)

Keane, Fergal *The Road of Bones: The Siege of Kohima, 1944. The Epic Story of the Last Great Stand of Empire* ISBN: 9780007132416 (Harper Collins, 2010)

Lake, John, Chris Davey *Osprey Combat Aircraft, no. 14: Halifax Squadrons of World War 2* ISBN: 1855328925 (Osprey, 1999)

Lamb, Richard *War in Italy 1943-1945: a Brutal Story* ISBN: 0719549337 (John Murray, 1993)

Lawrence, T.E see Ross.

Lewis, Norman *Naples '44: an Intelligence Officer in the Italian Labyrinth* ISBN: 0907871453 (Eland 1978)

Lunn & Arbon *Aircraft down III: RAF Riccall & 1658 HCU* ISBN: 0951125931 (Hardwick, 1989)

Ministry of Information *Bomber Command* (HMSO, [1941])

McLaine, Ian *Ministry of Morale: Home Front Morale and the Ministry of Information in WWII* ISBN: 004940055X (George Allen & Unwin, 1979)

McNeice, Louis *Meet the U.S. Army* (text) (HMSO, 1943)

Miller, Alice Duer *The White Cliffs* (Methuen, 1942)

Morton, H.V. *London. Being The Heart of London, The Spell of London* and *The Nights of London* [in one volume] (Methuen, 1940)

Nichol, John and Rennell, Tony *The Last Escape: the Untold Story of Allied Prisoners of War in Germany 1944-45* ISBN: 0670910945 (Viking, 2002)

Tail-End Charlies: the Last Battles of the Bomber War 1944-45 ISBN: 0670914568 (Viking, 2004)

Nicholson, Virginia *Millions Like Us: Women's Lives in War and Peace 1939-1949* ISBN: 9780670917785 (Penguin Viking, 2011)

Pack, Jeff *Love is in the Air: the Wartime Letters of Joe Pack and Margaret Dillon* ISBN:184683046X (Woodfield, 2008)

Petersson, Lars G. *Deserters* ISBN: 8788214702 (Pen Press, 2004; Danish Resistance Museum Publishing, 2005)

Knox, Hermione, Countess Ranfurly *To War with Whittaker: the Wartime Diaries of the Countess of Ranfurly, 1939-1945* ISBN: 0749319542 (Mandarin, 1994)

Rapier, Brian J. *Melbourne Ten* ISBN: 0950732613 (Air Museum Publications, York, 1982)

Renshaw, Michelle *Accommodating the Chinese: the American Hospital in China, 1880 – 1920* ISBN:041597285X (Routledge, 2005)

Ross, 352087 A/c *The Mint: a Day-book of the R.A.F. Depot between August and December 1922 with later notes* (Panther, 1969)

Rossiter, Mike *Bomber Flight Berlin: the Story of a Lancaster Bomber Crew* ISBN: 9780552162326 (Corgi, 2011)

Saint-Euxpéry, Antoine de *Wind, Sand and Stars: an Airman's Reminiscences* (Services Edition, 1943)

Smith, Graham *Norfolk Airfields in the Second World War* ISBN: 9781853063206 (Countryside, 1994, 2007)

Stark, Freya *Dust in the lion's paw: autobiography 19139-1946* ISBN: 0099728206 (1961) (Arrow, 1990)

Stark, Freya and Moorehead, Caroline *Over the Rim of the World: Selected Letters of Freya Stark* ISBN: 0719546192 (John Murray, 1988)

Steinbeck, John *The Moon is Down* (Library of America, 1942)

Sweetman, John *Bomber Crew: Taking on the Reich* ISBN: 0316727717 (Little Brown, 2004)

Swift, Daniel *Bomber County: the Lost Airmen of World War Two* ISBN: 9780241144176 (Penguin, 2010)

USSR Embassy, London *The Third Molotov Note on German Atrocities* (HMSO, 1942)

Wilson, Kevin, *Bomber Boys: the Ruhr, the Dambusters and Bloody Berlin* ISBN: 9780304367245 (Orion, 2006)

Wilson, Kevin *Men of Air: the Doomed Youth of Bomber Command* ISBN: 9780297853213 (Phoenix, 2007)
Yindrich, Jan *Fortress Tobruk* (Panther, 1956)
Zeigler, Philip *London at War 1939-1945* ISBN: 1856193845 (BCA, 1995)

Index

4 Gordon Square 4, 11, 12, 13, 30, 31, 71, 72, 75, 89, 93, 104, 107, 110, 111, 129, 133, 134, 137, 138, 147, 149, 150, 152, 161, 166, 167, 185, 196, 197, 198, 200, 204, 215, 227, 232, 234, 247, 258, 261
Adams, Derrick 57, 85, 86, 97, 103, 120, 121, 123, 124, 158, 165, 176, 177, 178, 192, 198, 248, 269, 290
Allan, P/O 119
Ayres, Sgt ... 179, 222
Bailey, Brenda Friedrich 22, 23, 261, 262, 263, 274, 303
Beaton, Cecil 239, 240, 259, 260
Beirut .. 240, 241, 246
Berlin 52, 59, 73, 76, 77, 78, 79, 88, 96, 97, 98, 99, 100, 101, 104, 107, 115, 143, 176, 201, 230, 247, 261, 283, 284, 292
Bethnal Green 77, 78, 233
Beveridge, Sgt 174, 176, 180, 208
Big City, see Berlin 59, 101, 115
bilherzie 227, 244
Bomber Command 38, 42, 43, 44, 50, 51, 52, 77, 78, 81, 96, 98, 114, 132, 133, 143, 154, 158, 201, 207, 208, 212, 264, 291, 292
Bremmen 43, 77, 81, 283
Brennan, Dan 42, 51, 54, 62, 81, 115, 118, 119, 168, 175, 211, 278, 280, 292
Brize Norton RAF station 47, 48, 53, 270, 279
Brown, Percy 224, 232, 258
Busby, Hubert 239
Butterworth, Jack 224
Cairo 18, 37, 52, 232, 234, 235, 237, 239, 240, 247, 249, 258, 261, 270
Carr, Air Commodore Roddy 198
Carter, Susie 253
Chevrons Club, RAF 87
Chieti, PG 21 270, 278
China, the China Convoy 12, 17, 31, 32, 34, 66, 134, 167, 204, 217, 218, 223, 227, 228, 234, 238, 262
Churchill, Winston 38, 43, 44, 68, 79, 114, 191
cinema, in London and York 19, 50, 68, 247
Cobb, P/O 119
Compton, Sgt 180
Curtis, E 119
Dahl, Roald 237
De Grey Rooms 4, 6, 7, 62, 63, 66, 73, 74, 85, 87, 89, 238
Debenham, Squadron Leader A.I.S 187

Dortmund 81, 168, 175, 180, 199, 200, 206, 208, 209, 210, 211, 214, 218, 224, 261, 283, 284, 287, 292
Egypt 4, 31, 33, 37, 235, 237, 249, 270
Embankment, Thames embankment 13, 66, 89, 90, 96, 112, 113, 202, 215
Essen 77, 80, 81, 82, 109, 114, 115, 121, 122, 143, 158, 162, 175, 176, 199, 212, 220, 261, 283, 284
Ethiopia 12, 17, 31, 32, 106, 161, 219, 227, 229
F.A.U. Friends Ambulance Unit 11, 12, 16, 22, 25, 27, 28, 29, 32, 34, 38, 39, 104, 109, 129, 160, 162, 163, 166, 171, 204, 227, 232, 233, 234, 235, 236, 238, 241, 247, 248, 249, 251, 252, 253, 254, 255, 259, 260, 261, 286, 292
flowers 75, 141, 152, 264, 265, 278
Frazer, Jack 236
Friends War Victims' Relief Service 11
Genoa . 50, 51, 52, 84
Green, Jack 229
Grimwood, Peter 41, 58, 60, 76, 85, 87, 92, 93, 122, 123, 135, 150, 156, 158, 165, 177, 178, 215, 243, 264, 289
Hadfield-Spears Mobile Hospitals 34, 109, 136
Handley Page Halifax heavy bomber 47, 52, 60, 70, 71, 77, 95, 100, 121, 125, 136, 178, 180, 183, 200, 209, 288, 289, 292
Happy Valley, see Ruhr 59, 122, 191, 208
Harrison, Maurice 119, 179, 193, 199, 289
Inglis, Ian Bethune 199, 289
Italy 4, 38, 51, 59, 115, 143, 234, 248, 250, 251, 253, 254, 257, 258, 262, 263, 278, 279
Jerusalem 18, 239, 240, 241
kala azar 227, 244
Kay, Norman 239
Kiel 110, 120, 124, 125, 127, 283, 284
Knight, Gwendy 170, 171
Lattakia 241, 242, 244, 245
Lawson, George 9, 40, 56, 60, 76, 87, 92, 97, 103, 120, 122, 139, 144, 147, 150, 156, 158, 160, 165, 177, 178, 190, 243, 268, 289
London Hospital Students Hostel, see Philpot Street 13, 150, 159, 180, 181, 188, 196
malaria 34, 227, 228, 229, 244
Marjorie Whittles 6, 7, 10, 12, 13, 14, 23, 24, 29, 41, 66, 70, 87, 90, 104, 105, 106, 111, 112, 134, 135, 150, 152, 182, 223, 225, 238
Maxie Sgt Steel .. 214
McBain, Alan 204, 217, 256
Melbourne, RAF Squadrons, 10 52
Melbourne, RAF station 8, 39, 40, 45, 49, 52, 53, 59, 62, 66,

69, 76, 79, 80, 82, 93, 96, 97, 99, 100, 101, 103, 109, 118, 121, 122, 123, 124, 125, 126, 127, 128, 130, 132, 133, 135, 139, 141, 143, 144, 147, 148, 150, 155, 157, 158, 163, 164, 168, 171, 173, 175, 180, 184, 191, 192, 194, 198, 208, 209, 210, 212, 213, 220, 221, 231, 266, 280, 289, 291, 292
Mills, F/S179, 180, 287
Naples234, 249, 250, 254, 256, 258
Narden, Sgt 168
Norfolk37, 38, 48, 59, 83, 84, 88, 140, 240, 268, 269, 289, 290
Norwich4, 37, 38, 47, 92, 134, 135, 136, 140, 213, 215, 219, 221, 265, 269, 290
Nuseirat 238
Oflag 79: Brunswick Boys Club 279
Operation Chastise, the Dambuster raid... 191
Palestine232, 235, 238, 240
Peace Pledge Union17, 23, 38
Peet, Stephen 154
Philip Rowntree16, 24
Pinkerton, Sgt 174
Play Centre13, 14, 21, 22, 71, 72, 135, 149, 153, 160, 182, 188, 202, 204
Plenderleith, Norman58, 60, 82, 121, 150, 156, 157, 165, 177, 183, 196, 212, 214, 215, 220, 221, 243, 265, 289, 290
Price, W/O, Captain119

RAF 10 Squadron32, 42, 43, 49, 50, 52, 53, 77, 84, 114, 118, 119, 124, 125, 132, 187, 194, 210, 211, 212, 230, 279, 288, 292
RAF 102 Squadron52, 58, 100, 180, 210
RAF 77 Squadron52, 58
Ramallah 241
Red Cross, British and International32, 224, 225, 231, 232, 248, 261, 286
Rome234, 249, 250, 253, 254, 255, 256, 257, 258, 259, 260, 261, 263, 270, 278
Ronald Joynes31, 32, 35, 182, 258
Rowntree's Cocoa Works11, 16, 24, 29, 69
Ruhr59, 77, 80, 81, 96, 116, 123, 125, 158, 162, 176, 179, 191, 210, 211, 212, 224, 261, 266, 268
Seaton Ross, see Melbourne 53, 54, 81
Shaw, Mary22, 78, 106, 135, 151, 238, 239
Shelters, air raid12, 27, 28, 72, 73, 78, 139
Sinclair-Loutit, Angela228, 229, 233
Smethurst, Margaret67, 187, 188, 219, 220, 225
Spears, see Hadfield Spears Mobile Hospitals34, 110, 235
Spray, Bill239, 256, 274
Stark, Freya234, 270, 296

Steel, Sgt., Maxie 6, 10, 15, 40, 41, 57, 58, 60, 61, 62, 76, 84, 85, 87, 92, 115, 119, 121, 123, 128, 139, 154, 156, 158, 165, 173, 177, 178, 179, 185, 187, 190, 192, 193, 196, 199, 213, 214, 215, 230, 231, 266, 269, 283, 289, 290
Stephen, see Peet 109, 136, 235, 282
Sugar Loaf, see Play centre 12, 21, 22, 27, 31, 104, 129, 138, 152, 215, 238
Swift, James, Acting Squadron Leader 174
Syria 4, 31, 227, 229, 235, 236, 241, 243, 247
Syria, see Hadfield Spears 12
Taylor, P/O. 157, 168
theatre, plays and musicals 28, 34, 74, 88, 95, 254, 255
Tobruk 3, 34, 240, 270, 278
Tribunal 23, 24, 25, 303
Turin 50, 84, 119, 143, 283
Unit, see Friends Ambulance Unit 115
Unit, the Unit, see F.A.U. 11, 12, 16, 17, 22, 23, 24, 25, 26, 28, 29, 30, 31, 32, 34, 47, 48, 49, 72, 93, 110, 111, 133, 139, 151, 153, 166, 170, 183, 219, 224, 228, 231, 232, 234, 235, 241, 246, 247, 249, 250, 252, 253, 254, 257, 258, 259, 260, 261, 264, 286, 292, 303
Wallis, Albert Wally 158

Wallis, Albert, Wally 40, 60, 76, 87, 122, 154, 156, 165, 178
Wallis, Wally, Albert 9
Wally, Albert Wallis 81, 86, 92, 139, 144, 147, 150, 160, 178, 243, 289
Wann, F/O 119
Wapping, London docklands 12, 13, 14, 17, 18, 19, 20, 21, 22, 27, 66, 71, 72, 73, 78, 87, 88, 149, 188, 189, 197, 223, 238, 247, 286, 303
Warvics, see Friends War Relief Service 31, 286
Whitechapel 7, 13, 17, 18, 19, 20, 27, 68, 87, 106, 107, 114, 149, 151, 161, 182, 198, 221, 247, 286
Whittles Marjorie 6, 67, 154
Wingham, Tom 100, 101, 210, 211, 291
Wright, Sgt. 157, 168
York 4, 6, 10, 11, 16, 41, 52, 62, 63, 64, 68, 69, 73, 74, 76, 84, 86, 87, 88, 90, 92, 95, 103, 109, 120, 126, 132, 133, 134, 142, 144, 148, 149, 153, 154, 155, 159, 160, 163, 165, 166, 169, 170, 171, 173, 182, 185, 187, 190, 191, 192, 194, 195, 198, 199, 201, 203, 205, 215, 218, 219, 224, 226, 234, 250, 266, 269
Yorkshire 4, 45, 49, 50, 59, 62, 82, 126, 178, 184, 194, 199, 272, 280, 303

Notes

[1] E.V.Morton's *London*, written in 1925 and revised in 1940, consists of a series of linked articles. It is atmospheric, especially sections which take place on the river.

[2] Tower Hamlets might consider adding a plaque mentioning Royal Jubilee Gardens near Hermitage Wharf.

[3] Thank you to Savills estate agents on the Wapping High Street for giving me an excellent map of the area. And thank you to the librarians of the Bancroft local history library, without whose help, I would probably have never found the exact location. It was very hard to find a good map of the area. Time after time I looked at maps of London, all of which ended at St. Katherine's Dock.

[4] P&J Bakers on the Wapping High Street. I was warned off the Wapping Constipater by another customer! I can recommend the Whopper, an enormous iced bun.

[5] Brenda Friedrich married Sydney Bailey, who was also in the Unit. We sat together in Friends House on the Euston Road to hear Clifford Barnard talk about his new book *Binding the Wounds of War: a Young Relief Worker's Letters Home, 1943-1947* (2010). Brenda's father was in Buchenwald KZ concentration camp. She has told her story in the history of her parents, *A Quaker Couple in Nazi Germany* (1996). When Brenda joined the Unit at 17 she cycled from Devon to Yorkshire for her training.

[6] According to Virginia Nicholson's *Millions like Us*, 257 women were imprisoned by Tribunal. She barely mentions the Quakers and does not mention the women in the FAU.

[7] The Kindertransport was arranged by Quakers, for instance, because they were aware of the danger to Jewish families obliged to

stay in Germany. German Quakers made sure their co-religionists were kept informed of Nazi atrocities.

[8] Memorabilia from Captain Hughes was shown to me by his daughter, my sister-in-law, Janet Wood.

[9] *Bomber Command*, ITV, 3rd July 2012.

[10] For example, Christopher C. Harmon in *Are we Beasts? Churchill and the Moral Question of World War II "Area Bombing"* records a 1942 meeting in Moscow between Churchill and Stalin. "Now, in conference with Stalin, Churchill presented the newest and most fearsome face of Britain's bombing strategy. He did not talk of seeking out factories while accepting German civilian casualties as collateral damage. "We looked upon [German] morale as a military target," he told the dictator. "We sought no mercy and we would show no mercy." "

[11] Radio speech, recorded in 1951: http://news.bbc.co.uk/today/hi/today/newsid_8930000/8930339.stm . Guardian transcription from 21st August, 1940: http://century.guardian.co.uk/1940-1949/Story/0,,128255,00.html . Quoted speech Reproduced with permission of Curtis Brown, London on behalf of the Estate of Sir Winston Churchill. Copyright © Winston S. Churchill.

[12] Ian McLaine in *Ministry of Morale: Home Front Morale and the Ministry of Information in WWII* states that Cecil Day Lewis wrote *Bomber Command* for the Ministry of Information but the dates of C. Day Lewis joining the Ministry and the publication of the book do not seem to tally.

[13] John Sweetman, *Bomber Crew: Taking on the Reich*, (2004), p. 55. Wellington's were crewed by six men, Halifaxes and Lancasters by seven. Often a second pilot was also on board and occasionally an observer.

[14] Jack's sister Sylvia found that her brother's log book had been destroyed in the 1960s, with so much government information, electronic storage systems being a thing of the future. Log books belonging to distinguished airmen, or of airmen who took part in the most important operations, were the only ones kept. In 1961 the government advertised the imminent destruction of all log books unless previously claimed but Jack's family did not see any of these advertisements. Maurice Harrison's family have his log book. Log books were kept by each member of aircrew and recorded each job done in detail. In order to decipher Jack's service record I found Michael Bowyer's books about air stations invaluable.

[15] Jack had not yet been posted to 10th Squadron at Lossiemouth when it took part in attacks on the Tirpitz but he was posted to Lossiemouth shortly afterwards.

[16] There is a description of RAF Melbourne here http://airfields.fotopic.net/c1489992.html .

[17] Sgt. Frank Jones served at Melbourne for a short time in 1944 but caught dysentery from the insanitary conditions in camp and once recovered, was transferred to Pocklington. Quoted in Kevin Wilson's *Men of Air: the Doomed Youth of Bomber Command* (2007, p. 213).

[18] Bruce Saunders in *Bombs Away* (Bowman, p. 121).

[19] See http://www.raf.mod.uk/bombercommand/h10.html .

[20] According to Mac's wife the Blacksmith's Arms in the village of Seaton Ross, renamed the Bomber's Arms and now closed, had a ceiling made out of two Mosquito wings and she could just see their outline through the plaster. Mac was a M/U/G in 10 Squadron and Iris was with signals and worked on the Knavesmire, plotting aircraft courses and whereabouts during missions.

[21] "You leaned against …" This description ends "later, in the end, we only grew to hate it, to hate all things that were near to or related to death."

[22] Day bombing missions almost stalled in 1941 because losses were too great compared to results achieved. Regular nighttime raids were made possible by improvement to Radar in 1942. In the early days relatively few bombers could be equipped with the new radar, so squadrons were formed using experienced crew and called the pathfinder squadrons. They flew in the vanguard with a Master Bomber and dropped target markers for the following heavies.

[23] "On big raids .." Numbers of aircraft on the 1 / 2 March raid are from MOD history web at http://www.raf.mod.uk/bombercommand/mar43.html . The route taken to the Ruhr varied and later in the war, once France was liberated, 10 Squadron aircraft flew down to Reading before turning East.

[24] The De Grey Rooms. "The impetus for the erection of the building was given by the Earl de Grey and officers of the Yorkshire Hussars who required suitable accommodation for their annual mess. It was intended to be used for concerts, balls, public entertainments and meetings"(York.Conservation.Trust).
http://www.yorkconservationtrust.org/properties/DeGreyRooms/DeGreyRooms.html

[25] Wings for Victory Week. See the Pathé news reel shot in Trafalgar Square at the beginning of Wings for Victory week.
http://www.britishpathe.com/record.php?id=12165

[26] The movie *Babes on Broadway,* (1941) directed by Busby Berkeley for MGM, includes the song 'How about you', lyrics by Ralph Freed and music by Lane Burton.

[27] Bethnal Green disaster. See
http://www.nationalarchives.gov.uk/releases/2006/january/january1/operations.htm

[28] Terror flier poster propaganda includes a warning to remember the blackout. The text is "Verdunkeln! Der Fein seiht Dein Licht!" = "Blackout! The Devil sees your light!" A skeleton rides astride a twin-engined bomber waving a wrecking ball in his right hand and aiming for a person way below him, standing in a lit doorway.

[29] On the old airfield at Melbourne there is a memorial. "This plaque is a memorial to all aircrews of all Allied nations who lost their lives in the surrounding countryside not least the crew of Halifax bomber JD105 10sqn Melbourne which crashed within half a mile of this May 5th 1943." Sgt. Peck crashed on the airfield itself exactly two months before.

[30] Scrub, now a common term, was RAF slang for having a mission cancelled once they were ready to fly or already in the air and meant that their names had been scrubbed off the blackboard.

[31] Jack's school, CNS, had rather fine tennis courts at the front, by the entrance. When, later, Jack and Freda are seen playing tennis, it cannot have been on these courts because they were seen from above, indicating courts at the foot of York city walls.

[32] Spilt beer. This famous incident in Wapping was described to me by Brenda Bailey and descriptions of it are also online.

[33] 'Till the Lights of London Shine Again' Joe Loss and his orchestra, sung by Chick Henderson. Lyrics and music by Tommy Connor and Eddie Pola (London, 1939). It is a slow foxtrot with a wistful chorus. Music available from Amazon: http://www.amazon.co.uk/Lights-London-Shine-Again-Henderson/dp/B0060T82J6

[34] "Here I am" – Freda was telling a story and exaggerating details, a typical line shoot or pilot's colourful but not really exaggerated account of being in a sticky situation: 'There I was, upside-down with nothing on the clock but the maker's name ...' Another example is 'The flak was so thick you could walk on it'.

[35] The Bomber Command diary for March is at http://www.raf.mod.uk/bombercommand/mar43.html

[36] The Anhalter. For Harold Swain's story see http://www.bbc.co.uk/ww2peopleswar/stories/88/a7212188.shtml

[37] The experience of walking from the Spree via the flak tower, which was grafitoed with skeletons, and over a park to the station ruins was so disorienting that I laughed uncontrollably in a restaurant afterwards, and I my apologies to the waitress were incomprehensible so I think she thought I was drunk.

[38] RAF Pocklington. Andrew Sefton's web is at: http://www.pocklingtonhistory.com/history/20thcentury/pocklingtoninww2/thatfatefulnight/index.php

[39] Tom Wingham writes in *Bombs Away: Dramatic First-Hand accounts of British & Commonwealth Bomber Aircrew in WWII*, edited by Martin W. Bowman (2010). For another account of this mission www.aircrewremembrancesociety.com/raf1943/dickinson.html

[40] The date on the letter written on March 26 was 1942. I thought initially that this was a sign of Jack's tiredness but looking more carefully at the writing, I see it is Freda's. She must have filled in the date when she was tired and upset, maybe when she was sent her letters to Jack and sorted them into date order.

[41] See New Zealand Evening Post, v.185:no.81, 6 April 1943, p.5. and http://www.wartimememories.co.uk/airfields/dalton.html . For the story of a child whose Kiel school was bombed in the spring of 1943 go to http://www.bbc.co.uk/ww2peopleswar/stories/61/a2904761.shtml

[42] Walter Scott *The Rover's Adieu*. The Oxford Book of English Verse, 1250-1900 (1919).

[43] Text widely available but I found it searching for information about the Bomber Command Memorial. The Hon. Anne C. Cools, Canadian parliamentarian, quotes the speech (http://www.parl.gc.ca/Content/Sen/Chamber/411/Debates/118db_2012-11-08-e.htm) Debates of the Senate (Hansard), 1st Session, 41st Parliament, Volume 148, Issue 118.

[44] Larry Donnelly in the 10 Squadron Association Newsletter no. 32: http://www.10sqnass.co.uk/images/stories/pdfs/n32.pdf

[45] Max Hastings, *Bomber Command*, (2010, first published 1979). LMF is described mainly in chapter 8: '76 Squadron Yorkshire 1943'.

[46] Freydis Sharland kindly gave me permission to use her words, which I transcribed from an interview in *Shooting the War: Women*, Tue, 9 Feb 2010, 03:00, BBC Four shown in February 2010. (http://www.bbc.co.uk/programmes/b00qjnmy#synopsis)

[47] Nobody from Melbourne flew on raids from 5th to 7th April, as the weather was too bad and on 8th Jack's usual aircraft was flown on ops by a different crew.

[48] A transcription of the letter is available at esdailecarter.wordpress.com.

[49] Freda's letter of 21st April and Jack's of 24th mention Feathered Friends. One of the advertisements for July 1943 can be found at http://www.flightglobal.com/pdfarchive/view/1943/1943%20-%201702.html

[50] June 28th, 2012, Green Park. During the dedication ceremony of the Bomber Command memorial, bomber aircrew sitting in front of me was heard to mutter about Butcher Harris, laughing to his neighbor, who was also a veteran: "Bastard, we called him".

[51] James Swift of 83 Squadron in Lincolnshire also raided Dortmund that night. His story is told by his grandson, Daniel Swift in *Bomber County: the Lost Airmen of World War Two* (2010). James Swift's log book records that there was "considerable heavy flak" that night (p. 186).

[52] On Freda's death, Sybil was sent her copy of *Knavesmire: York's Great Racecourse and its Stories* (1984). I looked at it when I visited Sybil in York and it includes an aerial photograph of the racecourse camp.

[53] Sgt Pinkerton was flying ZA-X BB324 when it crashed on 23rd June, 1943.

[54] FIDO the fog-busting petrol-burning runway marking was not introduced until later in the war.

[55] Sgt Compton fought off enemy aircraft on more than one occasion and it was with great pleasure that I noticed he was awarded the Distinguished Flying Medal in May 1943. It is noticeable on reading through the Honours and Awards section that Mid-Upper and Tail Gunners are the most often awarded of all crew, including Captains.

[56] One of many web sites which detail aircraft shot down is the Netherlands web at http://www.defensie.nl/media/verliesregister_1943_tcm46-154754.pdf ref T2305 .

[57] Roddy Carr retired in 1947 and died in Bampton, Oxfordshire in 1971. See http://www.raf.mod.uk/history.bombercommandcommandersofworldwarii.cfm .

[58] According to www.ww2aircraft.net this was the day Mengele became a doctor at Auschwitz.

[59] Bomb Load: – 2.1000lb. (A/C H.D.A.F.E.G. and C – long delay, remainder G.P.TD.0.02) 7. S.B.C. (90 at 4lbs) 6 S.B.C. (8 at 30lb). The letters denote the aircraft followed by their cargo. Each aircraft carries two 1,000lb bombs. Most of them are long delay bombs and the rest are G.P. general purpose T.D time delay bombs. They also carry incendiary bombs in their S.B.C. small bomb containers. The 90 4lb bombs were, I believe, magnesium and the 30lb bombs were phosphorus.

[60] "…two others were attacked by night fighters." I have not been able to confirm that Jack's aircraft was brought down by a night fighter. The three aircraft lost that night were ZA-Z W1217 in Holland; ZA-B DT789 and ZA-G HR696, both lost in Germany.

[61] Sgt. Dew's account is at www.tom.forbes.dsl.pipex.com

[62] Askham Grange is now a women's detention centre.

[63] Alan McBain was part of the China convoy, and having escaped the Japanese advance up the Burma Road, he was now stationed in Calcutta and at the time was battling monsoon and famine.

[64] I believe this is the correct name but cannot verify this. I think he was E. R. Curtis in ZA-N, JB960 which was shot down after the Essen raid on 27/28 May. The only reason I have for thinking this is that the records state that he was among the youngest pilots to die and Mary herself was only 19. There are six aircrew with E in their initials, three on ZA-N. Three crew with the initial died when ZA-W JB598 went down over Essen after colliding with a Lancaster.

[65] In the North of England, as it happens, it was traditional to use tiny cups after a bereavement.

[66] This is the edited section of a letter Freda wrote after meeting John, when they were both on holiday in Ibiza in 1953. John left the Hotel Bahía before Freda, and appears to have left her a note implying that she was flighty and insincere.

[67] Bilherzie, like Kala-Azar, is a usually fatal waterborne parasitic infection, closely connected to malaria.

[68] "The Conqueror" was stolen from the offices in Gordon Square on Monday 11th January 1945 and was mourned in this reminiscence in Chronicle 67 6 January 1945.

[69] Shepheards, a hotel famous among officers of WW1 and unofficially part of army HQ in WW2, off bounds to other ranks: http://www.shepheard-hotel.com/history.html .

[70] Stalag Luft were camps for air force prisoners of war. Stalag stands for Kriegsgefangenen-Mannschafts-Stammlager and officers were imprisoned in Oflags.

[71] 'The Last Days of Spears' *Friends Ambulance Unit Chronicle*, no. 74.

[72] Freda described her visit to Syria in 1996, *Visit to the Syria Sections (Hadfield Spears Mobile Clinics) – June 1944*, which she sent to interested friends and Friends. I have quoted from her original diaries.

[73] William Wordsworth, Composed Upon Westminster Bridge, 1802.

Earth has not anything to show more fair:
Dull would he be of soul who could pass by
A sight so touching in its majesty:
This City now doth like a garment wear
The beauty of the morning; silent, bare,
Ships, towers, domes, theatres, and temples lie
Open unto the fields, and to the sky,
All bright and glittering in the smokeless air.
Never did the sun more beautifully steep
In his first splendour, valley, rock, or hill;
Ne'er saw I, never felt a calm so deep!
The river glideth at his own sweet will:
Dear God! the very houses seem asleep;
And all that mighty heart is lying still!

[74] For further information see Michelle Renshaw on the holistic method in her *Accommodating the Chinese: the American Hospital in China, 1880 – 1920* (2005).

[75] Beaton describes people in Arabic Cairo: "The children filled their ewers and the water carriers inflated their horrible goat-skins at the tiled fountain. The women in black walked sloppily, without looking where they were going "and he describes Transjordanian costume as "fancy-dress".

[76] Transcribed from BBC4's documentary *Shooting the War: Women* (2009). Freydis Sharland, who kindly gave me permission to use her words here. See the earlier quotation in Chapter 4: April.

[77] Freda's discomfort at being expected to take advantage of her situation when she was in Cairo was mirrored by my friend Jenny Stanton and me when crossing borders between Israel and Palestine in 2004. We refused, except on one occasion, to use the fast track queue for foreigners.

[78] This report, Newsletter No. 9, includes a harrowing description from Gerald Gardiner of Belsen Concentration Camp. He inspected the camp for the Commissioner [Red Cross, I assume] six days after it was liberated by the 2nd Army in April. He comments that conditions were similar to those at Sandbostel, though on a greater scale. If ever there was a good reason for fighting and winning this war, by whatever means, then this is it. See Clifford Barnard's two books about his time at Sandbostel.

[79] Freda kept many issues of the Friends Ambulance Unit Chronicle but not this one so thank you to the Librarians of Friends House Euston Road for allowing me to read this issue, call number PERS B/F7/AMB/2.

> [80] Bill Spray, a marvelous inspirational man, worked with the F.A.U. in the Near East and France and at last in Germany. He was awarded the Croix de Guerre. I gave him a very early draft of chapter 1, when he made his comment about Freda.

[81] The Imperial War Museum interviews with Freda did not give me any new information but confirmed that she had added to Lyn Smith's understanding of the way the Unit worked. They can be ordered from the Imperial War Museum, reference IWM 10235/3/1-3.

[82] F.A.U. Chronicle 85 for 29 June 1946 records that Dortmund had a population of 538,000 before the war but by the time Germany surrendered "the population had dropped to almost half that figure". The countryside in the Ruhr was overrun by the starving population, "Travelling in the country in search of food has now reached vast proportions."

[83] Bomber Command Memorial was dedicated in June 2012.

[84] The Commonwealth War Graves Commission tell me that the crew's bodies were moved from the north cemetery in Düsseldorf to Reichswald on 4th October 1946. This happened "after the war" or "later" according to most information I could find so I am very grateful to the CWGC for giving me the exact date of when Jack's body was moved.

[85] Message boards, for instance, PPRunE.

[86] Sonnet 29 William Shakespeare

When in disgrace with fortune and men's eyes,
I all alone beweep my outcast state,
And trouble deaf heaven with my bootless cries,
And look upon myself and curse my fate,
Wishing me like to one more rich in hope,
Featured like him, like him with friends possess'd,
Desiring this man's art, and that man's scope,
With what I most enjoy contented least.
Yet in these thoughts myself almost despising,
Haply I think on thee, and them my state,
Like to the lark at break of day arising
From sullen earth, sings hymns at heaven's gate.
For thy sweet love remember'd such wealth brings
That then I scorn to change my state with kings.

Made in the USA
Charleston, SC
02 March 2015

161-162 omitted on reprints